D0439398

Walking in the Sacred Manner

*Healers, Dreamers, and
Pipe Carriers—Medicine Women
of the Plains Indians*

Mark St. Pierre
and Tilda Long Soldier

A TOUCHSTONE BOOK
PUBLISHED BY SIMON & SCHUSTER

New York   London   Toronto   Sydney   Tokyo   Singapore

TOUCHSTONE
Rockefeller Center
1230 Avenue of the Americas
New York, NY 10020

TOUCHSTONE and colophon are registered trademarks
of Simon & Schuster Inc.

Designed by Irving Perkins Associates

Manufactured in the United States of America

10 9 8 7 6 5 4 3

Library of Congress Cataloging-in-Publication Data

St. Pierre, Mark, 1950–
Walking in the sacred manner : holy women, healers, and pipe
carriers—medicine women of the Plains Indians / Mark St.
Pierre and Tilda Long Soldier.
p.   cm.
"A touchstone book."
Includes bibliographical references.
1. Indian women—Great Plains—Religion.   2. Indian women—Great
Plains—Medicine.   3. Women healers—Great Plains.   4. Indian
mythology—Great Plains.   5. Shamanism—Great Plains.   I. Long
Soldier, Tilda, 1962–   . II. Title.
E98. W8S7   1995
299'. 798' 082—dc 20   95-6393
                                    CIP

ISBN 0-684-80200-7

Contents

Dedicated to the Lakota women who try to live with the traditions through the struggles and hardships of today.

In honor of all who actively contributed to making this book a reality, including:

The late Madonna (Swan) Abdalla

Madonna Blue Horse Beard

Dora Brown Bull

Leona Brown Bull

Ethel Brown Wolf

Oliver Brown Wolf

Vivian Bull Head

Sheila M. Curry

Colleen Cutschall

The late Chauncey Dupris

Ray Dupris

Charlotte Gusay

Dr. Herbert Hoover

Sidney Keith

Carol Little Wounded

Mel Lone Hill

Oglala Lakota College Library

Orville Mesteth

Jessie James, Jr.

Stella Janis

Valentine Janis

Cecelia Looking Horse

Stanley Looking Horse

Arlene Marshall

Neva (Light In The Lodge) Paxton

LeVera Rose (South Dakota Historical Archives)

Mike Running Wolf

Belle Starboy

Steamboat Springs Arts Council

Dr. Ronald Theisz

Ted Thin Elk

Delia Two Crow

Tanya Ward

Roberta (Deer With Horns) Wolf

Ted Wolf

Jackie Yellow Tail

Cissy Young Bear

Darlene Young Bear

Mitchell Zephier

Introduction

What is important for us is that the old ways are correct and if we do not follow them we will be lost and without a guide. We must remember that the heart of our religions is alive and that each person has the ability within to awaken and walk in a sacred manner. The manner with which we walk through life is each man's most important responsibility and we should remember this every new sunrise.

—THOMAS YELLOW TAIL, Crow Holy Man 1903–93,
from his granddaughter, Jackie Yellow Tail

In the religions of the modern world, women are often relegated to second-class citizenship or worse. With rising frequency and intensity, women are asking, "Why?" and "Just where do we fit in these traditions?" For each of the religions of Islam, Judaism, Buddhism, or Catholicism, the answer would be slightly different. For many women the traditional responses are not likely to satisfy them or relieve their quest for a religion that can respond to their needs. It is not only women who question and search for the richness of a truly affirming religious experience: society itself seems to be on a spiritual odyssey. Ours is an era of great change and confusion, and perhaps it is a time in which people will finally listen to Native America and see that there are cultures that have not denied women spiritual equality.

Non-Indian people have been turning to Native American practices for years, as evidenced by the proliferation of the vision quest, the sweat lodge, and so forth. Some of what we know has come legitimately through or from native peoples; much has not. The recent commercial availability of tarot cards based on "Lakota Religion" is a good example of using aspects of a spiritual practice without really understanding it. Native Americans who are well versed in Indian religious life need to be listened to more carefully. This book is not intended to make converts or teach all there is to know about Native American religion. It is difficult for these belief systems to be taken out of context and practiced by those who do not deeply understand or live in that culture.

We work in a family-owned Indian art gallery in Steamboat Springs, Colorado. In the role of salespeople, we encountered many questions about native people's religions, and "New Age" writers became increasingly common. The idle curiosity and occasional blatant racism of the questions often provoked Tilda to comment, but generally, in typical Lakota self-effacement, she referred the questions to me or ignored them. These questions provided much of the motivation for Tilda's and my journey of discovery in the world of women healers of the Lakota.

A full-blood Oglala Lakota, Tilda was raised "out in the country" in what could be considered a physically arduous life. Home was a weathered, square-hewn log house on the homestead of Little Warrior, her maternal great-grandfather, in the Medicine Root District of the Pine Ridge Reservation, near the village of Kyle in western South Dakota. The house sat below a grass-covered hill capped by a protrusion of yellow sandstone. From the ridge top there was a spectacular view of the pink, yellow, and red striped, jagged badlands, which spread to the north and stretched from east to west as far as the eye could see.

Ozuya Cikala (Little Warrior) had been one of the last living survivors of the Little Big Horn Battle. In his adult years Little Warrior had been one of the most powerful medicine men of the reservation. According to Tilda's older relatives, he was able to "pull green herbs from the snow to doctor his patients." In 1950 he successfully treated the famous Black Elk for a stroke.[1]

Little Warrior died in the mid-1950s. When Tilda was born, in 1962, the shaman's separate little frame house had fallen into ruin. The main log house had changed little. Water was hand pumped from a well near the large one-room cabin. The sill and post log building had been an Indian dance hall, a place for gatherings and all-night wakes as well as a home.

A relative told us that "when Little Warrior was living, he would invite people over to feast and to dance. We loved to go over there. He was a kind and generous man who loved to laugh. People would come from all over and camp for a few days."

In Tilda's day, as in the past, kerosene provided light, and wood provided heat and fuel for cooking. Tilda reminisces,

We all lived in one room. Around the walls were dresser, bed, dresser, bed. There were ten of us, including Grandma.

I remember in the summer heat we would eat our evening meals outside. Grandma would sweep the ground on the shady eastern side of the house. Then she would sprinkle the ground with water on that spot, to harden the loose gumbo, and finally place a piece of canvas there for all of us to sit on.

In the summers she baked bread outside over an open fire. She would cook the soup indoors on a propane stove that sat next to our wood cookstove. When it was ready, we would sit and eat "Indian style." This was a happy time of day when people would talk and laugh and catch up on the news of the day. The conversation was always in Lakota.

At night, especially in the long, howling darkness of a plains winter, there were stories to be told. Wood crackled in the stove, and shadows danced in the lamplight. A dozen young ears would be poised for a new story, or an old favorite, about ancient spirits like Iktomi the trickster or Anukite the double-faced woman. Lakota morals, made real through Iktomi's failed schemes, were always easier to hear enhanced by the skill of a good storyteller and the laughter created by Iktomi's antics. However, by this time, Lakota creation stories, rich in important cultural and spiritual messages, had generally been replaced with that of Adam and Eve.

On Sundays Tilda would walk across the prairie, her hand securely in Grandma Sadie's, to the little Mediator Episcopal Church three miles away. "In those days the church would be crowded, and the singing of Christian hymns in Lakota seemed so beautiful," she recalls.

There was, however, always the influence of powerful beliefs that had existed since the beginning of time. By Tilda's birth in 1962, one hundred years of Christian missionary activity, including starvation and incarceration intended to create doubt in the old ways, had passed. All over Indian country, old cultural ways and traditional religions had often been lost or driven "underground." In many traditional full-blood families, respect for traditional ways was tempered with this missionary-inflicted fear for the spiritual consequences of attending or sponsoring "heathen Indian ceremonies and devil worship."

With the many stories that Indian converts and their ministers perpetuated about the potentially deadly results of the improper use of the awesome power of these older ways (witchcraft), the old religion came to be feared and even avoided. This fear often prevented whole families from attending ceremonies. Ideas about the devil from the Old and New Testaments, and, more important, Christian ideas about the roles of males and females had deeply permeated the religious life of the Lakota, creating imbalances in the rights and roles of men and women that had not existed before.

It is into this climate of doubt, suspicion, and oppression of the old native religion that Tilda and all other twentieth-century Lakota were born.

Tilda herself had little personal experience with holy women. Her knowledge of holy women and their importance to the people came from family stories.

One hundred years of concealing the old religion from the missionaries and agency officials has left many Lakota with an imperfect understanding of their own traditions—though many of its influences on character and personality remain strong, even on those many Indian people who are expressly Christian.

With all this in mind, important and troubling questions came to us concerning our impending search. Would people have forgotten? Would they still be reluctant to talk? Would they have been taught to forget their religious history, including that of holy women?

This quote from Orville Mesteth, a Lakota elder, gives profound testimony to why this miraculous legacy of powerful holy women was all but lost:

> It seems to me that early in this century, these women had to make great displays of their powers because the Catholics were still in their inquisition stage. Sort of like the Spanish Inquisition. They were doing all they could to defame our religion, undermine the medicine people, causing the people to be doubtful or fearful of our ancient knowledge, break down the people's faith. I heard this one story of a powerful Hunkpapa Lakota medicine woman. She was from up near Little Eagle, on the Standing Rock Reservation. The story was told to me by a Mrs. White Bull.
>
> About 1910, when the Catholics were trying especially hard to discourage the people from believing in the old ways, this woman became fed up. She was disappointed in the people for giving up their faith, living in doubt. In the middle of winter, with thick snow on the ground, she called a large group of people together and said, "I am going to show you something!" She walked into a thicket of plum bushes and snapped a branch off one of those bushes. She held that branch out and sang. Plums sprang out of that branch. She said, "Come eat them, they're real." But some of the people had already been so affected (by the influence of the missionaries) that they were frightened and would not eat the plums even though others said they were good and sweet. They had learned to fear their own religion from the Catholic missionaries.

Despite the rich Lakota lifestyle, language, and the old, simple living off the land that Tilda was raised with, her immediate family harbored many of these fears and avoided the ceremonies. So it was, and is, for many traditional full-blood families. In their hearts, however, and in the subconscious landscape of their dreams, the spirits still live and communicate with the people.

When Tilda was ten her beloved Grandma Sadie (Little Warrior's daughter) died unexpectedly. Without Sadie Crazy Thunder's powerful guidance, the family slipped into despair and alcoholism. Eventually the tribal courts intervened, and Tilda, along with one sister and two brothers, was placed in the home of Grandma Dora Rooks (Sadie's sister and Little Warrior's daughter). The other two boys were placed on another part of the reservation. Dora already had seven other grandchildren living with her. It was here, in Dora's home, that Tilda prepared for adulthood.

My [great aunt] Grandmother Dora was kind of strict.[2] She told us girls living with her that we needed to know how to do certain things if we were going to be Lakota women and mothers one day. It is here that I learned to cook, do beadwork, sew, and make quilts. She taught us many things that at the time seemed hard. But now I am so glad she taught us these things and that I paid attention. They have turned out to be very useful.

It was Grandma Dora who first brought Tilda to the ceremonies.

I went to my first sweat lodge when I was twelve, I think. I was probably thirteen when I went to my first house ceremony. It was a Lowanpi Ceremony. Both were run by [the late] Reuben Fire Thunder. I was in ninth grade when I went to the only Sun Dance I have ever attended. We kids were raised with such great respect for these things that I guess we felt only other Lakota people [more spiritually prepared] were worthy of participating.

Furnished by a life among her people, Tilda's contributions to this book on holy women come partly out of the very dichotomy of contemporary tribal life, which encompasses not only the dual exposure to and simultaneous pull of Lakota tradition and the white world but also, as a part of that, the contrast and occasional conflicts between traditional spiritualism and Christianity.[3] In recent years the Catholic church's attitude has changed, and it has come to encourage the old ceremonies. The Indian Religious Freedoms Act of 1968 also had a profound impact on the use of traditional ceremony.

Tilda participated in all the discussion that led to the narrative portion of this book, clarifying my written perceptions of spiritual concepts and ceremonies and correcting linguistic problems. Her ideas about dreams, ceremonies, healing, and death make up the core of those chapters. She also carefully edited the manuscript and further refined what I wrote. We conducted all the interviews together, traveling thousands of miles in quest of the information in these pages.

I was an assistant vice president of Oglala Lakota College when Tilda and I met in 1983, and we were married in 1986 near Kyle at Mediator Episcopal Church, whose cemetery holds the bones of Little Warrior, Sadie, and Dora.

After college in 1972, I helped start the Big Foot Community College in Eagle Butte on the Cheyenne River Reservation in 1973 and taught Indian studies at the University of South Dakota and Black Hills State University. I have also been constantly involved with Lakota religion.

I learned my lessons not from books but firsthand, from such powerful and knowledgeable Lakota elders as the late Lucy Swan, Charles Kills Enemy, Joseph Rock Boy, Pete Catches, and the still-living Sidney Keith. My closest ties were with my spiritual father, the late Kenneth Young Bear, an Assiniboine/Hidatsa/Santee who married a Minnecojou Lakota, Darlene Knife, and lived with her on the Cheyenne River Reservation. Madonna (Swan) Abdalla was perhaps the most dear to me of all.[4]

I have never taught a course on native religion or philosophy. We believe that if a Lakota or non-Lakota wants to know something about the Pipe (Old Lakota) religion he or she should go to the source—by living on a Lakota reservation for an extended period of time. We have decided to record this information because we feel, for the sake of searching women and all people, that contrary to New Age writings, the truth should finally be shared not as a how-to book but as an affirmation of the spiritual potential of all people, men and women. To share an accurate view of this spiritual world and its tribal context was our goal.

After we spent a number of years in the Native American art business, our contact with dozens of non-Indian customers—and, most often, women—familiarized us with many of the popular New Age writers and what they were claiming were true stories of Indian medicine people. Very seldom were these books about men, like the earlier, apocryphal Carlos Castaneda, nor did they present the truth; they seemed created to take advantage of women's needs for a spirituality that involved and spoke directly to them.

We were, perhaps, reluctant to react. Knowing that the commitment involved in providing a positive and accurate response to these often silly and always misleading books would be great, we remained silent. The books kept coming, taunting, each wilder than the one before. Customers literally pushed the books at us, telling us that we needed to read them, that they were marvelous, inspiring, and true, and the questions kept coming.

To commit oneself to writing a book requires tremendous time, self-discipline, and, of course, energy. For Tilda and me the energy came in part from anger. For Tilda this anger had a very genuine, personal origin. Her reaction to New Age writers is not an existential or academic reaction but the response of a modern yet traditional Lakota woman, fluent in her language and at peace with her identity. Her other source of energy came from a desire to see her people portrayed in a truthful light. She wanted people to know about the truth of holy women, not the unrecognizable images she was presented with in the books she had been given:

> Coming from a different culture and being a full-blood, I see these books as very misleading. I cannot begin to read them because they get me so angry.
>
> I felt that a true book should be written about holy women, a book that would set things straight, once and for all. . . .
>
> Anglo women would bring us books on New Age—crystal-clutching, so-called holy women—and ask us to read them.
>
> It seems ironic for Anglo people to shove these silly books in my hands and tell me to read them when I am very aware of my Lakota religion. I had grandmothers and grandfathers who were powerful medicine men and women.
>
> It is very frustrating for my husband and me when some of these people argue over the fact that they believe these writers actually had these experiences. In my opinion these books are wrong, very misleading.

My personal anger at these false prophets came from my academic love of truth, my adopted religion of twenty years, and my belief that true journey toward spiritual enlightenment and fulfillment is a human right. Tilda and I believe that information about Native American spiritual traditions, shared honestly, can provide genuine spiritual fulfillment for the seeker.

There are some Indian people today who are adamant that the kind of information in this book should not be shared with non-Indians. They forget that many Indian people themselves used books like *Black Elk Speaks* and *The Sacred Pipe* as they traveled on their own spirit journey.[5] There are, however, many more native men and women who feel the time is right, that the knowledge they still possess is critical to the very survival of our society and their own. This book is therefore both written for and in honor of native women. Jackie Yellow Tail, a young Crow woman trying to make the "Sacred Walk," said of this conflict,

I believe that our beliefs do need to be shared; I think that the color of people's skin doesn't make them any better or worse than anybody else. Everybody that's here is here for a reason, whatever the Creator chose. It's what's in the person's heart and mind. There's good and bad in everybody. The positive and the negative. Mother Earth has her North Pole and the South Pole. She's got her axis that keeps her centered. The way I see it, each of us is a small replica of Mother Earth. We have our positive and our negative, and the good works with the bad. It's just that there's an imbalance in a lot of people. They go too far either one way or the other. . . .

Life is a circle, the world is a circle. The Christian way of seeing the world is that within this circle there's a man called Jesus; on the outside is the trees, the rocks, the animals; all around the world are the different things that are on Mother Earth. In the center is man above all things.

The Indian way of thinking is that there is this same circle, Mother Earth, and around her are the rocks, the trees, the grass, the mountains, the birds, the four-legged, and man. Man is the same as all those other things, no greater, no less. I mean, it's all so simple; people make it so hard. That's why I say we're like Mother Earth: each one of us has that ability within us to grow spiritually, we're connected with the Creator from the top of our head, our feet walk on Mother Earth. It's within us; and why should we hold that to ourselves when we know, no matter what color that person is, that he has the same spiritual yearning we have? People are a little Mother Earth, they deserve to be treated with respect. They, in turn, need to treat us with respect, that give and take, that positive and negative.

So we were about to begin an important pilgrimage, in which many others would eventually share. Certainly, on the first of many thousands of miles, we were plagued by fears that we would not reach our destination. Would the trail have grown too cold? Would people share with us their memories? Would we find medicine women still practicing?

Our approach was to follow the early leads that had come to us over the years, to take a tape recorder and notebook and record firsthand the accounts of these women and the ceremonies they used for healing. We sought out living holy women as well as sons, daughters, and grandchildren of historic holy women. These interviews invariably led to new people to speak with.

Those who want to understand must travel into the world of native women, into the villages, into the dusty past and the paradoxical present of a very different culture. The traveler must be willing to journey into the dreams, minds, and souls of these powerful women.

In many ways we were to travel more deeply into this feminine Indian world than any chroniclers had done before. What we were to discover were the firsthand experiences of native women on their own journey of spiritual discovery and fulfillment. It is to them, and to those elders who shared their family legacy, that we owe our heartfelt thanks. This book is only a humble attempt to set a small piece of human history straight.

I believe that our people, and all people all over this earth, are going to be going back; . . . they are already searching for something, they don't know what it is they are going back to. It's the creator. The Native American people have been close to God, . . . and sure the young people are forgetting, as are some of the older people, because of Christianity, because of the materialistic ways, what I call cultural shock. It's what happened to our people when they were put on reservations.

They taught our people to think the way the non-Indian thought. They turned everything upside-down in our Indian world. We've forgotten who we were; and yes, maybe it's true that we can't go back to the days when the buffalo roamed the plains, but I believe that basically Indian people do still have their spirituality.

Whatever is coming, whatever is going to happen, there's definitely coming what some call "the end times." I've had dreams of these things. There are going to be people who will live through some of the catastrophes that are going to happen. There will be a need for spiritual people always, people who are close to Mother Earth and close to the Creator. Maybe it's not so much trying to keep our traditions alive, . . . that's only a part of it; mostly it's our prayer life and being close to the Creator that we wish to keep. Other people are looking to Native Americans, the indigenous people, because of those very things. They are going to continue to look toward the Indian people, especially in the times that are coming.

—JACKIE YELLOW TAIL,
Crow, traveler on the
sacred walk

1

Healers, Dreamers, Pipe Carriers: Communication with the Sacred

At a certain point in the ceremony while I am singing, I start to cry.
They are not tears of sadness or joy, but recognition. I cry because I
have the feeling, and I know "they" are there.

—WOUNYE' WASTE' WIN: *Good Lifeways*
Woman, Lakota[1]

If we look back far enough, we see that most cultures in the world had
something similar to what in English is called a shaman, a specialist in
communication with the spirit realm. Common threads in the fabric of
shamanism everywhere in the world include the belief that an ordered
spirit world exists, that all in creation, including man, have a soul that
lives after death, and that communication with these spirits—plant, animal, and human—provides important information to the living. All remaining forms of shamanism, which has also been called "the original
religion" and "the world's first and oldest religion," share certain ideas.
All shamans believe that through drugs, specialized ritual, self-denial, or
a combination of these a sacred altar can be created, a mysterious place
and time in which direct communication with the spirit realm can be accomplished.[2] In Latin this is called an *axis mundi,* or a central axis to the
universe, where the various layers or dimensions of creation and reality
are brought close together.

In some parts of the world shamanism remains a major force in the daily practices and beliefs of aboriginal peoples. In the Americas, Europe, Asia, and Africa, the hints of ancient shamanism remain in artifacts, cave paintings, and even regional variations of major religious denominations. Halloween is a good example of this blend of the Christian with the pre-Christian in our own Euro-American culture. The spirits of the dead—skeletons and ghosts, our ancestors by impersonation—come back on this special day to beg for their share of the harvest. The day is still celebrated, complete with the admonition of the spirits to abide by the ancient policy "trick or treat."

Sensing and Understanding the Sacred

The Sun Dance, in some form or other, is virtually universal to tribes on the northern plains. It is a ceremony in which men and women pledge one to four days of abstinence from food and water. They dance in the hot sun from morning until dark, even throughout the chilly night. Among the Lakota, the dancers may further vow to be staked through the skin of their chest or back to the Sun Dance tree (the stakes and cords representing human ignorance), or they may drag a buffalo skull or offer small pieces of flesh from their upper arm. These flesh offerings from the upper arm are generally a sacrifice made by women, although men may make it as well. The Cheyenne and Crow do not include flesh offerings in their Sun Dance.[3] Suffering is a vital part of a successful Sun Dance. If a few of the dancers are fortunate, they may collapse and experience a vision.

A vow is made a year before the dance in return for a spiritual favor or in petition for a favor, which may include such things as the healing of a sick family member or the safe delivery of a new child into the world. Although personal reasons for Sun Dancing vary, the community aspect of this ceremony is to pray for new life, that the (feminine) world might be green and bountiful with the male influence of rain. The outer arbor or shade of the Sun Dance lodge is round, made of pine or cottonwood boughs, or even plastic tarp, but always in the center is a tall cottonwood tree, specially selected by a party of male scouts, often including four virgins who count coup on the tree with sacred axes dipped in red earth paint to bless the tree. It is then cut, lowered to shoulder height, and carried back to the Sun Dance camp. Offerings, consisting of rawhide cutouts of a man and buffalo bull, as well as pieces of cloth into which tobacco has been tied, are tied into its upper boughs. These represent participating families' wishes for themselves and the collective world.

It is difficult to know how Plains Indians, whether Lakota, Cheyenne, or Crow, feel when they see the Sun Dance tree or attend a doctoring ceremony. To them the cottonwood tree is the cosmic tree, its limbs in the clouds, its spiritual roots spreading deep into Mother Earth and to the four directions. This tree is the center of the sacred universe during the ceremony.

Some anthropologists might say that is a procreative or phallic symbol. Certainly this is true in the sense that it is a central ceremony devoted to praying for the health and future generations of the people. This symbolic "fertility" is further enhanced by the rawhide cutouts of the man and buffalo bull tied into its branches of living green. The successful completion of the Sun Dance as a succession of smaller rituals including the selection and setting up of the tree, sweat lodges of purification, the specific songs, ritual gift giving, flesh offerings, and so on, in turn affects the people and their immediate future.[4]

Spiritual beliefs and definitions are also set in a specific language. This language then shapes symbolic concepts that are shared with those who speak that language. It is difficult in a book like this to translate spiritual languages, and the broad concepts they represent, from one language to another. It must be remembered that all conversations and scenes related by the tribal peoples in this book were experienced in that tribal language.

The symbols of the pipe, drum, sweet grass, eagle feathers, and parts of or representations of animals like buffalo, wolf, or elk carry deepseated, shared meaning acquired by Native Americans from birth. It is critical for the traveler into the world of medicine women to understand that Indian culture shares numerous internal symbols, concepts, and ideas that these people have been exposed to from the earliest stages of their life. As a Hopi friend wisely said, "Our children feel and hear the drum before birth." The drumbeat is likened to the heart of the people and, because it is useful in restoring vitality, remains a part of Lakota healing rites. The touch of an eagle feather carries a spiritual residue from the eagle that transmits a healing force. A dream of a bear might call a man or woman to be a healer or, more specifically, to become an herbalist. Of course, these dreams are not in English, or in symbols shared universally with the dominant society.

Each time a story is told in oral form only the intention, nuance, and mood of that rendering is captured. Each story retold during a cold winter night, whether from tribal tradition or family history, reflects what the teller wishes to highlight in that one telling. It is difficult if not impossible for those not raised within a culture to participate meaningfully in those ceremonies or understand them entirely. In the Indian community it is the shamans, the special holy men or women who understand and can interpret the deep meaning of these ceremonies because of their specialized training and ritual practice.

Power   As in all belief systems, faith in a spiritual reality beyond this physical world is essential. Plains Indians often speak of the "power" of their religion. "Power," in the modern, physical world, could be defined simply as the ability to get things done. Power has the same meaning for Plains Indian people in their perception of the spirit world. As Neva Standing Bear Paxton, a Lakota spiritual leader in the Denver native community, says, "When I am asked about my religion, I talk about being Episcopalian, but for my spirituality, I go with my Indian ways."

In this context Neva suggests that "religion," which to her is Episcopalian, is a system of thought and rituals that, though they may be concerned with salvation, are relatively powerless to affect changes in the conditions of this world, including the restoration of a person to physical health. When Neva wants to do this she turns to the old traditional Lakota system and its very different understanding of spiritual power.

Power may occur on any number of levels, from the power to sense danger to the power to call spirits into a ceremony to doctor a patient.

The manifestation of power can come through a shaman's diagnosis, "treatment," or prediction of the outcome of an illness. A modern shaman may address other problems, such as locating a missing person or solving family problems such as alcoholism. No matter what the problem may be, the holy person must accurately predict the future and tell the patient what is needed in order to achieve this cure or avoid future problems. This is risky business, and not only because it places the shaman or "soul" traveler in potential spiritual danger when he or she flies into the spirit realm to recall a lost aspect of the soul but also because the shaman may have to challenge the spirit helpers of a "witch" who has created this trouble for the patient. Eventually the shaman may diminish his or her own spiritual powers through a lifetime of use and dissipation. It is also treacherous in that the journey may take the shaman into a strange world of trials and danger where he or she may be hurt. It is also dangerous because in a tribal society the shaman's reputation rests on the accuracy of his or her "predictions." Positive results also reassure the faithful and remind them of the mysterious and tremendous powers of creation.

Shamanism   Many religious scholars believe man's primeval form of "spiritual contact" comes through some form of transformation in which a spirit takes over the body of the trained and initiated holy person or shaman. This transformation may be brought on by fasting or be drug-induced, or the practitioner may be catapulted into the sacred or entered by spirits through the use of ritual. With practice, the shaman may also achieve this state spontaneously. In this state, the shaman may, as in the following story related by Madonna Swan about a Bear spirit helper, acquire the posture, movement, and voice of another being.

> When I was eight years old, we went to the Fourth of July in Faith. My dad was going to take us to the rodeo. A real rodeo! We were all excited, but that time I had a real bad toothache and was really suffering with it. Dad had a car then, and I was lying in the back seat.
>
> I was too sick to go to the rodeo, and I was disappointed; I just cried. There was a woman from Bridger who was a good herb doctor. Her name was Mrs. Blue Hair, and she was a real, old-fashioned Indian woman. Mom saw Mrs. Blue Hair and her family camped not too far from us at the Faith Fair. Mom went to talk to Mrs. Blue Hair about my toothache. "Yes, I can help her, at least until she has it pulled or fixed. Lay her down on the cot in your wall tent then pull the flaps down. I'll be over in a minute."
>
> Soon Mom told me to get in the tent and pull the flaps down. "Why? What for?" I asked.
>
> "She is going to try and doctor that tooth so you can go the rodeo," Mom said. Mrs. Blue Hair came. First she sang and prayed in Indian with her hands outstretched to each direction. When she had finished the medicine song, she bent over me. She sounded like a bear was in her chest. Mrs. Blue Hair took some white powdered medicine from a little buckskin sack and rubbed it all over my tooth. It looked like chalk. When she was finished it hurt less. By the time the rodeo was ready to begin, my tooth was much better. So in a way it was Indian medicine that got me to my first rodeo! Robert Blue Hair, the old woman's son, had that gift until he died a few years ago.[5]

This communication or temporary possession by spirit helpers is done through what is called "shamanic transformation," in which shamans become ecstatic, literally "leave themselves," and, in a trance state, are infused with and take on the actual behavior and personality of the helper spirit, or enstatic, and go inside themselves to contact the spirit helper. In a milder form, the shamanic medium communicates with a spiritual visitor to the ritual altar or participates in "spirit flight" into the land of shadows and the spirits or across great distances in the physical world. These last two are the types of shamanistic transformation still primarily used by Plains Indian people. The following passage from Tanya Ward, a full-blood educator from Cheyenne River Reservation, speaks of the Lakota reality of soul travel:

I first met Mrs. Kills Enemy when I was five years old. I lived that summer with my grandmother, Nellie Hump, in Red Scaffold. My grandmother had a lot of visitors that summer. These people were called by relationship, not by name.

It was late afternoon when my grandmother began pitching another tent outside and moving furniture into the tent. It was a time of excitement. My grandmother used to sit outside and look either south, west, or east because these were the directions that the roads ran. My parents lived to the east, my cousins lived to the south, and my great-uncle, John Hump, and his family lived west.

Grandma used to say, "They are coming," and someone would arrive. She seemed to have a sense of people coming to visit. Soon there were many pots cooking, and the log house smelled of bread baking.

Grandma kept saying, "They are going to be here soon." I used to wonder in later years if my grandmother knew folks were coming because she received mail, or did she have one of the feelings once again. I used to ask her, "How do you know?"

She would say, *Slolwaye* [I just know].

It was near evening when a car drove up to the house. My grandmother ran outside to receive the guests. There were several people in the car, but only one woman emerged. She was of average height. I know this because Grandma Hump was very tall, and she stood over this woman. The visitor was stately in stature, and her skin was light in color. My grandmother was very dark because she was always outside. The woman wore a dark, long dress. On her head she wore a dark flowered scarf that was pulled over her face, making her face barely visible.

She came inside and took her shawl off, placing it on the back of a chair, along with her scarf. Her hair was shiny and black. It was braided in two braids, one on either side of her face. She sat down at the table and began looking around. She turned and looked at me and asked, "Who is this sitting on the bed?" My grandmother began explaining who my parents were and why I was there with her. Our Indian names were given first, then our English names.

The mysterious woman had a very good command of the English language because she stopped speaking Lakota for a moment and said, "You can call me Mrs. Kills Enemy." When she looked at me it was as though she could see right into my head and read my thoughts. It was a piercing look. I wasn't afraid of her, but she appeared as though people should be afraid of her. She invited me to sit beside her and eat with her. She asked me questions about how old I was, and "Are you in school?" "Do you have any brothers and sisters?"

I said no.

She said, "You will have a sister when you are older."

I asked her, "Why did you come?"

She said, "Your grandmother is ill. She is really sick, but she won't stay in bed. I came to get her well."

"How are you going to do that?" I asked.

"Well I am going to pray with the pipe and give her some medicine. When we have done that she will be well."

Then I said to her, "I didn't know Grandma was ill. How did you know my Grandma is ill?"

She replied, "I came to see her because I saw her in a dream, and I saw that she was sick." Much of what that woman and my Grandma Hump spoke of did not make any sense to me until recently. There were speaking about "mind travel" or "soul travel," and they could do it. Mrs. Kills Enemy struck me as someone different than anybody I had met. I think that she possessed special powers that made her different. To me as a child, it seemed that she exuded an aura of mystery. This was my first impression of Mrs. Kills Enemy. She was a very different person. She created a feeling in me that is very hard even yet to describe.

For traditional practitioners, these journeys are undertaken only under the most dire circumstances and are thought to be very dangerous. This power may also be perceived as finite. When it is expended, so, in a sense, is the life force of the holy person who possesses the power. The Lakota believe that prayers or ceremonies used to *Hgmuga,* to intentionally hurt others (using black magic or witchcraft), may actually result in damage and destruction to the family of the holy person who loosed these powers.

Danger for a shaman may include the pollution, weakening, or complete loss of their own life force, of their very soul. The shaman may be judged finished or in decline if he or she has serious health problems. Holy people in this situation are even avoided altogether. It is not uncommon, then, for holy people to feel abandoned at the end of their lives. When he was dying of cancer of the spine, Chauncey Dupris, a Minnecojou Lakota holy man, said, "When they need to be doctored they come and get me, any time day or night. Now that I am sick, no one comes over here to doctor me. There is no rest for me, no retirement until I pass from this earth."

The Shaman's Role in a Tribal World

That man can successfully communicate with the spirit realm was not foreign to the ancestors of most people of the world, including Euro-Americans. Despite the spread of the Holy Roman Empire and Catholicism across Europe, much remains of older beliefs. Shrines and votive candles are still used in the Catholic church by the faithful seeking the divine intercession of a patron saint. In Ireland, offering cloths are still left at special springs.[6]

All practitioners and followers of shamanic traditions share the belief that the soul has multiple aspects and that spirit flight is possible while the living body is left behind. Most share the idea that it is the shaman who helps maintain a spiritual equilibrium in the human world and in man's relationships with the spirit, plant, and animal worlds.

The shaman must be familiar with the often treacherous journey to the world of spirits and be skilled at interpreting their messengers. He or she must be able to construct an *axis mundi,* or altar, and, through ritual, journey to the spirit world at will or be able to "hear" the spirit messengers who journey to this side of the veil. The shaman must then interpret sacred information to the patient, the patient's family, or, on some occasions, the community.

Lakota call this altar the *Hocoka.* In all shamanic religions, the common people believe that the shaman is the receptacle and fountain of sacred knowledge for the community. The shaman is also the source of sacred songs, art, philosophy, and ritual. The shaman is thus shaped by his or her unique tribal tradition but also, in turn, continues to shape the ongoing tradition through the eventual sharing of their own rituals, songs, and sacred experiences with apprentices.[7] All traditions, even ceremonies of shamanism, are vital and, as living things, must help the people in the times and conditions in which they live. There are, for instance, no buffalo hunts today; thus some of the rituals used to speak with the buffalo nation have been lost as modern shamans deal with the problems of modern tribal people.

Tribal groups differ in how the shaman is selected, but the belief that these people are exceptional is universal.

<u>Wiyan Wakon</u>: Holy Women

Women appear in critical roles in the creation stories of Plains Indian people as both "positive" and "negative" characters. Some had the capability to be both. These people accepted and honored the female side of creation in all its manifestations.

Among Plains Indians, special people receive messages of "divine selection" through their dreams to a calling as a healer. Because men and women are equally capable of sacred, profound, and complex dreams, the elevation of a lay woman to holy woman is always possible.

The Northern Plains Indians were subsistence hunters who gathered plants for medicine and food and intercepted the great migrations of buffalo and elk. Winter snows, drought, changing animal migration patterns, tornadoes, disease, and occasional starvation were facts of life. The successful interaction with the creator and the spiritual forces of the natural world helped the humans to survive.

Through their dreams and visions, certain men and women could predict changes in weather or even, with the proper prayers, change threatening weather. Movements of animals like the buffalo were predicted or even guided by proper communication between the humans and the spirits of the animals they relied upon for food. Special people who had dreams of these animals became sacred interpreters and petitioners to these animal grandfather spirits. They became shamans.

Beyond the childbearing years—beyond menopause—is when many opportunities for spiritual service to their people open up for Lakota women, including the central one here, the calling to help those who are suffering. Whatever the woman's calling—to doctor through the spirit or with herbs, or to prophesy—this is when her powers become manifest, mature. It is the point in life into which all the women healers in this book, living and dead, passed before they became holy women. The dreams may have begun earlier, as might apprenticeship in the ritual ways, but fulfillment was virtually always postponed until the woman was beyond childbearing, and her awesome female powers had mellowed.

Like men, Plains Indian women may be called to a number of distinct if occasionally overlapping roles in the spiritual service of their people. The term *holy woman* is as vague as is the term *healer.* Native terms are much more complex and numerous than clichés like "medicine man." Understanding these names in the context of Indian people and the language they come from is critical to an accurate understanding of the approach and role of the holy woman in her contact with the realm of spirits.

Ihan'bla: To Dream

Plains Indian children raised close to tradition learn to listen to and interpret the dream world, which is the lasting and sacred world. The ability to acquire the clear memory of dreams, to discriminate between significant and insignificant dreams, to remember them in detail, and to interpret them satisfactorily must be acquired in childhood. The amount of time it takes to interpret or understand a dream might be moments, or it might be a lifetime. Most of the traditional crafts of Plains Indian women are tedious and repetitive, leaving a great amount of time for reflection and contemplation. Both men and women use dreams to learn about the sacred world. For some it is a lifetime of exploration and learning the truths of the universe.

Some women in their special capacity as "dreamers" are called upon, by the clarity and regularity of their dreams, to warn people of impending problems and to predict and possibly alter the outcome of events by understanding what their dreams are about. The dream of a buffalo might cause the dreamer to feed the people as the buffalo does, for example. Dreams of lightning might call upon the dreamer to put on a *Heyoka* (Clown Dance) in which the flesh of dogs is used to restore the dreamer to his or her old self and extend health to the sick and elderly. A tribal culture's notion that dreams themselves can hold tremendous power to affect the dreamer and perhaps his or her family or community as well gives dreams this central significance in daily life.

Other dreamers may be called upon to start a society, or act out in public ritual, their *ihan bla'* (dreams), such as the performances of Elk Dreamers or *Heyoka* (Thunder Dreamers), or perhaps to lead a ceremony such as a Sun Dance. Only a few women are selected by their spirit dreams to be medicine women or holy women. Dreaming of certain spirits may call women to a variety of specific vocations or talents.

In the nineteenth century, before the reservation system began to alter the traditional social fabric, young women were invited by older women to join craft societies related to the spirits they dreamed about, such as the quillwork societies, or lodge sewing societies. All women, however, were and still are expected to be aware of cultural ideas and values that command respect in the eyes of the community. After the turn of the nineteenth century these craft and dream societies began to die slowly with the passing of members. Although these societies no longer exist, many of the beliefs and attitudes about dreams and spiritually derived talent for traditional crafts remain. This is certainly true of porcupine quillworkers. This art form, perhaps even more so than in the past, is considered sacred.

Women who become "doctors" are in essence no different from any other woman in the community except that they have an additional role to fulfill. It is important to realize that they are not considered strange or necessarily exceptional. Though the power of their ceremonies may command deep respect, in most instances their roles in family and community life are the same as those of other women.

> *They [other women] didn't know how [to deliver their own families' babies], so they were very afraid. So when they came after me I would go and do it.*
>
> —LOUISE PLENTY HOLES, Oglala, Lakota midwife

Wapiye': To Work with Spirits

In Lakota, *wapiye'* means to doctor or conjure the sick. Both men and women can *wapiye'* the sick. Even a *Wasicun Wakan* (literally, "mysterious white man," or physician) has this ability. It is important to point out that the "doctor" in a sense falls outside the central religious world of the common people.[8] Most Lakota will attend a doctoring ceremony in their life, but very few will conduct them.

Among the Lakota there are seven central religious rites that may be used by the *Ikce'* (common) man or woman as they progress from the beginning of their earthly journey to its end. These are the *Inipi,* or Sweat Lodge; *Tapa Wankayeyapi,* or the Tossing of the Sacred Ball; *Isnati Ca Lowan,* or Women's Coming of Age; *Hanble'ceya,* or Fasting for a Vision; *Hunkapi,* or the Making of Relations; *Wanagi'Yu hapi,* or the Keeping and Releasing of the Soul; and the *Wi Wanyang Wacipi,* or Sun Dance.[9]

Two of these, the Keeping and Releasing of the Soul, and the Tossing of the Sacred Ball, are no longer, or only rarely used. Some of the functions and spirit of the Keeping and Releasing of the Soul have generally been incorporated into modern memorial feasts. To be useful to the faithful, ceremonies must be alive to the needs of the people. Ceremonies have actually come and gone, incorporated into the needs of the times, whereas core beliefs have remained fairly constant, allowing these systems to remain meaningful without the dogmatic structures found in many other religions.[10]

The calling to doctor, and the ceremonies associated with healing, form a distinct and exceptional vocation. There are three types of ceremonies that involve doctoring. These are the *Lowanpi* ceremony, or "Sing"; the *Yuwipi,* or "they tie them up" ceremony; and a less formal, more idiomatic or generalized *Wapiye'* ceremony used by many of the holy women who also are herbalists and may choose this as expedient depending on the nature of the illness and the complexity of putting on either a *Lowanpi* or a *Yuwipi.* A woman who uses the *Lowanpi* ceremony would not likely use the *Yuwipi* ceremony, or vice versa, for certain spirit helpers dictate the type of ceremony to be held. Some women may have a variety of spirit helpers, and the patient's problem or illness may prescribe the details of the ceremony and the specific spirits to be called upon.

A fourth method of doctoring involves no ritual at all, and the women who practice it are thought of as *Pejuta Win,* or herb women doctors, and heal the sick principally by means of traditional pharmaceuticals. The plants used as remedies may need special songs learned in dreams to unleash their healing power; without the songs they are just plants.

Some women's dreams call upon them, depending on the needs of the patient, to utilize one or more of these methods. All are *wapi'yekiya,* using Indian medicine; and in today's parlance they are also Pipe Carriers—literally, followers of the old religion in that they generally own and use a prayer pipe not only to pray but also as a physical representation or symbol of their participation in the pre-Christian religion.

All *wapi'yekiya* (Indian medical practitioners) make or apply medicine. In the Native American context medicine can be an herb taken orally, the touch of a spirit or a feather, a sacred song, or even a handshake.

The differences in curative methods lie in the belief about what causes disease. In the Western world, disease has rational, scientifically provable causes. These pathogens include viruses, bacteria, old age, cancer, inherited defects, and accidents. In the Western medical model we may speak of stress or depression as a source of illness, and even accept that depression can cause sickness and possibly that some ailments may be psychosomatic, or caused by the mind.

Many Westerners, in their devotion to science, do not accept that illness may stem from a problem of the soul, or one of its parts. Yet this belief is at the essence of fully half of the Lakota belief about illness. The health and well-being of the soul, even after death, is a primary concern and the motivation for much of the ongoing ritual life of plains Indian people.

Wapiye' Win: Spirit-Calling Woman

A *Wapiye' Win* (ghost- or spirit-calling woman) holy woman is someone with a special vocation. She is someone who knows how to access the sacred—who, through the use of spirit helpers, or direct flight into the spiritual realm, receives important information about the problem at hand and how it might be remedied.

Madonna Swan passed away in October of 1992. Her memory, intelligence, and knowledge of Lakota culture made her a natural person to ask about holy women. On a snowy, late October visit to her home in Eagle Butte, South Dakota, it seemed to me that Madonna's gestures and eyes told us "Ask now, I won't be here much longer." Here, in part, is what she said on that last evening we spent with her:

In 1958 we went to Kyle. I had heard of a woman there who was said to be very good at curing the sick. I had been having trouble breathing. At a certain time every year it would become like pneumonia. The woman's name was Louise Kills Enemy.

In 1958 I got sick again, so I went down there to Kyle with Marceline Swan, Charles Little Shield, and Mary Swan. I wanted to be doctored, to see if I could keep from catching this cold.

She had the ceremony in a house. All the windows and doors were covered. There were four others to be doctored as well. And I think also at that time there was a young man that was going to *Hanble'ceya* [Fast for a Vision].

She told me, "Whoever is going to doctor you is going to come in from the south, so when you go in, face south." Then the ceremony began. All the people came in, and the singers, male singers, came in and sat down. She handed me a pipe and said, "They [the spirits] will try to take it away from you. Don't let them."

Mrs. Kills Enemy sat inside her altar. It had four direction colors (red, yellow, black, and white) on tall staffs in each corner. The whole altar was surrounded with tobacco ties [tiny sacks of tobacco linked by light string], and in the middle was a sand painting. They bolted the doors and windows. She sat in the middle of her altar with her head down. It seemed as if she were talking to someone all the time. I guess that's what you call *Lowanpi*.

After they blew all the lights out, the singers sang a spirit song. Then she said, "First the Black-Tail Deer will come in. He's going to walk around the room to the left. If he stops and does not go completely around the room, that's no good; someone in that house [a patient] is going to die. If he circles the room and goes out, that's good, because all the patients are going to live." Pretty soon that deer spirit came in, and you could just hear his hooves and hear him snort. Mrs. Kills Enemy said, "It's good! He went all the way around."

She doctored the patients one at a time. When it was my turn she said in Indian, "You need air, so an Eagle is going to come in from the south; don't be frightened. You will feel the Eagle's wind; it's wind above you. When you feel that, breathe deeply."

Pretty soon this thing flew in from the south. I could hear it coming. All the air came over me. She said in Indian, "Whenever he flies over you and makes that wind, try to breathe it." He came in over me four times, and each time I tried to breathe in.

Then she said, "Next, the White Owl is going to come. He has lots of air, too." And here they were, singing, and those owls came in over me like that. Ooh, it was just scary, too. Like the eagle, the owl came in four times and made a noise each time, and then went out.

When the kerosene lights were put on, she told me, "You won't get sick anymore. You will be able to fight off infection." After that I never did get that again. I was cured. I imagine she was about sixty then.

What Madonna gave us is absolutely singular in the literature about Lakota women. Louise Kills Enemy's type of ritual is called a *Lowanpi,* or "sing," and it identically follows the patterns and practices that a male *Lowanpi* priest would use.

. . .

Mrs. Kills Enemy's ceremony included a Deer, an Owl, and an Eagle spirit helper and her own retinue of male singers. Her *Hocoka,* or altar, contained a border of cloth tobacco ties. Four thin wooden staffs stood at the corners, from which hung sacred colored flags, one for each direction, each of the four winds. In the center was a sand painting, consisting of a simple disk of sand, onto which was drawn a sacred design whose meaning was known only to her. Her "claim" as "one who could sit at the altar" was justified; the prognosis was fulfilled. She is the same Mrs. Kills Enemy whom Tanya Ward recalled for us.

Today, the help most often sought is from a *Wapiye' Win* (ghost- or spirit-calling woman) and is for a spiritual remedy.

<u>Pejuta Win</u>: Herb Woman

There is some overlap today, and perhaps always has been, between the role of holy woman, *Wapiye' Win (Wapi' ya* means to conjure the sick in the Indian way), and that of medicine woman, *Pejuta Win,* wherein the holy woman's rituals involve the contact with the sacred but may also include administering a traditional medicine as well, hence the term *Pejuta Win* (medicine or herbal woman), or, literally, a "woman who uses herbs." Only certain women used both, but both are considered *Wapi' yekiya,* using Indian medicine to *wapi' yechi,* or make someone sound or well, to bring them back into balance or harmony.[11]

Mrs. Dora Brown Bull related the following story about her son and a medicine woman from Kyle, named Millie Lays Hard:

> When Vernal [now in his fifties] was a little boy, about one and a half or two years old, he got real sick. My mom and I weren't sure what was wrong with him. He almost died. He got real skinny. He couldn't gain any weight, so finally Mom brought Mrs. Lays Hard back. She made some tea out of a root. She told us to give him this tea until it was all gone.
>
> When we got done covering all the windows, she got a sheet and wrapped herself in it from her head to her feet. Then the lights were put out, and she was placed at her altar. Then she went from one end of room to the other, making owl noises. Mom held Vernal during the ceremony.
>
> When she was all done, she told my mom and me that Vernal's grandfather's spirit had been trying to get him and take him to the spirit world. And that's why he was getting sick. Mrs. Lays Hard said she took care of it and told us not to worry about it anymore.

Mrs. Lays Hard was paid with Bull Durham [sacks of tobacco]. This took place about 1939. The lady at that time was in her late sixties. She was said to be a *Wanagi Wapiye'* [using the spirit to heal].

Although on our last visit Madonna seemed very weak, it was obvious that she wanted to talk, perhaps to distract her from her knowledge of impending death. Many years before, tuberculosis had claimed one of her lungs and half of another. Numerous bouts with pneumonia had weakened her remaining lung, and she had spent twenty years living on oxygen. Still, she had long outlived all the medical doctors' most hopeful expectations. That night she joked, "This time the doctors gave me only six months, . . . but I'm already into my seventh. They've been wrong before." But somehow it seemed to me that she knew her time was close, and she died one week after our visit. Madonna recalled for us her mother, Lucy's, experience with a *Pejuta Win,* a medicine or herb woman:

There was another medicine woman from Kyle; her name was Mrs. Emily Hunter. She was an *iyeska* [mixed-blood]. She was a very quiet lady, and she doctored in that manner. She would come in, and whoever was going to be doctored, she made them lie down and covered them with a cloth.

My mom was sick. At that time [late 1930s] we were living in Bridger, and Mom got so sick she couldn't get out of bed. Dad went after Mrs. Hunter, and they brought her back. Mom's stomach was hurting her. "I'll be well soon," she kept saying, but she didn't get well.

So they brought Mrs. Hunter back. "What's wrong with you?" she asked in Indian. Mom told her, and she said, "No, that's not where it hurts you." She said she had to have some kind of root, so Dad and them went out looking for it. They had to use a flashlight because it was at night.

Soon they brought back that root. Mrs. Hunter made a tea out of the center part of it. She made a big pot of tea out of that. She said to drink it, and she said, "If that doesn't work, we'll have to try something else." About four in the morning Mom went out and went to the bathroom. Mrs. Hunter said, "You see, she had a kidney infection." So Mom had passed her first water in days, and Mrs. Hunter had cured her.

That Mrs. Hunter was a half-breed, and she was light-complected. She spoke only in Indian, and she was from Kyle.[12]

There were also women who doctored without ritual, who cured the sick primarily by using physical remedies like Mrs. Hunter used on Madonna's mother, Lucy. These treatments might have been revealed to them in dreams or even passed down from one generation to the next.

The following story is from Jesse James, Jr., an Oglala/Creek who told us of his grandmother, a former wife of Crazy Horse.

> My grandmother, Mrs. Laravie, treated her grandmother for cataracts. She took cottonwood bark and burned it in a very hot fire until it was just a fine white powder. She took that powder and put it in her grandmother's eyes. The old woman's eyes swelled shut. In four or five days, her eyes opened, and that cataract was cracking, breaking up, and she could see again. She didn't have a ceremony; she just knew about these things and did them. As Grandma told me this story, she laughed easily, her eyes were alive with faith.

The knowledge of traditional herbs is shrinking. The total number of *Pejuta Win,* herbalists who have learned how to gather, prepare, and administer herbs is very small, perhaps no more than one or two on any reservation. Thus, the number of herbs, including roots in common use, has also declined, but the use of *sinkpe' tawote'* (sweet flag root) for colds and sore throats, various berries and teas as diuretics, and braided *wacanga* (sweet grass) as a spiritual fumigant is very common. Many people have their own "traditional" remedies for adult-onset diabetes, which has become epidemic in the Indian population. Often these include a tea to which certain kinds of *Peji hota* (sage) might be added.

Modern tribal people live in what we might call a cultural continuum. This imaginary curve would, at one end, include the practices and beliefs of the most traditional full-blood, who speaks the language, lives in accordance with the old religious obligations, and maintains an extensive set of relations and family responsibilities. On the other end of the spectrum would be the mixed-blood who may not look Indian and who, as the full-bloods believe, "is Indian only when there is some monetary benefit to it." Most modern Indian people inhabit an area that lies between these two extremes. Day-to-day life is a blend of very old and very new. Jackie Yellow Tail, a Crow woman, said it well:

> *Sometimes I feel like I'm running through this world with a jogging shoe on one foot and a moccasin on the other.*

Modern Holy Women

Plains Indian men and women are aware of an oral legacy of holy men and women unknown to outsiders. Memories of ancestors and their spiritual accomplishments are combined with personal experience to shape a view of the spiritual present. Holy women who were ancestors continuously came to light during the two years of our journey. No matter what household we visited, stories of medicine women emerged.

We have known Roberta (Deer with Horns) Wolf for many years, but until now she did not think to share her memories of her own grandmother. Tilda and I sat up talking with her and Ted, her husband, late one evening, telling them about the long research trip we had been on, when she said,

> You know, my grandmother was that way, a medicine woman. Her name was Alice Deer with Horns. She was *O'ohenunpa* [Two Kettle], from near Laplante, South Dakota. I remember that she used to send us little ones outside when she wanted to pray. One time I peeked in at her. I was about eight years old. Even though I was behind her she noticed me and said, "Okay, you can stay, but you must sit perfectly still and be quiet. Don't say a word."
>
> She had all her things spread out on the floor. It was a long time ago, but I remember she had many little sacks with herbs in them, her pipe, and a little wooden bowl with *wasna* [crushed, dried deer meat] in it; there were many things. She smudged all those things with sweetgrass. Then she sang and loaded her pipe. Then she prayed.
>
> When she was done praying she smoked her pipe, and then she touched it to my lips. Later I asked her why she did this, and she said it was a more powerful way to pray. She was going to teach her ways to my oldest sister, but my sister died of diabetes when she was sixteen. When my grandmother died, my mother burned her medicine bundle. I don't know why she did that, but she did.

For the tribal peoples of this land, this balancing between two worlds can be very precarious, both spiritually and physically. What many of today's medicine men and women do most is help people who are "injured" by living as a colonized tribal people. In effect, they doctor depression, lack of positive identity, suicidal behavior, drug abuse, alcoholism, family crises, spouse abuse, and stress-related illnesses that are effects of colonization. They also doctor "standard" types of illnesses such as cancer as well, but most "obvious" problems are left to run their course or are treated by a white physician.

Popular American culture loves to borrow things from American Indians. Although it is possible that such "ceremonies" as Indian drumming and sweat baths help people to get back in touch with the natural world, they are imperfectly lifted from a continuum of religious ceremonies that carry Plains Indians from birth, through life's struggles, to death and beyond.

To understand, at any level, the meaning of these ceremonies and their relationship to the religions from which they are borrowed requires a fairly deep understanding of their true cultural context, which includes knowing those mythic stories of creation, ancient gods, and tricksters that are used to shape and teach the young in the Indian world. We must understand and, as much as we can, share a context acquired by the Indian person over a lifetime, presented here in just a few pages. These include Lakota ideas about creation and the birth of their spirit world, their ideas about life and death, their dreams and everyday life.

A seeker of spiritual understanding would not be able to understand Judaism, and the beliefs and ceremonies that go with it, without reading the Old Testament. We must understand the origin of the metaphors acted out in the ritual, to understand the place and use of that ritual within that particular belief system. For Indian people, the beginning is told in their own unique tribal creation stories.

2

All That Is, Set in Motion

With a visible breath I am walking;
I am walking toward a buffalo nation,
And my voice is loud.
With a visible breath I am walking;
I am walking toward this sacred object.

—SACRED CALF PIPE
WOMAN

Children in the nineteenth century heard stories about the origins of their people and ways of life many times from before they could speak, until and even after they became adults. They had years to absorb the subtleties and nuances of these stories. These stories are the skeletons upon which the flesh of understanding is hung. They form the basis of Lakota society and spiritual practices. To understand how Lakota people view the spiritual world it is necessary to share in their oldest stories just as they did as children, and to start at the beginning:

LAKOTA CREATION STORY

Iyan, the rock, existed in a void; it was dark and lonely there. Iyan wished to create something other, so that he would not be lonely and so that he could have some power over something other than himself. He pierced himself, and his blood, which was blue, flowed out until he was shriveled, hard, and powerless. What came from him formed *Maka Ina* [Mother Earth]. The blue also formed the oceans, but the released powers could not reside in the water, so they formed the blue sky dome and called it *Mahpiyato* [blue sky].

The energy given up by the rock, now hard and powerless, is *Taku Skan Skan,* that which moves all things. This power was now diffused into the female earth, the male sky, and the waters.

Sky, *Mahpiyato,* creates *Anpetu Wi,* the Sun of the day, and *Hanhepi Wi,* the Sun of the night, or Moon, to share his world with him. They marry, and there is constant daylight. He creates *Tate',* the father or "chief" of all winds.

Created next are the *Pte' Oyate',* humans who live under the ground. They are created to serve the gods. They are called the *Pte' Oyate'* or Buffalo Nation; they became us, the Lakota. Their chief is *Wazi* [Old Man], and his wife is *Wakanka* [Old Woman].

They have a daughter, *Ite'* [face], who grows up to be the most beautiful of the Ikce' people. Ite' is admired by Tate', the Wind, and eventually marries him. Wakanka is not satisfied that her daughter is married to a god, Tate', and that her children are the four winds. She wishes her beautiful child to be married to Wi, the Sun. She wishes for herself, her husband, and her daughter to have the power of gods and conspires with Iktomi, the Spider [trickster], to get what she wants.

He promises to help them, if they help him in his plan to make people look ridiculous forever. Iktomi tells Wi that he should have a feast to show everyone how proud he is of the Pte' woman Ite'. He then helps Wakanka construct a magic charm for Ite', so she will soon become so beautiful that it will make Wi fall in love with her human daughter.

Later, Iktomi sees Hanhepi, clothed in all her beauty, heading towards the feast. He tells her that Ite' has been invited and that she has made for herself a special dress. He encourages the Moon to return to her lodge and put on a more beautiful dress. Afraid to be embarrassed by a mere human, she agrees.

According to Iktomi's plan, this puts Ite' at the feast of the gods before the Moon. Iktomi tells her that the empty seat beside Wi is for her, and she sits down next to the Sun. Then Wi, the Sun, takes one look at her and falls in love. Soon Hanhepi arrives to find her husband staring longingly at Ite', a mere human. Ite' sits with Wi, ignoring her own husband, Tate', the Wind. The Moon is shamefaced and storms off.

Angered, Mahpiyato, the Sky, calls the spirits together and punishes them for their foolishness. He banishes Ite' to the earth, making one side of her face forever ugly, and tells her, "From now on you will be known as *Anukite'*, Double-Faced Woman!" She is pregnant by Tate' with their fifth child. Because of her mischief, *Yumni,* Whirlwind, is born playful and childlike. He will never grow up. Sky sends Wakanka and Wazi to the far edges of the world, where they will wander forever. Tate' is given custody of all five "wind" children and sent to the face of the earth, where he is to await a messenger, who will be *Whope',* daughter of Mahpiyato himself.

Wi is told that because of his betrayal he will never see his wife again. Hanhepi is told that because of her shame, she will constantly turn her back on her husband and will never look at him directly again. This begins the second time, night, and initiates the day-night cycle, and the third time, the "changing moon" or months.

Over time, Anukite' comes to be lonely for her Ikce' or human nation. In spite of Mahpiyato's admonition that she never reside with her people, she begins to scheme. Drawn both by her desires and by his own for a little mischief is Iktomi, also banished to earth for his part at the great feast. He is tired of teasing the animals and wishes to have more fun, if only he and Anukite' can entice the *Pte' Oyate'* [humans] to the surface of the world. They decide that the smell of freshly roasted buffalo meat will entice them out of their cave. Anukite' kills a buffalo, prepares the meat, and decorates the tanned robe with the quills of the porcupine.

Iktomi changes his form to that of a wolf and, with the wondrous tanned and quilled robe of the buffalo and some roasted meat, heads for the cave known to connect the surface world with the underworld. He will leave the buffalo robe and meat near the entrance to entice the Ikce' people to the surface.

Tokahe' [First Man], chief of the Pte' Oyate', or Buffalo Nation, asks the spider to lead them to the surface world, where he finds the wondrous gifts and brings them back underground and shows them to the People. Six men and six women are convinced that Tokahe' has found a better place to live and follow him and his wife to the surface. Here they become the ancestors of the *Oceti Sagowin* [Seven Fire Places] that make up the Lakota, Dakota, and Nakota peoples—the People who are today called Sioux by the whites.

Soon the seasons changed, and the People wished to escape the cold that was sent by North Wind to torture them. They searched for the cave entrance but could not find it. Tokahe', no longer Pte' People but now only *Ikce Oyate'* [Common People], became frightened and ashamed; he cried for help. Wazi, now called "the Wizard," and his wife, Wakanka, now known as "the Witch" because of her ability to predict the future, will take pity on the humans, teaching them many things that they will need to know to live on this changing earth. Thus the people learned to make their homes on earth. (Originally told to Mark St. Pierre by Colleen Cutshall, Lakota artist and educator.)

A Female Messiah

In Western—and, in fact, most Eastern—traditions, men are not only the central characters in creation stories but also millennial transition characters like Mohammed, Buddha, and Jesus. These male avatars, incarnations of the sacred, come along and transform the belief system.

For the Lakota of the mid eighteenth century, recently displaced from their woodlands home of the Great Lakes to the endless and treeless prairie by the Chippewa, whom the French had armed, life was hard and full of new challenges. Without the plants and animals they had come to rely on, the people were poor and hungry, both physically and spiritually. Changes in their worldview were necessary if they were to survive. During this difficult time of transition from woodlands to high plains life, a "messiah" appeared in the guise of a woman.

In Lakota belief, Whope' (Falling Star), the daughter of Mahpiyato (also called Sky), reappeared before the Lakota as the Sacred Calf Pipe Woman. I first heard this story in 1971, from the late Manuel Red Bear, a Hunkpapa/Itazipco, while living in Bear Creek, an Itazipco (Sans Arc) village on the northern part of the Cheyenne River Reservation near the Moreau River in Northwestern South Dakota. He was, without my knowing it, taking me to Green Grass, also an Itazipco village on the Moreau River, and the permanent home of the Lakota "Holy of Holies," the Sacred Calf Pipe Bundle.

I am going to take you to a very special place, and as we drive there, I am going to tell you why it is so special to us Lakota. . . .

A long time ago, before the people had horses, the camp of Standing Walking Buffalo was having a hard time. Standing Walking Buffalo was from the Itazipco [Sans Arc, or bowless] band. They were hungry because the buffalo had not come near their village in a long time.

The chief sent out two young hunters to scout out the buffalo and return with news of where the buffalo were.

They had been out for some time and had walked a whole day's distance from the village. Far out on the prairie, one of the young men saw something moving. It was too far away to see it clearly. As they approached they could see that it was a very beautiful young woman. She had very long white hair, and it covered her naked body like a robe. In her hands she carried sage, and on her back was a bundle. The two men were amazed at finding a young woman so far from any village. One of the young men said that this must be a *Wakan Win* [sacred or mysterious woman] to be out here all alone. He turned his eyes away, because she was naked and obviously Wakon.

Now the beautiful young woman was very close. The other young man thought, "I will have *tawi'nton* [sex] with this woman. There is no one to protect her, and I will have my way with her."

The woman was a sacred woman, and she could read his thoughts. She said, "Come ahead and do with me whatever it is that is in your mind."

Immediately the man with bad thoughts went forward, and the woman lay down with him. As soon as they lay down a mist descended from the sky and covered both of them. The other man fell to his knees in amazement. The sounds of locusts came from that cloud, and when it lifted, the young woman was standing there unharmed, and all that was left of the bad man was his skeleton. Snakes slithered in his rib cage. Now the good man was very frightened.

The woman addressed him and said, "Do not be frightened; you are a good man, and you had good thoughts about me. To your village I will bring a sacred relic. Go now and tell them to prepare for me. I will come at first light with a great gift to make their lives easier."

The man ran back to his village, which was a long way away. When he got there the people asked where his friend was. He told them what had happened. The family of the bad young man asked what had happened. When he told them they were angry and accused the one who had returned of killing their son. Standing Walking Buffalo believed the young man and said, "Let us prepare for this woman and see if she comes as he said."

They prepared the village and put up a large council lodge in the center, covering the floor with sage. The next morning, very early, the camp crier announced that someone was approaching.

Across the prairie toward the camp came the beautiful woman. Only now she carried the large bundle in her arms. She seemed to be floating in a cloud. She sang a song as she approached:

> With a visible breath I am walking;
>   I am walking toward a buffalo nation,
>   And my voice is loud.
>   With a visible breath I am walking;
> I am walking toward this sacred object.

The people were all dressed in their finest buckskins. The men didn't look at her because she was naked, so a woman led her into the council lodge. They were so poor that all they had to offer her was water. She took it and drank it.

Next, she told the people that she had been sent from the Buffalo Nation. She gave them many instructions about how to live. She told them that she had brought them a sacred pipe. She also promised them that if they followed her advice and lived with respect for one another and followed the ceremonies they would always have plenty. She told the men how they were to live, how to do the Sun Dance, how to fast for a vision. She instructed them in the Sweat Bath, or Inikagapi, and the Taking of Relatives, or Hunkapi. She reminded them that they were to treat women with respect.

She taught the boy children how they were to live, and next the girl children. She told them to listen to their parents and lead good lives, not to have thoughts like the bad man.

Last, she addressed the women, telling them how to live, how to be good mothers and grandmothers. She told them it was their job to take care of the dead and taught them how to conduct the spirit-keeping ceremonies. She taught them how to remember her in the White Buffalo Calf [Coming of Age] ceremony and the Throwing of the Ball rite and how this would help the young women to have good lives.

Then she turned to Standing Walking Buffalo and said, "Your people, the Itazipco, are humble, and so I have honored them above the rest. It will be up to you and your descendants to take care of this Pipe." One of the men was jealous and wanted the Pipe; a fight broke out, and an ear was cut off in the fight. The White Buffalo Calf Maiden picked up the ear and attached it to the pipe stem. She told them this was to remind them of what jealousy does to people.

She stayed with the people for four days, teaching them many things. On the last day she lit the Pipe and, smoking it, offered it to the sky and then to the east, south, north, and west and then to Mother Earth. Next, she handed the Pipe to Standing Walking Buffalo and walked to the edge of the camp. She told them they could now look at her.

As she walked away she rolled on the ground like a buffalo and turned into a yellow buffalo for the east. Then she rolled and became a black buffalo for the south, then again she rolled on the prairie and became a red buffalo for the west, and finally she rolled again and turned into a white buffalo for the north and disappeared. That is the last the people saw of her, but we still have the Pipe, and it is still kept by the Sans Arcs in Green Grass, South Dakota. That is where I am taking you now.

This is the most powerful story in Lakota religious life. Many versions exist, but the core is always the same, involving bravery and long-suffering, generosity, humility, honesty, and respect for all things in creation. Each aspect of the story has meaning on many allegorical levels, including the woman's age, beauty, virginity, and apparent defenselessness, the death of the immoral hunter, and the respect shown to her in the camp of Standing Walking Buffalo. Other values taught or reinforced by her, such as industry, humility, proper parenting, and vanity, are still influencing Lakota belief and behavior.

These examples given by the Sacred Maiden are the essence of the Lakota personality. She brought, or altered, all the rituals that took the Lakota on the passages through life. All religions must do that—create meaningful passage through ritual, from one stage of life to another. For Lakota women, these stages correspond to those of Mother Earth herself: the rock age, the bow age, the fire age, and the pipe age. These four stages for humans are childhood, adolescence, adulthood, and old age. Reincarnation is one possibility for the Lakota after death, so it might be said that this cycle could "end" in rebirth, or that it never ends.

It is her sacred character that Lakota women are to emulate if they are to live a good and respected life. Whereas all agree that she exists, not all Lakota agree on who this person was. Some say she is a reincarnation of Whope' (the falling star), the beautiful one.

In an earlier epic legend central to concepts of Lakota life, she was sent by Mahpiyata, the Sky, to live with Tate', the Wind, and his five sons. When asked by Tate' who she was she said, "The Sun is my father, the Moon is my mother, and the stars are my people." Eventually she came to marry *Itokaġa,* the South Wind. In the lengthy stories about her stay with Tate', she in turn tests each of the males in the household as they try to win her hand in marriage. Yumni, the childlike Whirlwind, loves Whope' as a child loves a mother.

This is one scene from the story told by George Sword, an Oglala, to James R. Walker, a physician on Pine Ridge, at the turn of the century. Tate' had instructed his four normal sons that soon they would be sent out to stay permanently in one of the four directions, thus creating the fourth time, which we know as the seasons. Before they left, each stopped by to speak with Whope'.

"My sister, would you give me something to drink were I thirsty?" said Yumni.

"Little brother, you shall never be thirsty, and you shall never be cold, and while I am your sister you will always be merry. There are many places in the world where there is no water. When the directions are made, you can go to these places and dance upon them without thirst or weariness," she said.

"You tell of only good for that little one who can do no good for himself or for any other. I am the oldest, firstborn, and I am strong. I can travel far, and I can do much. I have the right to the first and the best of everything. You should give to me that which is good," said *Wazi yata* [North Wind].

"You have much to do, and I will help you doing it. When this work is done and there is the fourth time, then we will prepare for the future," she said.

Yata went and sat at his place, and Tate' said, "My son, it is the will of the Great Spirit that the oldest brother should counsel and lead his younger brothers and should be first in all things as long as he is worthy. But if he should be unworthy, then another brother may be chosen as the leading brother. You will soon begin with your brothers the work for which you came into being. You will lead this work, but remember that the Mysterious Beings are everywhere all the time, and if you prove to be unworthy, it may be that you will be displaced and one of your brothers given the first place. Prepare yourself well and do the work I have given you in the best manner that you can, and you will hold your place as the first of the brothers and have the first direction in all future references to the directions."

"I now care not so much for the directions as I do for Whope', and I wish her for my wife. Why not let my brothers make the directions and let me stay at the lodge and take her as my woman," said Wazi yata.

"The Great Spirit has willed that you do the work that I have given you to do. His will must be obeyed, and if you resist it, you will only bring upon yourself his displeasure. Then, when there is the fourth time, if Whope' is willing to be your woman, you may take her. If she is not willing, then, my son, beware of what you do," said Tate'.

When it was evening *Eya* came gently to the door and said, "Whope', I would always have you for my sister. This day I have gone and come as gently as the sun travels over the world. I have disturbed and broken nothing. You made me happy, and I will forever love you as my sister."

Yanpa strolled to his place, and Whope' said, "Yanpa, my brother, are you weary? Is there something I can do for you?"

"I am always tired and always hungry. I wish I were refreshed and had something to eat," said Yanpa.

Whope' took from her pouch a wisp of sweetgrass and gave it to him and said, "I would always have you for my brother, and as long as you regard me as your sister whenever you are tired or hungry, place sweetgrass on the burning coals, and the incense it makes will relieve you of your weariness and hunger. But when you forget me, you will be fretful and unpleasant to everyone. Remember that when the Mysterious Beings smell the incense of sweetgrass, they will be pleased and will give their help to you."

Itokaġa came and laid down the carcass of an antelope at the feet of Whope' but said nothing to her. She neither looked at him nor spoke to him. He sat at his place and gazed at the fire. Yata watched them and smiled. Eya watched them and rubbed his head.

When the three brothers were in the tipi, Okaga went and sat by the water. Long he sat and gazed at the stars. Then quietly he played on the flute and sang.

Yumni said, "Sister, I think you like music; when Okaga plays and sings you look very happy. When you smile as you are now smiling, you are very beautiful, and I love you very much."

"I love you very much, and I wish we could always hear that music," said Whope'.[1]

Tate' is a good and wise father setting challenges for his sons so that they may prove themselves. Wazi yata, North Wind, is boastful, selfish, demanding, mean, and too quarrelsome; Iwiyohiyanpata, East Wind, too lazy; and Wiyohipeyata, West Wind, too unsure of himself, suspicious and jealous. Okaga is chaste, humble, kindhearted, industrious, generous, honest, open, intelligent, and courageous. He has warmth and a sense of humor. Each wind is allegorical to the Lakota definition of a good man, and the lengthy stories serve to teach both boys and girls. Whope' ends up selecting Iyokaga, South Wind, as her husband, and Yumni resides with them forever.

In these most ancient of *Ohukankan* (creation myths), Whope' is the embodiment of feminine ideals. This is why the most common identity of the White Buffalo Calf Maiden is thought to be Whope'. The date of her arrival, recorded in numerous winter counts, is thought to be about 1780, a time of great crisis, hardship, and change in Lakota life. She then also symbolizes hope in a better future and survival of the People. Perhaps this is why, in these present hard times, her memory has become important once more.

Less orthodox believers think that she was the coming of the Virgin Mary to the Lakota; others do not wonder who the White Buffalo Calf Maiden was at all. It is important only that she did come and that her legacy lives on in the collective consciousness of the People, shaping modern beliefs and behavior.

The following passage, from the book *The Sacred Pipe,* gives further insight as to the importance of this sacred woman in Lakota thought and philosophy.

The *Winyan Wakon* (Mysterious or Holy Woman) touched the foot of the pipe to the round stone that lay upon the ground and said: "With this pipe you will be bound to all your relatives: your Grandfather and Father, your Grandmother and Mother. This round rock, which is made of the same red stone as the bowl of the pipe, your Father, *Wakan-Tanka,* has also given to you. It is the Earth, your Grandmother and Mother, and it is where you will live and increase. This Earth that he has given to you is red, and the two leggeds that live upon the earth are red; and the Great Spirit has also given to you a red day, and a red road. All of this is sacred, so do not forget! Every dawn as it comes is a holy event, and every day is holy, for the light comes from your father, Wakan-Tanka; and also you must always remember that the two leggeds and all the other peoples who stand upon this earth are sacred and should be treated as such.

From this time the holy pipe will stand upon this red earth, and the two leggeds will take the pipe and send their voices to Wakan-Tanka. These seven circles that you see on the stone have a meaning, for they represent the seven rites in which the pipe will be used. The first circle represents the first rite that I shall give to you, and the other six circles represent the rites which will be revealed to you directly.[2]

The White Buffalo Calf Maiden is, at the very least, a feminine messianic figure who helped the Lakota make the transformation from the woodlands of Minnesota onto the great plains. The sacred maiden either brought or changed the seven rituals used by the Lakota for their survival. Two rituals, the *Inipi* (Sweat Lodge) and the *Hanbleceya* (Crying for a Vision), existed before she came. She added a pipe ceremony to these. The new rituals were the *Wanagi Gluhapi* (the Keeping of the Soul), the *Isna Ti Ca Lowan* (First Menses, or Ceremony of Isolation), the *Hunkapi* (Making Relatives), the *Wiwanyag Wachapi* (Sun Dance), and the *Tapa Wanka Yap* (Throwing of the Ball).

The Sacred and Ritual Metaphor

Most Lakota ceremonies act out in dramatic physical metaphor patterns that were revealed to them by the very process of creation. All the spirits banished to earth continue to act out their basic natures. Anukite', who made the first quilled robe, continues to influence Lakota female artisans. She is still very dangerous to men and can influence women to be promiscuous as well as artistic. Iktomi is everywhere, sometimes appearing as a human, sometimes in another form, always ready to make fools of mankind.

The Lakota see themselves as *Unsika',* pitiful, and must *Wacekiya',* pray or cry to this mysterious constellation of powers for help if they are to survive on this earth as a distinct people. The interaction of humans with the sacred mystery is believed to be necessary for the continuation of all life, and that includes all the races on this earth. This is the very essence of Lakota and other Plains tribes' ceremonial life.

The word *Wakan-Tanka,* sometimes mistakenly translated as God, does not in fact refer to a character like Yahweh of the Old Testament, who is often given male characteristics, but instead means literally "the great mystery" and is a metaphor for the very mysterious forces that caused the universe to come into creation. It has aspects that reflect both male and female human traits. All of creation, the Rock, Four Winds, the Sky, Mother Earth, the Sun, Moon, Lightning, the Human, Buffalo, Bear, and Plant and Animal Nations are aspects of Wakon-Tonka. These are considered the good spirits.

Since all things in Plains Indian life are balanced between good and evil, so are the spirits. The Mysterious Beings, which may inhabit the land, water, and forest, are evil.

Each of these spirits, good or bad, has a "personality" and is capable of manifesting human qualities, such as fickleness. The changeable personality of these ancient spirit forces is often addressed in ceremonies or in prayers to change the weather to break a drought or protect the people from famine or flood, for instance, or perhaps cure a sick person.

Tunkasila, "grandfather," used in ritual prayers to address the spirits and may refer to one or *Tunkasilapi,* all of the spirits, including those that have existed since the very beginning of creation.

Lakota Ceremony

In the Winwanyag Wachapi, or Sun Dance, the four-day ritual brought to the people by the White Buffalo Calf Maiden, the Sun is honored, along with Maka Ina (Mother Earth), Tate' Tobe (the Four Winds), and Wakinyan (the Thunders), as the forces that will cause the continuation of all life on earth. They, with Mahpiyato (Blue Sky), bring forth the seminal *Maga ju* (rain), which impregnates Mother Earth with the feminine potential for new life and, through her bounty, nourishes and helps create new generations of plants, herbs, and animals that are harvested for the good health of the people. *Mni* (water) is essential and seen as connecting all life. It is viewed as having sacred powers of healing. Water is used in conjunction with almost all ceremonies as the most precious and basic of gifts. Thus Lakota People generally pray for only two basic things: *Wicozani na Wiconi Cage'* (health and generations). *Wa* (snow) is sent by the *Waziyata* (North Wind) to prepare and purify the earth for this sacred renewal of life.

As part of the Sun Dance altar, the buffalo skull painted with symbols of lightning, hail, or rain is used to represent a number of ritual metaphors including the Buffalo Nation (of which the Lakota consider themselves a part), the White Buffalo Calf Maiden, and the contract between man and the Great Mystery to "exchange prayer for sacred help," in the form of rain or food and shelter, provided by the buffalo.

A sacred woman selected for her good character sits near the sacred altar and fasts along with the dancers for the full four days. She represents the female side of creation. Generally she is past her childbearing years. The Sun Dance leader, or *Itancan*, is a person who has certain dreams that have led him or her to lead the dance. Each Sun Dance, and the details of ritual (e.g., when and how long the dancers will dance, what the arbor will look like, and so on), are dictated by the dreams of the Itancan. Because each Sun Dance leader falls back on his or her own dreams, the use of this sacred woman is not universal.

In the Cheyenne Sun Dance of the past and present, the woman is younger and literally acts out the procreative act with the Sun Dance instructor. Should a child be born of this union, it is considered a special child and a wondrous sign.[3]

Hunka Lowanpi: Making of Relatives It is not just the humans who may take each other for relations: it can also be the ritual joining of the souls of young humans with all of the Great Mystery, or creation—hence the most common of all Lakota prayers, and the one that follows all ritual acts, is *Mi' takuye' Oyasin,* literally, "I acknowledge everything in the universe as my relations."

Isna Ti Ca Lowan: Sing, or Ceremony of Isolation at First Menstruation (Girls' Puberty Rite) The "new woman" is instructed as to her responsibilities to her family and creation. The help of the White Buffalo Calf Maiden is called upon, including her legacy of wisdom, to ensure that this girl will be able to live up to these standards. This ceremony is so strongly related to Whope' that it is also known as the White Buffalo Ceremony. In the old days the material used to absorb menstrual blood was wrapped up and placed in the branches of a plum tree to keep it from the schemes of Iktomi, the trickster.[4]

Ini kagapi: Sweat Lodge Water is placed on hot rocks; thus once again the power of Iyan (the rock, the first physical being) is released in the form of steam, or *Taku S'kan s'kan* (the original energy in all things), taking the faithful back to the beginning of time.

In the sweat lodge, as in all Lakota ceremonies, the wisdom and help of the four directions—winds—are called upon by name for help and wisdom. *Mi' takuye' Oya' s'in* is uttered at various times during the sweat, reinforcing the idea that through the mysterious act of creation all things in the world are permanently related, as is a human family.

It is said the sweat lodge itself is formed in the shape of ribs (Mother Earth's), and when the faithful emerge they do so as spiritually renewed people. Again, the health of the *wana'gi,* the everlasting, intelligent soul—the permanent part of the human—is the principal concern.

The Role of Women

In Lakota society, the spiritual and economic powers of women were not only acknowledged but well respected. When a man took a wife, he lived in her camp. When the Lakota traced their ancestry, while acknowledging and respecting their father's relatives, most took the band name of their mothers. These patterns still exist.

Because Lakota society is more balanced with regard to the male and female forces than other societies, it is little wonder that there are two commonly told legends about the end of the world—one female-based, the other male. Here is a female version told to me by the late Lucy Swan, a respected Lakota elder, in the mid-1970s.

> There is a very old woman who sits on the edge of a tall bluff. She is quilling a beautiful design on a buffalo robe. The woman is very old, so she tires easily. Beside her sits an ancient dog. He is so old that he has very few teeth. Even though he is old, he is still playful.
>
> Every day the woman quills that buffalo robe. Soon she is tired and falls asleep. When she rests at night, the dog unravels all that she did the day before. If that dog forgets to unravel those quills, or gets too old, the old woman will finish the robe. That will be the end of the world.

This is a male version that Tilda heard from her grandmother, the late Dora (Little Warrior) Rooks, in the 1970s.

> At one time there was a young [buffalo] bull. He had four strong legs. As the first three ages passed, he lost three of his legs, one by one. Every year he loses one hair.

Grandma Dora told me, "The white people are descended from the spider people. The have learned to use electricity. That electricity once belonged only to the *Wakinyan* [Thunder Beings].

To do this they put up wires on poles. They send these wires all over. As electricity covers the earth, it creates a huge spider web. One day this spider web will cause a great fire. This will cause the buffalo to lose its last leg and fall to the earth. This will be the end of the world.

There are versions that do not refer to electricity, but always the buffalo is brought down by man's mistake. Grandma Dora's version gives clear insight into beliefs held by some Lakota. One is that white people are heavily influenced by the spider Iktomi. The spider created human technology and culture. White people thus are believed to be clever when it comes to technology.

Another part of the preceding story reveals the Lakota attitude toward the Thunder Beings. They are to be respected and not played with, because they can be very dangerous.

This idea that certain races have certain predispositions was seen in a vision by Good Lifeways Woman, an Oglala Lakota.

Once I dreamed I was in a room like a Gymnasium; it was broad daylight. I was called to the corner of the room, where I found a peculiar light. It was in the form of a medicine wheel. From one quadrant of the wheel came a red light. It represented the Red Man. It came to me that the Red Man's contribution to the whole [of mankind] was spiritual insight. From another quadrant came a dark light; it represented the Black Man, and it came to me that his gift was in the expression of emotions, expressed physically in things like music and dance. In another corner was the white light, it represented the White Man. It came to me that the White Man's gift was in bringing ideas into physical reality [technology].

In another quadrant was a yellow light; it represented the Yellow Man. It came to me that his gift was in mental powers such as meditation and the ancient wisdom that produced acupuncture. Each [color on the sacred wheel] has a gift to share with the whole, none can exist without the other; all people must have a balance in themselves. Neither should one be too powerful and ignore the importance of the other, in this way all things will be balanced.

Oscar Howe was a Dakota full-blood and is considered by many to be an important twentieth-century American artist. He pointed to a design in his painting and said,

That was the first design that came to us. I call it *Tohokmu*. The humans learned it from the spider people. We are close to the spider people because some say it is they [trap-door spiders] that led us to this upper world. A very long time ago, close to the beginning of our time on the [surface of] earth, a young hunter was out looking for game. He had very poor luck and grew tired and hungry. Soon the night fell, and a wind came up.

The boy found a cave just big enough to squeeze into. That night it stormed. The rains fell, and lightning lit up the cave. When the hunter woke in the morning, right over his head was a beautiful spiderweb. The mist from the rain and the morning light made it sparkle. In the center was the design we call Tohokmu—the oldest design.

In the web was a spider soon to deliver her offspring. She told the hunter, "Since you saw the beauty of my web and did not harm me, I will tell you a secret." She told him of a hill made by her people. This hill was made of arrowheads that her people had created. She told him that these arrowheads could be very useful to hunt with. Then she told him how to use them. He thanked her and went back to his people.

On his way he stopped by and took a bag of these perfectly shaped stones with him. The people were very surprised and impressed at what he brought them. These arrowheads changed their lives. The spiders are clever. They are the inventors of technology.

The Lakota word for spider is *iktomi*. In the Lakota creation story, Iktomi is also the name of the famous trickster.

There are many standard Iktomi stories that were traditionally told, but they may also be invented on the spot, for these are fun stories meant to impart a lesson about morality to the children. As electricity, extending light and work hours, and television have invaded Lakota homes within the last twenty years, the telling of these stories has greatly declined.

Iktomi is a god and therefore capable of many marvelous things, including the ability to change his appearance. He is always out to make part of the creation, its plants, animals, or Ikce' Oyate' (humans) look foolish. He is generally the one who falls victim to the prank.

There was a time when Iktomi was walking along the riverbank. He was about ready to eat a dinner of prairie chickens he had captured and killed with his cunning. About the time he was ready to stop and eat, he heard a strange sound.

The sound was a soft moaning, like that of a beautiful woman. In fact, Iktomi was very vain and thought the woman was calling his name, so he strained to hear better, but he could not make the words out. Soon his curiosity got the better of him, and he strained his eyes to see if he could spot the woman. Because it was a human woman he figured he'd better make himself resemble a man, so he did.

Soon, across the rushing river he thought he saw the woman. He imagined she was naked and swayed gently as she moaned. Now, Iktomi thought, perhaps she is bathing, and if she sees me she might be frightened. So he decided on a plan to have her.

He commanded his male part to grow very long and stretch across the river all the way to that woman. Just as it was about to do so, a coyote came along. "What are you doing, Ikto?" the coyote asked, secretly eyeing the sack full of prairie chickens.

"Why, there is a beautiful woman across the river. It is rushing very hard, I'm not much of a swimmer, and I can't reach her even though very likely she is in love with me." With that he extended himself, striking that woman where he wanted. When he pushed he was stuck tight. The beautiful woman was only two twisted cottonwoods, the moaning simply the wind rubbing the trees together. Iktomi pulled and screamed but could not get free. The coyote laughed at his unfortunate friend, picked up the sack of birds, and moved off a short distance to eat in peace. By the time Iktomi pulled free, his dinner had been eaten!

This typical tale of humorous irony was told to me by the late Joseph Rockboy. The moral is obvious to any young male who might have heard it.[5]

Another legend which reflects traditional attitudes about the power of women to seduce men is about the woman who changed herself into a deer to entice men into becoming lost. Women who have this power over men are thought to be influenced by Anukite', who is a principal in the creation story. This is one of the *Wakan* (mysterious) powers of Anukite' and is important not only because it shows the importance of the creation stories in understanding behaviors and beliefs but also as a cautionary tale for Lakota men and women down through the ages.

White-tailed deer are thought to have a special relationship to courting men and are said to be manifestations of the influence of Anukite' in punishing men. Two passages follow, the first from Lucy Swan and the second from a famous Northern Cheyenne family, the Black Wolfs. Although the Lakotas' principal military allies, the Cheyennes, may not have had a spirit like Anukite', their ideas about the power of deer spirits are very similar:

We believe that certain women can appear to men as deer. Sometimes this can be dangerous. If a man is out hunting alone and he sees a doe, he shouldn't follow her. They can be tricky. She might be a spirit deer and try to fool him. She will smell very attractive and might even appear to him as a beautiful young woman. She may make him follow her by using her deer perfume.

He will follow her a long way, and when they stop to lie down together, she will turn back into a deer and run off. This will make him confused, crazy, and he could wander until he freezes or starves to death.

George Bird Grinnel, an early ethnologist who lived many years with the Cheyenne, tells of a young Cheyenne man, Black Wolf, who journeyed two days to visit the girl he loved in another camp. In a river valley, in thick grove of willows, he saw some tipis, one larger and more impressive than the rest. He approached this one and looked inside.

There was a light within, and he saw standing near the lodge a young man playing on the flute, as if in courting. In the lodge he could hear people playing the finger-bone game. He determined to enter and ask the people there where he should go to find his relatives in the camp. He peeped in through the door and saw within a number of beautiful girls and fine-looking young men, some playing the finger-bone game and some the seed game. Some of the girls had on striped Navajo blankets, and some painted robes—all very pretty. The young men too were finely dressed. The young people outside stood about, wearing their robes hair side out. When he saw all these girls, he felt bashful, and did not go in. Presently he went around to the back of the lodge to think what he should do. There he stopped and considered, and taking courage, started back to the door, intending to enter; but as he was walking he turned his head, and for a moment looked away from the lodge, and when he looked back, the lodge was not there. Instead all of these beautiful girls and men, there were deer, going off through the timber. He wondered to himself what had happened, and went down through the timber and continued on his way, often looking back and fearing lest something bad might come to him before he could get away.[6]

The following version comes from Tilda's childhood and refers to her grandmother, Sadie Crazy Thunder.

When I was a little girl, living out in the country, our grandma would call us in before dark. She would point up behind the house where there were bushes and say, "You better come in or Anukite' might come down and take you away with her." I don't know whether she was just scaring us so we wouldn't try to stay out longer, but she would say, "Don't let Anukite' catch you, because she cooks little children and eats them!"

Anukite' (Double-Face Woman) belongs to a class of spirits that existed almost from the earliest creation. She loves to taunt and even punish men. As Lucy Swan says, some Double Woman Dreamers are considered bad, loose, or immoral, always chasing someone else's husband, and others are principally good, whereas a few have both aspects to their nature: "If you dream of twins or are born a twin, you will be a good quill worker. Anukite' has this power to influence artists. . . . A little girl born with two swirls on her head will be a good artist."

In a culture whose ancient stories place women on a par with men, both good and evil, women were also allowed to act out their dreams in rituals of all kinds. Women who had certain types of dreams often formed or belonged to longstanding dream societies, *Okolakiciye,* just as the men did. *Wipata Okolakiciye'* was a society of women who believed themselves to be under the guidance of the Double Woman herself, Anukite'. They came together to share their handicrafts and sing and feast. Since early anthropologists and ethnographers often slighted investigations on the female side, very little is actually known about the ceremonies of these women's societies. Two rare songs related to the Double Woman Dreamers are perhaps all that remain. The first was left by the late Lucy Swan, whose knowledge of Lakota women's music was perhaps the best of her generation; this is the first time these songs have appeared in a book.

Cepansi ku wanna tuwa leciaya	Cousin come over here. [Now] someone is waving a shawl at you.
sina micoze	All right, look over this way.
Howe wayankaye, tuwa leciay sina micoze.	Someone is waving a shawl at you.

Another set of words comes from the late Severt Young Bear, a revered Oglala Elder and expert on Lakota music, through his grandmother.

Oyate ki wamiciyankape ogle	People behold. This beaded shirt my husband will display [wear]
Ksupi kile	As he does
Wicasa mitawa ki un otanin kte	Something of importance.[7]

The following is a very rare narrative of a modern Double Woman dream. It was an experience that Nellie Two Bulls, now a greatly respected elder, had as a young woman. Only eleven or twelve years old, she had been troubled by the feeling that three spirits had been watching her, and the feeling had progressed until she was afraid to leave the house:

The first time that happened to me, my cousin and I were playing. You know, she went back to her house and I was coming back to mine. All of a sudden, it seems like I am hearing voices behind me, I started walking back and kept looking back, but I didn't see anyone. But then again I heard some women talking, and laughing. I didn't know what they were talking about, they were laughing, so then I was almost running and went into my house. My mom was sitting there beading and I didn't tell her right away, you know. I kept it a secret for a long time; I didn't even want to tell.

That was the first time I heard those voices and three days later, I heard those voices again, laughing and talking. I'd stand and listen. They were talking about something, but I never knew what they were talking about. Pretty soon I even heard them at night or when I was home from school and I'd try to do my school work on the table. I'd start hearing them. Then pretty soon I saw three persons run right by my window. Pretty soon I was scared to go outside in the daylight alone, even to go to toilet. And I'd tell my mom, "Mom go to toilet with me." She'd say, "How come? It's daylight, and you're scared to go out?"

And here one night while I was sleeping—I had a small bed, my mom sleeping on the other side of me in our little bitty house. Then, all of a sudden, I heard something so I got up and I sat up, you know I woke up from my sleep and I opened my eyes to see three women standing before me. Right next to our bed they were standing and looking at me. And here this one lady, she was really tall with long braids and a red dress on. She had a white shell necklace too. The other one was middle size, not too tall neither too short. She wore a blue dress and had some shells and braid strings with quillwork on. And the last one was short and small and kinda fat. She has braids and coal black hair. And this woman was real jolly, and you know full of laughter.

She said, "We've been wanting, you know to talk to you for all this time but you're scared of us. And now we want to tell you many good things." They said, "We want you to see this. We brought all our work and we are going to display it." And they each got a bundle of their work and put it on the table for me. That first tall one, had all beadwork, and the middle one, all her quillwork, and the third one didn't display her work. "Do you want this?" she said. "I am Blue Bird Woman and this bag is full of songs. I am going to give a voice. If you'll want this, you'll get this. You will make lots of people happy and your voice will sound like a bird and nobody will have this voice except you. I will give it to you. Do you want it?" So I sat there, you know. I didn't even answer—thinking. "You want all this talent? We are going to give it to you this day and from this day your name is Blue Bird Woman. All the songs you will think about you will sing."

The others didn't tell me their names, but just her. She said she would give me her name and that day they would give me their talents, they said, "Everything you make you can make without a pattern or blueprint. You'll think about it and make it right away and if you think you can't finish it or it is too hard all you have to say is, 'My cousins, come and help me!' and we'll be there and your work will be finished in no time." That's what they said. "We're going back now." And they shook hands and said, "Well, this talent you got from us, you have to share with others, among your people. Don't have it all to yourself."

So the next day when I got up I felt even worse, you know. I didn't even want to eat. My mother cooking breakfast said, "My daughter, something is bothering you and I know because I am a medicine woman. Right from the beginning I knew but I wanted you to tell me yourself. I am not going to ask you, but I think this has been going on long enough and now your ways have really changed." So I told her you know. . . . And here my mom said: "You know, you're a dreamer of the Double Woman, but good thing it's in a good way, because there are two ways of being a Double Woman. One is you're going to make lots of people unhappy by taking their men. You could look at a man and get him right away and that's bad. But this other way, you're a Double Woman in a good way. Everything you do will not be for yourself. But there's lots of things that go with this so I'm going after your grandfather who's a medicine man and see what he says."[8]

Her grandfather put her on the hill to fast and pray. When she came down, her mother, a very wise medicine woman, also told her many things she was to remember. Nellie Two Bulls' dream provides precious insight into some important truths about dreams of calling. Dreams of calling were very bothersome to the dreamer; they made her sick and fearful. These dreams were persistent, not something acted on at first impulse. The dreams persisted until she accepted what these women had to offer; she could not escape her calling.

Another important point is that this dream was unwanted and unexpected—certainly not something Nellie sought. The dreams demonstrate how easy it is for spirits to communicate with those still "living." Quill-workers who have dreamed of the Double Woman play a significant role in the sacred world of the Lakota, for it is they who will make much of the "equipment" used in all the important rituals. The most important aspect of these dreams is how they always transform the dreamer's life. There is a cause and effect between the spiritual world and the physical world that provides the faithful with concrete evidence of the sacred.

So powerful is Anukite' that a man who dreamed of the Double Woman might become a *winkte'*, or transvestite, and dress as a woman, devoting himself to the decorative arts of women.

Nellie grew up to become the most famous Lakota female singer of her generation, perhaps of the twentieth century. She has continually looked for ways to share her talents, as she was instructed. She has been married to the same man all her life.

The Double Woman in Lakota thought and behavior demonstrates how aspects of the creation story persist in the oral tradition and are still experienced in the dream world to this day.

There are many directions, or callings, from the sacred ancestors that call women to various roles—some simple, used in everyday life, and others complex or deeply personal, to be acted out in a public display like the Clown Dances or the Horse Dance. The *Taha Kpanyapi,* hide softeners, one of the common guilds, came together to cooperate in the construction of lodges. Even they followed sacred traditions. A well-respected older woman, known to have lived all her life with one man, would be asked to sew the smoke flaps on. It was thought that if this was done by a lesser woman, the tipi would fill with smoke.

A modern correlation to the old dream societies might be the *Sina Wakan Okolakiciye',* or Sacred Shawl Women's Society, organized to provide shelter and support for battered women and help in rebuilding Lakota families damaged by colonialism and boarding schools. It too came out of the vision of a woman.[9]

Another type of story that might fall under what Lakota people call *Ohun'kankan Ehankehanni* (old-time stories) is this one from Ray Dupris. It is considered to be historical fact, and although the name of the woman is not remembered, the woman is, and the story is kept alive to be told late at night. Its purpose is to preserve events that tell something of the nature and beliefs of Lakota people. Ray, who was raised speaking Lakota, is an Itazipco from Iron Lightning, a tiny community on the northwestern edge of the Cheyenne River Reservation.

> There was a time before the white man came into our country, when the people occasionally lived in earth lodges. Sometimes if the *Saones,* northern Lakota people, were to be camped in one place for some length of time they would build these large winter lodges out of earth and logs, like the Mandan and Arikara tribes that lived along the *Oahe'* [Missouri] River. These houses had a square smoke hole in the top and were dome-shaped. Some were large enough to bring the horses inside.

There was a village made out of these and, one by one, the small children from this camp began disappearing. This made the parents and grandparents grieve, and the people were frightened. They put the men on guard. No one left the village, and after a time the people ran out of food. Soon the bravest men left the village. They searched nearby for this unseen enemy but found no sign.

A long time ago before the Oahe' River was dammed up and changed into a reservoir by the colonizers, the area near its banks was called Oahe', or "makes tracks." These tracks were made by *Untehi,* giant snakes that came out of their holes only every one hundred years. Only those who studied sacred ways or kept the history of the people remembered these stories.

These snakes are very large, perhaps two or three feet thick, and very long, perhaps one hundred feet.

For some time the men stayed close to the village trying to protect their families from this enemy that was stealing children. Finally the people grew so hungry that two brave men decided to go out hunting. They were hunting for some time and were separated by a small distance. One of the men heard a noise he had never experienced before.

Along the banks of the river willow trees and choke cherry bushes were being torn up, thrown about, and even tossed into the air, but the man could not see what was causing it. In the distance he saw flashes of light. They were similar to the ones the people made with flat pieces of sheet mica to signal and communicate with each other.

Soon the man became frightened and went looking for his friend. What he saw frightened him. His friend was lying on the ground. His body was all swollen and turning black. The man looked dead, but his friend cared for him greatly. He quickly made a travois and started to drag him back toward the village. He hadn't gotten very far when he heard the same noise. Trees were snapping, and choke cherry and plum bushes were being crushed and tossed into the air. A great cloud of dust was coming up along the riverbank. Frightened, the man struggled to pull his friend to the safety of the village.

As he came around a small rise in the land, the horrified hunter saw what was destroying the riverbank. It was a giant snake, returning to eat its victim. As it moved, its giant tail was twisting back and forth, uprooting trees and shrubs, throwing them as it went. As the brave hunter struggled with his companion, he looked at the snake. A yellow light came out of the snake's eyes, and the man immediately felt as if he too had been poisoned. His head and face began to swell, but still he struggled to help his friend.

That giant snake moved toward its victims, and the man, now weak and swollen, knew they were to be eaten. By the time he got close to the village he fell, his body now black and swollen like his friend's.

There was a woman in that camp who was a powerful Wapiye'Win [medicine woman]. She told the people she had heard of these giant snakes from her grandmother. She asked the warriors to make a loud noise and not look at the eyes of the monster. Soon the giant snake was frightened off and the unconscious men brought to the holy woman. They appeared to be dead.

She performed a *Yagopa* [sucking] ceremony. First she sang a sacred song over the men. She then leaned over and sucked the poison from the men using a buffalo horn. Then she coughed up ugly green bile. It was thick and smelled awful. She did this for some time. Soon the swelling went down, and it was clear that the men would live. She told the people, "These snakes come out only every one hundred years, and when they come out they are very hungry and will eat anything." They don't have to bite their victims, she said: "Their eyes send out a light that knocks them down and poisons their victims." This is where the missing children had gone, eaten by that snake.

These snakes still exist. Their dens have been covered by the Oahe' Reservoir, but people still occasionally see them now swimming in the Oahe'. There have always been medicine women, and I share this story to make that point known.[10]

Although this is just a small sampling of the many ancient stories still kept by the Lakota and Cheyenne, it is obvious that feminine nature plays a central role in that spiritual legacy. Female spirits, like males, are both good and bad, balanced. It is little wonder that a people whose oral religious tradition is inhabited by both powerful male and female forces has produced such remarkable holy women.

3

Lakol Wicohan: Being Raised in the Indian Way

Somewhere to the south there is a large camp in which beauty and peace abide. There is a council lodge, and inside it sits one they call Grandfather. One day he calls out to a man and woman, and both of them come sit in his lodge.

And he says to them, "You are now going to make a long journey, so do the best you can. Someday in the future you will come back here again. And then you will be asked to tell about how your journey fared. So go now, both of you. But never own more than you need."[1]

—Admonition of the Creator to New Travelers

To understand the beliefs, personalities, and motivations of holy women and healers, it is essential to understand how they were raised as women—as participants in their society—and how they learned their lessons, which are reinforced in everyday living and in the ceremonies of passage.

Plains Indian life is not neatly segmented, as some anthropologists like to think, into the sacred and the profane. Indian people do not have one way of perceiving the sacred that they use at home and a different one in church, requiring two sets of behavioral codes. Certainly in public ritual there are more formal behaviors, but day-to-day life is very much involved in the sacred mystery.

For a culture, a way of life, to remain vital it must change and be added to as social, environmental, and technological changes take place around it and some practices are left behind. The symbols and core beliefs that explain a people's place in creation must, however, be preserved and reinterpreted in these changing rituals.

Early Childhood

When a baby girl is born, the Lakota say, *Wicincala wan icimani,* "a female traveler has arrived." She is often immediately given an Indian name, a name by whom the spirits will know her. In the past this always took place; today it may or may not be done. The decision of whether this "naming" will take place depends on the *Tiyopsaye',* or extended family, their ties to traditional culture, and their financial ability to undertake the necessary feasts and *Wi'hpega* (give away).[2] If the child is given a name known only by Indians, it will exist alongside her Christian, baptismal, or legal name, for government purposes.

It is said that in the old days a hole was made in the baby's moccasins, and this would give the spirits notice that this soul was too poor to travel and had to stay with the family, lest it be enticed to wander away with them.

If the little girl was sickly, she might receive a special name from a *whinkte'* (male transvestite). This name was considered to have strong protective powers. This holds true not only for the Lakota but for many other Plains tribes, like the Crow and Cheyenne, as well.

The earliest name a child received might be based on something surrounding the circumstances of the birth or something or someone the child reminded the parents of. Adult names given later in life were not invented or chosen at random. Names had to be either ritually transferred from someone living who would forever give up that name, reverting to an older name, or else chosen by a "grandma" (an older female relative who had lived a good life—in some sense a family holy woman).[3] The name was often that of a deceased, very well respected ancestor. Darlene Young Bear, now in her fifties, tells of her naming:

> A Hunkapi ceremony was held for me when I was very young. I was just a baby. Grandma Louise is the one who explained this to me later. She said, "When you make relatives, you do it with all the spirits—the whole universe and all the spirits in it."
>
> That's why Grandma Lucy Short Bull wanted me to have that name first: "This will be how the spirits recognize you." She had that naming ceremony first, and then she spoke and told the people, "The reason I am going to pray and give Darlene a sacred name is that I am not going to live very long. I am old, and I want this little girl to carry on that name." It was a sacred name that was given to her by her grandmother. Grandma Lucy did not live much longer. She died in 1948.

She said, "My granddaughter will grow up and be able to do anything she wants to do. Anybody who wants to put her down in any way, she will get all the more stronger."

I believe that because some people were jealous when I started to sing with the drum groups, somehow instead of being weakened [by their jealousy] or losing my voice, I sang better.

Even now, if we're at a pow-wow, giveaway, or memorial and I have been asked to sing, I will make a prayer that I will sing well and that the people will enjoy it. That's when I found out it was true, what my grandma said. It was wished on me that I would have a good life, and it came true.

When she had this Hunkapi ceremony for me she said that it was going to be good. And that ceremony seemed to be strong, because I could have become a drunkard or had a lot of illegitimate babies, things like that. But somehow it seemed like those things went by, and [the spirits] prevented me from getting a crush on somebody and just jumping into bed with him. The spirits made me feel that I shouldn't do that to myself.

When you look around you see that too much, and I would see everybody my age or younger getting married. I wasn't married, and I was twenty-eight. Everyone was teasing, "You're twenty-eight, and no sign of Mr. Right!" That November I was going to be twenty-nine. That's when I met Kenneth, and we went off and got married, and then things just happened. After that I just kind of thought that I have been watched and have been guided by all of those spirits.

I think back to when I was very young and my Grandma Louise was telling me that all the spirits, good and bad, will watch over me. She said, "Because of this naming ceremony, all the spirits will watch over you. They will recognize you," she said, "in your heart. If anybody wants to do something bad to you and they ask that spirit they will say no, because they know you, and you are related to them and have respect for them. And you are supposed to have respect for everyone and everything. Whatever God has created that has a spirit, that's what he expects."

In my old age—I'm not old yet [laughing]—but this far I know I'm still fortunate that I realize those things and respect things and try to live good and try to raise good women and men who carry on all these ways of life that were good a long time ago . . . instead of pushing it [Indian religion and culture] aside and trying to live under a different culture that was not ours. Grandma said, "This is always ruining the people and ruining the Indian society. It's pitiful, the way we're going, because we're trying to be something we are not."

Central to the traditional attitudes held by the Lakota is the belief that through ritual Hunkapi, one could be made a relative to all physical and spiritual beings and that this sacred name would affix itself to the soul to be used in times of ceremony. Even though Darlene is a Catholic lay minister, her Lakota beliefs underlay the core of her personality and worldview. Her expression and obvious belief in these principles is typical of most full-bloods who participate in a Christian denomination while still adhering to traditional Lakota belief, behavior, worldview, and spiritualism.

The following historical naming scene comes from Frank Linderman's interviews with Pretty Shield, a Crow medicine woman, in the 1930s. The Crow Indians were traditional enemies of the Lakota and Cheyenne but share many cultural similarities as High Plains peoples. The term "wise one" is what the Crow called a medicine person.

"Little Boy Strikes with a Lance, my father's father, gave me my name, Pretty Shield, on the fourth day of my life, as was our custom. My grandfather's shield was handsome; it was big medicine. It was half red and half blue. This war shield was always hung on his backrest at night. In the daytime it nearly always hung on a tripod in back of his lodge, which of course faced the east.

"No woman's name was ever changed unless when she was very young she did not grow strong. If she was weak, and her parents were afraid that they might lose her, they sometimes asked one of her grandfathers [also great-uncles] to change her name for her."

"Do women ever name the children?" I asked.

"Yes, sometimes," she said. "A wise one, even though she be a woman, possesses this right. I named my own children, and all of my grandchildren. My Helpers, the ants, gave me all the names. I listen to the ant people, even to this day, and often hear them calling each other by names that are fine. I never forget them."[4]

In the nineteenth century little girls were treated much the same as little boys, allowed the run of the village, free to play with boys or girls of the same age. They were considered to be very intelligent and had many of the rights and responsibilities of adults. In the daily work of a nomadic village, children were expected to be polite to all adults and to share in the work as they were able. According to oral tradition, the children, girls and boys, were addressed together by the Sacred Calf Pipe Woman.

My little brothers and sisters: Your parents were once little children like you, but in the course of time they became men and women. All living creatures were once small, but if no one took care of them they would never grow up. Your parents love you and have made many sacrifices for your sake in order that Wakantanka may listen to them and that nothing but good may come to you as you grow up. I have brought this pipe for them, and you shall reap some benefit from it. Learn to respect and reverence this pipe, and above all lead pure lives. Wakantanka (the Creator) is your great-grandfather.[5]

Patterns of parenting in the Plains Indian community were not so clearly defined as in Western society. It was generally accepted that the mother's sisters would discipline and teach their sisters' children; their mother's brothers performed much the same role for boys. As Lucy Swan once related, "There is a lot of wisdom in this, because parents sometimes are short with their own children. The aunts and uncles could teach the children without getting upset, and that left the relationship with their mother and father a good and loving one."

The Crow medicine woman Pretty Shield gives great insight into Indian concepts of family and parenting:

> About the time when I came to live on this world my aunt, Strikes with an Ax, lost two little girls. They had been killed by the Lakota; and so had her man. This aunt, who was my mother's sister, mourned for a long time, growing thinner and weaker, until my mother gave me to her, to heal her heart. . . .
>
> This separation from my mother and my sisters was in fact not a very real one because the Crows come together often. . . . My aunt's lodge was large, and she lived alone until I came to stay with her. She needed me, even though I was at first too young to help her.[6]

"Family," to historical and contemporary Plains Indian people, involves a large number of relatives. Knowing who you are related to and how you are related is central to the girls' identity. How you are to act and show formal respect toward those relations is learned by example from birth. For example it was not considered respectful for men to speak directly to their mother-in-law, and women would not converse directly with their father-in-law. Sisters sometimes would not directly address their older brothers. This "respect" for relatives was spoken of by many contemporary Lakota. It is feared by many Lakota that this system of respect is breaking down. Oliver Brown Wolf, an elder from Cheyenne River, said,

> When we were children [in the twenties and thirties] we never referred to people by their name. Each relative has a specific name or term that describes his or her exact relationship to us, so that is what we used. *Scepansiya* is Ethel's [Oliver's wife] female cousin on her mother's side. She would refer to her sisters [female cousins] by the order in which they were born: her older sister she called *Cuwe,* older sister, and the youngest she called *Tanka.* I was an only child so my mom called me *Chaske',* which means oldest, or firstborn boy.[7]

Like the ripples from a pebble dropped in a calm pond, this learning goes on for a lifetime and includes tracking the births, names, and ages of scores of children. This sense of extended family extends to hundreds, or thousands, of significant people considered relatives.

Today reservation and urban grandmothers have assumed many of the roles once filled by a wider sphere of relatives. Grandmothers and grandfathers are most consistently available to help care for their grandchildren.

It is taken for granted that a Lakota will be aware of hundreds of people and their specific relation to him- or herself. Keeping track of ancestors is a consequence of a system that may have evolved in part as a way to ensure that people who are closely related do not marry or *Wogluze'* (commit incest). More important to everyday life is a code of respect that determines appropriate behaviors, including formal politeness shown to many spheres of relatives.

The wisdom of this pattern is remarkable. Children are not the sole property of one parent; they belong to the community. They have very adultlike rights as soon as they are born. Children are cherished and, with good health, are considered the two most precious gifts in Lakota life. This has not changed. It was believed, and still is, that children should be where the best things can happen for them. This is perhaps one reason that missionaries are able to talk so many parents into sending their children to mission boarding schools. All the "parents" watch and observe a child, and it is one of them—aunt, uncle, or grandparent—who might first discuss the child's special traits, including her closeness to the Great Mystery, leading the child to be exposed to and encouraged in the ways of the sacred. Her dreams may have a special quality; her unusual behavior might indicate her close relationship to the spirit world. This is watched and commented on.

To be a child in virtually all cultures is a special time; to the Plains Indian to be a father or mother was considered to be the ultimate blessing from the Creator. The following statement gives poignant testimony to the love of children and their place in the lives of the People.

> I was very fortunate; I had eight children born to me. That's a sacred number, you know. Well, I lost one. So many years later, when I saw that Dora Lee needed a mom, we adopted her. It did not matter that she wasn't perfect [she suffered from fetal alcohol syndrome], we wanted her and could love her, give her a home. Then I had my sacred number again. (Cecelia Looking Horse, Lakota elder and mother of the Sacred Calf Pipe Keeper, 1993)[8]

Children, particularly well-cherished ones, may be raised by a succession of relatives. This creates a rich childhood experience in which they can be exposed to many role models. These respected relatives may have a wide range of personalities, behavior, and talents, creating a powerful and extremely effective learning environment. This system also provides a safety net today for children whose natural parents die or for some reason (often alcoholism or divorce) can no longer care for them.

In the nineteenth century, little girls generally took the band identity of their mothers and spent a good part of their childhood in the village and lodge of their maternal grandmother.

Today, as in the past, all children tend to identify more strongly with their mother's relatives, although they do know and recognize with ritual respect those to whom they are related through their fathers. Today the practice of sending the oldest boy (*Chaske'*) and girl (*Winona*) to live with and learn from Grandma and Grandpa still persists among many traditional families.

In Plains Indian families birth order is critical. Among the Lakota, the firstborn male child (Chaske') and firstborn female child (Winona) are treated differently and raised with more ritual training and responsibilities than their younger siblings, even somewhat deferentially. It has always been this way. This stems from the ancient instructions of Tate' to his oldest son, the North Wind, that these firstborn children will one day lead the family in wisdom and ritual life, including at wakes and funerals.

Tilda, a second female child, remembers one of the ceremonies held for her older sister:

> When I was a little girl—quite young; I barely remember—my sister had her ears pierced in a sort of ceremony. [Grandma Dallas, daughter of Little

Warrior] was called over. She was someone the whole family respected. She prayed and said something, and with needles they poked holes in my sister's ears. Then they tied threads through the holes so they would not close up. This was the old way, not like the little machines they use now.

My grandma used to take little coins and tie them on buckskin thongs for the end of my sister's braids. I used to wonder why she always got these things and I didn't. I guess she was a year older and the firstborn.

In the time since Tilda's childhood, a formal public ceremony for piercing a little girl's ears has emerged. This ceremony, which involves a holy person, generally an older woman, consists of piercing the ears of the little girl with a sharp object. Sinew is then tied into the ear with the earring to ensure that it will not close up. The sinew is a symbol for the old way. The actual ceremony is a physical statement by the family that they follow the *Canku Luta,* or Red Road (Pipe Religion), and intend to bring their daughter up in it as well. This ceremony, *Nakpa Pahloka,* is now done more often in public, with an attendant feast and giveaway. It is often done during a Sun Dance, so that the child may symbolically show her support for the dancers. Little boys may have an ear pierced at this time as well. A talk is given by an older relative about the meaning of this ceremony and the responsibility of the child to the tribe and its parents.

Children are not as protected from the realities of life as are most Euro-American children. Knowledge of life on this earth and its temporary nature is made clear to them at an early age. "Only the Earth lives forever!" is a common admonition.

Often children hear prophecy about what their future will hold. Certain older relatives are well known for this talent and often share what they have "seen," even if it is negative.

Because children are thought to be very intelligent, perhaps even ancient souls who have returned for more time on this earth, there seems to be no prescription for protecting children from bad news or critical observations by adults.

When we were just teenagers, my Grandmother told us one time that she had seen in the future and knew what life would bring us. She told my brother that he would live with another tribe. He would live as a bum [not have his own home], along the railroad tracks.

She told me that I would have only one child, that I would live in a nice home, be married to a good husband, and have everything that I wanted in life. She told my younger sister she would marry a man from our tribe and that she would have lots of children, and that they would be sickly.

She did that for each one of us, including the cousins who lived in that house. It is strange that she could know how things would turn out for each of us. (Anonymous Lakota woman)

This gift and the women who have it are thought to be influenced by Wankanka, the witch and mother of Anukite'.

Adolescence

The Lakota believe themselves to be *Pte'* People, very close relatives of the Buffalo Nation. It was the sacred White Buffalo Calf Maiden, after all, who brought their principal cultural values. Being a good mother, wife, sister, neighbor, or grandmother is expected first.

Turning to the women, she said: "My dear sisters, the women: you have a hard life to live in this world, yet without you this life would not be what it is. Wakantanka intends that you shall bear much sorrow—comfort others in time of sorrow. By your hand the family moves. You have been given the knowledge of making clothing and feeding your family. Wakantanka is with you in your sorrows and joins you in your griefs. He has given you the greatest kindness toward every living creature on earth. You he has chosen to have a feeling for the dead who are gone. He knows that you remember the dead longer than do the men. He knows that you love your children dearly."

When a girl has her first menstrual period certain social changes take place that forever transform the girl to the role of a woman. In this ceremony of *Isna Ti Ca Lowan*—literally, the "Sing of Isolation"—a well-respected older woman was selected as a kind of godmother who would instruct the girl. This might be a relative or someone close to the family. The following statement comes from Mitchell Zephier, a Lakota silversmith and philosopher:

Well, that older lady [see bottom photo on third page of photo section], the way I understand it, she is the personification of the White Buffalo Maiden, and if you think about it, the White Buffalo Maiden brought the Lakota cultural values.

This older woman that's in the tipi with this young woman who's just had her coming of age [first menstruation], or her Buffalo Ceremony, is assuming the role of the White Buffalo Calf Maiden, and she is imparting the ways in which a Lakota woman should conduct herself. That's what I understand.

She tells her many things, and I think she's like a sponsor. She's a virtuous woman. She's well recognized, well thought of. She's recognized as a woman who has all the Lakota cultural values that a woman would want to strive for. She's like that, very maternal.

I think there's an invitation stick that's quilled, and they give this to this older woman or they put it in the ground in front of her home. If she takes that stick she's accepting the role. It's almost like a godparent. That was my understanding of it.

She has to get up in front of all the people who are working on or attending this ceremony. For instance, this young girl will be there with a lot of other young girls, maidens, or young women.

The older lady will remind the child of the family she is from, naming her ancestors. She will exhort them to live in service of the people, to strive to be like the White Buffalo Calf Maiden on earth, because the White Buffalo Calf Maiden brought certain—I wouldn't say commandments, but certain ways of living.

She brought the people rituals and a code of living. These values come from the very first contact she had with the People. These two men came in contact with her, and one of them had impure thoughts about her and went toward her, and he was covered in a mist. He was just bones when the cloud lifted. See, right there is a lesson in how men should respect women. She stayed with the people, and not only did she give them the ceremonies but it was my understanding that she gave them four of the cardinal virtues for men, and of course they are a little different for women. I understood that when a woman completes this ceremony she parts her hair in the middle, they paint the part of her hair with red paint. That implies that she was walking on the Red Road. That's just the way I heard it—that she was recognized as a virtuous Lakota woman.[9]

The menstrual ceremony, despite the banning of ritual by the federal government and the admonitions of Christian missionaries, held such central metaphor and symbolism for the continuation of Lakota life that the ceremonies were continued in semisecret, though they slowly diminished in frequency as the twentieth century progressed.

In the last twenty years a new ceremony now called "Hunkapi," replacing the older Hunka Lowanpi, or "Making of Relatives," has been combined with elements of the older *Isna Ti Ca Lowan* (Ceremony in the House of Isolation) to assume the place and most of the symbolism of what were once two separate ceremonies.

 The following is the most complete description of a modern Isna Ti Ca Lowan puberty ceremony we have ever heard; it comes from Madonna Swan:

Among the Lakota people, we have a way of marking a ceremony, for young women when they have their first moon, or monthly cycle. The day that I got my first moon, we were living west of Cherry Creek. Mom and Grandma closed off a little space for me to stay with ropes and blankets. I moved in Grandma's little cabin and that is where Grandma said I must stay for the next four days and four nights.

Grandma Julia instructed me not to look out the windows. I was not to stand at the door and peek out, or let my thoughts go outside that little enclosure. She said, "You are to stay busy doing something all the time, if you are not cooking, washing or cleaning the house you should be sewing or beading. Whatever you do if you are sewing and you make a mistake, you should not rip it out (teaching me self-confidence and persistence). If you do, you will be that way the rest of your life. If you do rip it out, it will be your habit in all things during your lifetime. So just keep going and the next time do it better," she instructed.

I didn't have to try very hard because Mom or Grandma were there to remind me and show me the right way to do things the whole time. I made a doll with a cloth Indian dress, beaded moccasins and leggings (that I may provide for the needs of my family in a symbolic way). I had never done beadwork before. I sewed buttons on all my Dad's and brother's shirts. I sewed all my Mom's old dresses. I sewed up and patched up bib overalls.

Then Grandma Julia cut some quilt blocks and I made them up into two quilt tops (to teach me thrift, beauty and industry). She taught me how to cook (provide hospitality) in the old ways that her mother had taught her (using a stomach pouch to put hot rocks in to cook soup, and to use her pounding and grinding stones).

Grandma told me, "Within these days you are not to have a bad disposition, or think bad thoughts about anyone or anything. Try to be happy and not to get angry or else that will also be your way in life." She told me not to scratch my head, or itch myself anywhere for these four days. Grandma had made me a stick, I had to clean my nails or scratch with that stick.

Every day she prayed over me, but before she would pray, Mom and Grandma would bathe me in water in which they added sage and green cedar. Then Grandma High Pine would pray. "Grandfathers above and in the four directions, make Madonna a good woman. Help her to treat guests with hospitality. Grandfathers, help her to be a good worker. Grandfathers, and Maka Ina (Mother Earth), help Madonna to be a good mother.

"I pray that the food she cooks in her life, will be good for those that eat it. Grandfathers, help her to be a good wife and live with the same man all her life. Grandfathers, bless her with healthy children." These are the kinds of things she asked of the Tunkasila.

During those special days, Grandma would take me outside and teach me. She told me everything in life is sacred. She said, "You should never curse things out or say *siceyala* (no good!), or anything like that. Those things, even if you don't like them, were created for a purpose. Everything is sacred. All the things you learn during these four days are important. These teachings will help you for a lifetime. You should try to learn all you can so that when you take a husband you can do all these things."

In these four days as in the past, Grandma instructed me in many things. She would teach me things by reminding, "We should always thank Wakon Tonka for all that he has given us, all that he has done for us. We should thank him for our health. You should never forget to pray to him when you are in trouble, or in need of anything."

Unci also told me, "The Sun, Wi, is Wakan Tanka; we pray to him, we also call him Tunkasila which means Grandfather. I have prayed with the Peace Pipe since I was a young woman and my father gave me a pipe."

When Grandma prayed, she held the mouthpiece pointed towards the sky to the Wi Tunka'silaya (Grandfather Sun), next she held it to the four directions, Wiyohiyanpa (East), Waziyata (North), Wiyohpeyata (West), and Itokaga (South), then to Maka Ina (Mother Earth).

She would say, "The directions are also our friends; we pray to them in time of need or necessity. The Earth is our grandmother, Unci to us all, to all living things. Hanwi the Moon is also our friend, and Tate' the Wind, and Whope', the beautiful one. She was the Buffalo Woman, the Buffalo Calf Maiden that brought us the Calf Pipe.

"Wakinyan, the Thunder, is also your friend, and Tatanka the Buffalo, and the Bear Hu Nunpa. Tate' Tob the Four Winds, the whole universe. Each spirit also represents something. The Tatanka Sicun (Buffalo Spirit) represents the energy of life as food and shelter for the Lakota people."

She also taught me about the Four Great Virtues, which govern the conduct of the Lakota people. They are generosity, bravery, fortitude (long suffering or patience), and moral integrity. She instructed me, "Watch out for Iktomi, they can appear as bad people or show themselves in other tricky ways. Some deer can transform themselves into people. If you like a person or have a secret crush on someone, the Deer People can know your thoughts and appear as that person and lead you astray. They can make your mind go crazy. You should be fearful and respectful of all these kind.

"There is a man for every woman, in time that man will come along. You won't even know each other. You will just meet one day and know this is the man for you." These are the kinds of things she told me and reminded me of during those four days.

At the end of the four days, I again went back into the regular world, but things were different now. About two days later they made a feast and invited everyone in Cherry Creek. Then they gave away what I had made, and many things they had been making and put aside for this day. Grandma gave a talk about what had taken place, instructing other women to do the same with their daughters, so that they could have good lives. Then she prayed and fed all the visitors and gave them a gift of a shawl, a quilt, or food.

Many things were different for me after that. I was a young woman now. It was hard for my brothers to understand. I could no longer play with them like I used to. I used to climb trees, play ball, and all those sorts of things. Grandma had instructed me that I was not to play with the boys like I had before, after I came out. I couldn't run around, climb trees, or play with my brothers anymore. I was thirteen years old then.[10]

Modern Rites of Womanhood

The tradition of marking the first menstrual flow with ceremony is still strong. During the ceremony red paint is applied to the part on the girl's head (signifying her dedication to truth and the Red Road), her forehead is painted red, and three marks may be painted on her chin, signifying that she is now a woman. A white vent plume from a golden eagle is tied to her hair, signifying virtue. She is allowed to wear these symbols in public, but today only the feather is generally seen in public.[11]

The mysterious powers that create new life are, as always, essential to the survival of the people. Unlike in the prereservation days, menstruating women no longer isolate themselves for four days each month. Today fewer young women go through the public ritual, but even that has been changing. Large public Hunka ceremonies, with attendant ritual giveaways, are being held, but generally, as in the case of Madonna, for only the oldest daughter. Still, within the household, instructions to all girls take place, and the central metaphors remain the same. This is what Tilda remembers of that time in her life:

When my cousins and I had our first period, my grandmother took us aside and spoke with us. She said, "When you have your period, your first moon, the way you are at that time is the way you will always be." She said, "During this time, don't sit around, clean house or sew or something. Don't sit around: if you do it will become like a habit. Being a wife and mother is tough. There is always so much to do, and these are hard things. If you are to be a good wife and mother, what you do in these first days is important.

"Don't cook, because your hands are dirty; scratch yourself with a stick if you need to. Don't do quillwork, and don't chew on your nails, because they are not clean at this time.

"When you have a husband or children watch out for the males when things like their clothes are on the floor; don't step over them, because you'll make them sick. When you have your moon, wash your own clothes separately.

"This is the time you learn all these things. Do all the good things in life, work at being a wife, a mom, and have a good home."

The "new" ceremony of Hunkapi has in recent years marked this critical change in young people's lives. Because the term *hunka* actually refers to one's ancestors and is a joining together of families both living and in the spirit world, it is a very serious undertaking. Both boys and girls may Hunkapi. A ritual leader is chosen, usually a well-respected older male who knows the family history of each child. The ceremony is announced by the family a year ahead of time so that relatives can assist in gathering all the traditional foods and gifts to be distributed to the helpers and visitors.

The use of the term *Hunkapi* has changed, as Darlene Young Bear stated in the preceding: to be Hunkapi was to be made a relative to all of creation. The new ceremony has acknowledged some of this older philosophy.

When we were going to do that for Joanne, my oldest daughter, my aunt told me how to go about that. Her Hunkapi ceremony was held at the cultural center. That was when it was first built. I put on a feast and a giveaway, and I had Joe Flying By come over and do that thing [perform the ceremony] for her. Joanne was ten. Unlike what people are now calling a Hunkapi, she did not take a [human] relative. That's why I said, "When you make a relative, that's another ceremony. You don't go through the Hunkapi ceremony to take a relative. Making relatives like, when you want to take someone for a sister, you have this ceremony where you both hold the pipe, stand there, and pray. You could draw blood and mix it together. That's actual adoption or making a relative."

And Hunka is when you make a relative to the whole universe, with spirits. The spirits are the ones that recognize you as a relative. At that time, you know, there are going to be sponsors who will be there. They are the ones who are going to talk to you, and tell you, and instruct you . . . like how to conduct yourself and all that kind of thing. So that doesn't mean that you're taking them as relatives. They may take an older person [who has lost most of his or her relatives] as a relative if they want, I suppose.[12] Even though I cry a lot of times, it has been a real good life for me. That's all the spirits guiding me.[13]

The modern Hunkapi ceremony is held shortly before or after the girl has her first moon, menstrual flow. It may be held as part of a larger gathering, such as a Sun Dance or powwow in the round brush arbor or as a separate ceremony, but it is still held outdoors if possible.

Each child chooses a sponsor, an older person loved and respected by the family. In this ceremony references are made back to the Calf Pipe Woman and to what she had to say to the young people. The children, if there are more than one going through the ceremony, are seated in a chair of respect covered with a star quilt.

The man conducting the ceremony will remind the child or children of many things, including that they are first Lakota and that they are to live as good Lakota People. Their ancestors are mentioned, and the children are reminded that they come from a proud family; their lineage and the accomplishments of their deceased relatives are mentioned.[14]

Ritual foods, including choke cherry juice and *wasna* (pemmican), are offered to the Grandfathers and Mother Earth and passed out to the elderly in attendance. Then each child is given a name. They may, as indicated by Darlene Young Bear, also adopt an older relative at this time. This adoption is public and formal and is considered permanent; it includes all the relatives of the adopted person.

The children may be given a new "spirit" name at this time, one that is more grown-up than their childhood names. As with most Indian names, these names are usually selected by older relatives from the names of deceased ancestors who had qualities useful in life. These new names are thought to be ritually attached to the child's soul and are used in all ceremonies for the rest of the child's life and, though seldom spoken, will be known to many friends and relatives.

When the ceremony is completed a large ritual Wihpeya (Giveaway) is held in honor of each child. The child's relatives, principally the females, will sew, bead, quilt, and purchase utilitarian items, towels, dishes, bolts of cloth, blankets, cigarettes, and the like for a year or more. These are dispersed in a specific protocol agreed upon ahead of time by the child's closest relatives, and shared with the *Eyapaha* (official master of ceremonies) to be announced over the public address system that is now a part of all modern powwow grounds.

A successful or proper ceremony provides all the visitors with a gift. There should be so much food dispersed that all who have come must eat until they are very full, then produce containers for the remainder, which they have brought with them. This leftover food is considered in a subtle way to be special or sacred and is symbolic in its relationship to the "life" of the people. The containers are filled to overflowing with *Wateca* (leftovers). In this way the feast goes on, and relatives or friends who were not able to attend may share in its restorative power.

Many non-Indians who hear of menstrual isolation and taboos fail to understand the significance that Plains Indian people attribute to menstrual blood. It is believed to be the manifestation of female capacity for creation and the powers that mystery contains. Some elders are concerned that even Lakota people misinterpret this ancient belief.

The late Joseph Rockboy, a revered Yankton/Sicangu Sioux elder who lived from 1900 to 1984, told me:

> People will say that a woman who is having her moon should stay away from the ceremonies because she could ruin them, but they don't understand or know why this is. It is because a woman is the only one who can bring a child into this world. It is the most sacred and powerful of all mysteries. Certainly the man must be there to plant the seed, but his part is simple and relatively unimportant.
>
> In our way we pray for only two things—'*Wicozani*' [health] and *Na Wiconi Cage*' [generations]. Everything else is up to man.
>
> Some people focus on the Sun Dance and the male power of the sky, but it is to bless Mother Earth with new life that the dance is held. When we pray in the sweat lodge or in our ceremonies, we always remember Maka Ina [Mother Earth]. We get our health from Mother Earth and the herbs that grow from her. We use some for food and others for doctoring.
>
> When a woman is having her time, her blood is flowing, and this blood is full of the mysterious powers that are related to childbearing. At this time she is particularly powerful. To bring a child into this world is the most powerful thing in creation. A man's power is nothing compared to this, and he can do nothing compared to it. We respect that power.
>
> If a woman should come into contact with the things that a man prays with [pipe, rattles, medicine objects] during this time it will drain all the male powers away from them. You see, a woman's power and a man's are opposites—not in a bad way, but in a good way.

Because of the power a woman has during this time it is best that, out of respect for her men and for their medicine things, she stay away from them. In the past they would build a little lodge for her, and their other female relatives would serve on her needs. She would get a rest from all her chores. It was not a negative thing like people think now. So you see, we did this out of our respect for this great mystery, out of respect for the special powers of women.[15]

Sacred Virgins

Another spiritual role as holy women that some teenage girls may be asked to act out is that of Hoks' winla (virgins) in the opening rites of the Sun Dance. Here, traditional ideas about chastity and virginity are still idealized, reinforced, and given ritual significance. At "traditional" Sun Dances, as in the past, four virgins are honored with a special role. They are taken by the "scouts" to a selected cottonwood tree. There, each girl "strikes coup" on the tree with a sacred hatchet or coup stick that has been purified and painted with red earth paint. This must be done before the tree can be chopped down and used in the center of the Sun Dance arbor.

In all ceremonies the ideals of purity and virginity are linked, recalling the nature of the Buffalo Calf Maiden herself.

A memory of Madonna Swan offers a child's-eye view of this tradition:

> I asked Mom, "What are those men going to do?"
> She replied, "They are going to take a sweat bath. One of those men has not been feeling well and they are going to pray to the Grandfathers to find out what is wrong with him."
> "When are they going to do that?" I asked.
> "Probably this evening at dusk," she said, and went on peeling and braiding the wild turnips she had dug that morning.
>
> The men didn't have their sweat bath that night. As Mom fed them, I overheard one of them say they couldn't have the sweat until another person arrived. I asked Mom what they were waiting for.
> "They are waiting for a virgin, either a boy or a young woman who must carry the rocks into the sweat bath so everything will go well for the sick man they are praying for. They are waiting for Swift Bear's granddaughter."

Swift Bear's granddaughter came that evening, they had the sweat bath the next day. When they were finished, and eating a feast Mom had prepared, I asked Grandpa, "Lala, why did you wait for Swift Bear's granddaughter?"

He answered, "Not everybody or just anybody can bring those rocks in there. You must approach sacred things in the right way. We needed a virgin to help us."

"What is a virgin?" I asked.

He replied, "It is a man who has not taken a woman, or a woman who has not been with a man. All things must be done properly if you are to gain benefit from these ceremonies."

Grandpa taught us a lot. He liked to talk about religion and ceremonies, about the proper way to approach these things and the Grandfathers in heaven.[16]

4

Adulthood

A nation is not defeated until the hearts of its women are on the ground.

—Cheyenne proverb

Certain longstanding ideas about the proper role of women in Plains Indian life have remained. Some are expressed in aspects of the traditional regalia worn at the powwow. As Lucy Swan explains, "They wear an awl case to show they are industrious. They used this a long time ago to make clothes and tipis, everything. The little pouch is for a fire striker, to show they are hospitable and can make a warm home for family and visitors. They wear the knife case to symbolize generosity and the feeding of people. Today they might not have the awl inside [the little beaded case], but it means the same."

These items attest to the message of the White Buffalo Calf Maiden to the women. It is very true that in the old days it was the woman who earned and kept the family's status. Her industriousness, cleanliness, truthfulness, humor, wisdom, courage, and generosity elevated her family in the minds of the people. The Lakota woman owned the products of industry and used them, traded them, or disposed of them as she saw fit. Her hard work earned her status in the eyes of fellow women and the community at large.

Within the oral tradition there are slight variations in how the words of this sacred woman are remembered. One variation we found comes from Mitchell Zephier, who got it from his grandfather, Bill Buck, who was born in the late nineteenth century.

They're the same as your values [brought by the Sacred Calf Pipe Woman] for men, with the exception of truthfulness for women. Truthfulness, I don't know—maybe it's something that gets lost in the translation. I've always wondered about this, but my grandfather Bill told me this because my aunts were gossiping about somebody.

At the time he told me this, he was in his seventies and had lived back when the people still lived in tents. He came to me and said, "That's not a good way for women to talk about people because when we were young we were taught to talk well about people, especially women, because in the tipi days people lived very close together. Their talk could cause serious trouble."

If you think about it, in the wintertime you're living in a small enclosed space with a lot of people, and you've got to have a certain decorum in order to keep that harmony. He said, "When the men would go off hunting or whatever, you know there were even instances when feuds started between women, like fighting over a buffalo kill—that type of thing. Truthfulness is one of the primary female virtues that they strive for, and bravery, fortitude, wisdom, and generosity, so you shouldn't be gossiping or causing trouble for others."

You know, those were the kinds of things that this elderly woman would say to those gathered for the Hunka, or puberty ceremony. This older, well-respected woman who had been chosen to be the sponsor of this young lady would stand up there and talk, and she would say, This is who you come from, this is the way you're supposed to be. Maybe she belonged to a certain woman's society, so that she was just expected to live a good life.[1]

Courting, Marriage, and Family

It is expected that all women will become mothers. This is expected even if the woman does not "stay" or live with the father. If the mother stays with the father—"marries" him either in the Indian common-law way or legally in the white way—so much the better. A woman who successfully fulfills these roles is greatly respected. Elders were expected to impart these values to children.

In the nineteenth century, courting was a formal process. Girls from proper families, after the *Isna Ti Ca Lowan* (in some ways the Indian equivalent of a debutante ball), were assigned an older female guardian to ensure propriety in courting. In most cases single women participated in social or athletic activities with other women. This practice continued even after marriage. Men would line up outside the lodge of the eligible young woman and wait for a turn to speak with her. With the young woman's feet planted in the slanting doorway where an older female relative could see them, the man would cover their shoulders and heads with a special courting robe and make his case.

If the woman seemed interested, her suitor would approach her oldest brother and speak with him. If the oldest brother considered the young man worthy (capable of supporting a wife and family) he would give his permission. In theory a girl might end up with a man she did not care for. If, however, after a time she could not grow to care for him, she could quite easily divorce him.

Lifelong marriage is a Lakota ideal but, as in most cultures, is actually achieved by few. In true egalitarian fashion, the Lakota actually made divorce quite easy for either party, and a type of serial monogamy is actually the reality for most women. The woman owns the house and all the equipment associated with it. Before the Anglo institution of "legal marriages" there was no need to stay in an unhappy or abusive relationship.

A Lakota woman was free to act as she wished and "belonged" to no one but herself. All she needed to do was place the dismissed husband's clothing outside the door, and divorce was official. Plural marriages were acknowledged, but for more than 90 percent of Lakota people the problems and expense involved tended to preclude polygamy. When a man did have more than one wife, the wives were often sisters—women who were used to sharing the same household. This arrangement might be made at the insistence of the elder wife, to make her life easier.

In the days before Christian missionaries and the treaties with the U.S. government, there was no marriage ceremony per se. This is not to say that "marriages" were not acknowledged or culturally revered. The marriage ceremony consisted of smaller ceremonies and covered months or years. Gifts had to be offered to the family of the girl. Anthropologists call this payment "bride-price." It might be virtually anything, but the most appreciated were horses. A contemporary Oglala Lakota last name, Her Many Horses, is a poetic reminder of those times.

Indian people resent the idea, perpetrated by books, that a woman was purchased and instead considered the exchange of gifts to be part of the ritual and, if done properly, a compliment to the family of the girl. This might be called a reverse form of dowry. Girls from high-status families were expected to marry boys from the same background. It would be unusual for a girl to marry beneath herself. The number and type of gifts offered by the suitor served notice that the boy was responsible and from a good family.

The man, if well-off, went to live in a tipi erected near that of his new in-laws. For at least a year he would live near them. Perhaps, if he was very poor, he would reside in the same lodge as his in-laws. Despite the close quarters, the old rules of in-law avoidance held, however.[2] What communication did take place with his new in-laws, including his sisters-in-law, was of the teasing and joking variety. All Lakota are well respected if they can tolerate teasing without becoming upset or, conversely, can make people laugh at their jokes.

Over time, many of the old ways of courting became obsolete—older brothers no longer make the decision about whom their sister should marry, and horses are not generally given as gifts—but much also remains. Like other Indian ways, this practice of giving gifts has fallen out of use, but its place in Lakota collective memory and oral tradition has remained.

To be a mother and later, grandmother and—Wakan Tanka permitting—great-grandmother was considered the ultimate blessing, and the highest calling for a Plains Indian woman. This passage of Lucy Swan's, about her own marriage in the early twentieth century, reflects many of the older practices and beliefs.

One of my friends sent a letter that spring to a male cousin of hers. She told him she had found the perfect wife for him. She told me that she had the perfect husband for me. She said, "His name is James Hart Swan. He has been to school in Chilloco, Oklahoma, and he even had two years past high school in Lawrence, Kansas. He is very educated and very handsome and comes from a good family; his father was a chief."

I didn't think much of what she said, but one day my friend ran over to where I was working. "He's coming! He's coming!" she yelled.

"Who?" I asked.

"My cousin, James. He's coming to meet you. If you're right for him, he wants to marry you!"

"Marry me! Oh no, I thought. I'm just a little girl! Why, just last summer I spent most of my time riding from powwow to powwow on the reservation with my sister," I told her.

Oh, what fun we had though. We stayed with older relatives. Whenever we needed money, I would cut a tooth off the elk-tooth dress that Mom let me use. I would sell the elk tooth, and then we would have money. It still makes me laugh when I think about how angry your grandma High Pine got when she saw the dress! Still I told my friend, "I am too young; this man will never want to marry me."

Well he came, and he was handsome—and so old, I thought. He asked me if I could sew. "Yes," I said.

"Can you cook?"

"Yes, I can."

"Do you know how to hitch a team?"

"Yes, and I can do beadwork, and make moccasins and . . ."

"Never mind all that!" he said. "If you marry me, you won't have to worry about any of that!"

"But I'm just so dumb. I'm only a sixth-grader," I told him.

"That's okay, you don't have to be educated. If you can read and figure and speak English, that's plenty," he said.

Soon he left, and I never heard from him until I got a letter from my brother. He said James had gone to Rosebud, to White River, and spoke to him about me. In the letter he said, "This man has no wife, and he has gone to high school and even beyond that! He seems like a good man, and I am sure he can take care of you."

Mom didn't like the idea at all. Still, my brother was the man of the family, now that my dad was gone, and he said to marry this man.

My friend helped me make a wedding dress and many presents for me, even for a baby! They teased me so much—we would just laugh, imagining what it would be like to be married. About two weeks after the letter came, James came to the school with my brother George, and we rode back to Cherry Creek on horseback in August of 1918. We were married at a Catholic church just south of Eagle Butte, South Dakota.[3]

In the old days, before the reservation system was imposed, arranged marriages were the most common type, although romantic marriage was certainly known; and occasionally couples eloped. Marriages today are no longer arranged, but church marriages are rare. Most people are married by a justice of the peace or live in a so-called Indian or prairie marriage, which is recognized by the community but not by the government except as common-law. Lakota attitudes toward married life were far more egalitarian than is commonly believed by non-Indians. This included, or perhaps started with, attitudes toward sexuality. Among the Lakota, the woman owned her body and all the rights that went with it.

By honoring her husband with fine clothes and a beautiful lodge, the Lakota woman built, inch by inch, the reputation and status of her family. Generosity with the fruits of her industry was extended to all who visited her home. When her husband or son came home from battle, it was the women who danced in his honor.

There have been stories that if a woman was sexually unfaithful to her husband he would cut the tip of her nose off, permanently marking her as a loose woman, but this has never been documented or photographed among the Plains Indians, since women owned their sexual life as well.

Women nursed their children for up to five years, both because they felt it was right to do so and because they believed it acted as natural birth control, spacing out the children. It did, in any case, act as a social form of birth control. Husbands were expected to respect a nursing wife and to avoid sexual contact with her. For a nursing mother to become pregnant too soon was considered a disgrace for the man. This may have been another reason for plural marriage.

> *While the white man was calling the Indian woman a drudge, old He Dog, at ninety-two, told me: "It is well to be good to women in the strength of our manhood, because we must sit under their hands at both ends of our lives."*

> —MARI SANDOZ[4]

Childbirth, Child Rearing, and Midwifery Louise Plenty Holes is perhaps the last living Lakota elder with the knowledge of midwifery. Midwives had a special kind of calling, no different from or less important than women called to doctor with spirits or herbs. In fact, some women doctored with spirits and herbs *and* practiced midwifery. It is unfortunate that references to them have been all but omitted from literature on native people. Tilda's translation of Louise's words gives direct insight into how Lakota people dealt with childbirth in the days before white hospitals. The midwife was not a nurse assisting a doctor but rather a type of *Pejuta Win,* a medicine woman delivering the new "traveler" herself.

We lived near Rocky Ford until recently. Back then there weren't any *Wasicu Wakan* [white doctors] over there, so we used to deliver the babies. There wasn't anyone to deliver the babies, so we stronghearted ones would go and help them deliver their babies. We haven't lost one yet. I delivered Herbert Pourier's children and his grandchildren—and even six sets of twins.

As I remember, there was just my mother. My mother was the only one who did it. I helped her, and that is how I became good at it. . . .

When I was twenty-three I delivered my first baby and cut the umbilical cord. There were these little paring knifes, and there were pocket knives by then. She would sharpen it very good and put it in the boiling water I had prepared. When the baby's head was exposed she took the knife out and lay it down, to be prepared. When my mother had delivered the baby I would wash the baby and cut the umbilical cord. If the cord was cut too short it would contract and go back into the baby and cause the baby to bleed to death. She would take the cord and tie it off in several places with *takan'* [deer tendon] so it wouldn't unravel. Then when the string was invented we used it; but Mom was afraid, so she used *takan'*. I usually cut them long and put ointment [buffalo grease] on them. Then I take a piece of material and wrap them with it.

When we first deliver a baby we take them by the feet and hold them upside down and spank them lightly. They have this little piece of what looks like gum in their mouth. When that comes out, they cry.

They [other women] didn't know how [to deliver their own families' babies], so they were very afraid. So when they came after me I would go and do it. I would stay for five days, until the mothers are well and the babies are nursing well. The babies didn't use bottles then. They nursed them. For three days [after delivery] we gave them [the babies] warm tea till their stomachs get well. The mothers nurse them. But afterward, if the mother is not feeling well, we gave them tea until the mother feels better. When the mother's belly is hurting we wrap them tight with strips of sheets. When they are feeling better they can nurse their babies again.

When I first get there, the first thing I do is heat some water, and then I examine the woman. If the baby doesn't turn in position yet, we make the mother walk while I get everything ready. I wash my hands very good and clip my nails short. If I don't do that I might scratch the baby.

They used buffalo grease. The woman would wash, and we'd wash them and put grease on them. There was no medicine then, so that's what they used. . . . About the last ten I delivered, I used Vaseline.

When the baby doesn't come we reach up inside and get the baby, or we would turn them around. If one has its feet come first, we would take their feet and push them back in. If the [woman's] belly is way up there, they haven't turned yet. If you rub and push while she holds her breath, the babies turn, and the belly goes down right away. Then they start hurting really bad. They start contracting.

Some of them [expectant mothers] are very scared, and some are very ornery. We would talk to them. Some would try to run away. Now, here at the hospital, they strap them down. We didn't do that. We would hold them down, and their legs. We'd wet a towel and put it between their lips or wipe their face with it. And also we'd have them bite down on it; otherwise they would bite their lip.

We never give them any medicine. There were no medicines [painkillers]. The husbands would leave because they were afraid. They would stay outside. They would pace. Sometimes the rest of the family would come in and carry on. The mother would hold her breath, and that causes the baby not to come right away. So, when the family stays quiet and stays in the other room, the baby comes a lot quicker.

I usually take a young woman with me who holds the mother down, because some could be ornery while I deliver the baby. The young mothers usually have their babies a lot quicker than the older mothers. When the water breaks long before [delivery], it is harder for the baby to come out, but some come right after the water breaks, and it is easier.

I examine them and see how much they dilate. When I can see the baby's head, that's when the pain is really bad. I tell them, "If you lie still, the baby will come good and the head will be okay. If you talk a lot and breathe wrong, the baby's head will be long. So if you lie still, hold your breath, and push, the baby will come out a lot quicker, and the baby's head will be round. Even if you think you will die while holding your breath the baby will come nice and perfect." But if they keep holding their breath [too long] it cramps around the baby's neck, and that's bad. So then we put our hands in there and grab the arms and pull the baby out. When they keep breathing [without holding and pushing] the baby can't come. If the baby is blue, it is very hard.

No matter how stronghearted they are, and if they breathe a lot, even if the woman is small, she delivers naturally. There was no baby powder in the old days, so there was these little white things on the prairies. If you walk on the prairie you'll find them. They are about the size of a quarter. If you tear them open you'll find some brown powder. If we sprinkle that on the umbilical cord, it heals very good and never gets sore.

We also pray. When a woman is suffering, we pray. We ask the great spirit for help. When we pray the baby comes well and nothing bad happens. These are the things my mother taught me.[5]

This account may be the only one of its kind. As roads improved and automobiles became more numerous in Louise's area, expectant mothers could drive to Pine Ridge Agency and deliver their babies in a hospital. The time-honored and well-respected calling of midwife faded almost into history.

To counter some aspects of popular literature that portray native people as stoic or create characters who speak pidgin English, we are pleased to be able to include some poems that give tender insight into the world of a Lakota mother. The fact that they were written by the late Isabelle (Ten Fingers) Kills Enemy, a respected Lakota holy woman whom I first met in the early seventies, reveals a deeply touching side of a holy woman.

Isabelle's daughter Valentina Janis explained that during the years when her mother was most active as a healer, she was not around her much and went to only a few of her ceremonies. Valentina shared what she could and then said, "You know, there is something about my mom that not very many people know. She loved to write poems and songs, and she even wrote her own music." Here is a poem on the loss of a child:

SINGING TO HEAVEN

On a moonlight
In a dream, little darling
Dream denotes so you will be gone—gone—gone
From this whole wide world of living.
Just memories you are leaving
Singing, winging your way to heaven
Singing, winging your way to heaven
In this dream world
We're happy, little darling
Missed you soon from our midst you're gone—gone—gone
In vain your name we were calling
Searching then we heard your singing.

RISING WIND (ISABELLE TEN
FINGERS), 1906–84

Mother, daughter, granddaughter—these holy women we met or learned of were not the isolated, childless crones of popular literature. Valentina also showed us a set of songs her mother had composed on staff paper. Not only could this woman, a reservation full-blood born on April 18, 1906, write poetry in English but she also had acquired all the skills involved with songwriting. Cultural anthropologists tell us that shamans were the first poets, artists, and songwriters of the human race. They further point out that high intelligence and being multitalented were almost prerequisites to this sacred calling. At the end of her life, Isabelle wandered into the Badlands near her home. Her body was not found for some time.

BEAUTY OF MY MOTHER'S PRAYERS

My dearest memories of Mother
As she trod along life's way
Serenely she paused and stood there
At the altar knelt and prayed

There's a sweet strangeness when
Mother prayed for you and me.
And the peace and love on her face
Was like the glowing dawn of day.
The sunlight seemed brighter
Round her
When my mother knelt and prayed.

Like rainbow o'er the flowers that grow
Beauty of my mother's prayer
Like singing or a river that flows
Beauty of my mother's prayer

Like breezes o'er my fevered brow
When life is low, and the joy of love on her face.
Was like the glowing dawn of day.
The sunlight seemed brighter around her,
When my mother knelt and prayed.

—RISING WIND (ISABELLE
TEN FINGERS), 1906-84

Medicine dreams and callings to serve the Great Mystery were put aside until the active years of life had past and the onset of menopause had begun. Until then, mothering preoccupied women's lives even in their subconscious landscape. After an attack of pneumonia, in a near-death experience Madonna Swan (Abdalla), unable to conceive because of damaged ovaries, had the following dream:

I must have fallen asleep or something, because I saw Levi In The Woods come into the room.

It was so real, not like a dream. He always used to wear a blue shirt with a tie and dark pants, and that's what he had on. He was standing there, just looking at me. I couldn't believe it was him. He was supposed to be dead, and yet here he was, I thought.

He said, "I come to see you." He rattled that plastic tent and smiled, then he opened it and peeked in and said, "You've been wanting this for a very long time, so we brought you one."

"So what is it?" I asked. They rattled that plastic tent again, and Levi's mother opened the tent.

She brought a bundle in and laid it right beside me, and she said, "Look at him, he's just cute!"

So I looked down like that, and it was a little baby boy! "Oh," I said. "You're right, I always wanted one!"

"Yes, I know," Levi said. "So we brought you one." I lay there looking down at my new baby, and I was so happy.

Then I must have come to or woken up, and I looked and the baby was gone—there was nothing there! I started to cry.[6]

Menopause: A Time for the Sacred

The role of grandmother is greatly anticipated by Plains Indian women. It is a time of great responsibility, because grandmothers, as in the past, do much of the childrearing. It is a time to impart wisdom to the young, ever mindful of the kind of adults they will be. It is a time to prepare to enter the spirit world and be Wica' hunkake, an "ancestor spirit." It is the time of being in charge of rituals such as Isna Ti Ca Lowan, as sponsor of a Hunkapi or the preparations for funerals and the memorials that follow for four years on the anniversary of beginning of the soul's journey.[7]

To be a grandma and past the time of childbearing is the time when many who have been called in their dreams or visions early in life fulfill their spiritual destiny and are finally able to answer the sacred calling to help those who are suffering.

The last ceremony that Ted Has Horses had while he was alive was mine. I had a thanksgiving, and I asked him something; I saw something. I don't remember now what it was, and I asked him what it meant. And the answer that *Pejuta Yuha Mani* [a spirit named Walks With Medicine] gave through Ted was, "A woman cannot work with the sacred until her menstruation has stopped," and that was the answer he gave me, and I was so angry I thought, "I didn't ask that!" I was embarrassed. I was angry because I was embarrassed. I thought, "Do you think that I came here asking to be a medicine woman? Now I'm embarrassed you said that in front of everybody, and now they think that I'm asking. I know that. I already know that about menopause," I thought.

And then when I went to Pete about the last time I was there, he said, "They said to tell you that you are now *winu'hcala* [an old woman], that you're over it [menstruation]." So that was it. I never had it [my period] again.

Then this same man talked to me again. I was driving to Pierre, and there was this medicine plant that I saw. It was off in the ditch, and I looked at them and said, "Oh, that's what the medicine man said to gather. He had said, 'Now's the time to get them, because they're in their true ripeness. What you use on it is the root, and all the growing stuff is gone now, so the sap is down below. And this is the time you take it.' He said, 'They are like women; these plants are like women you see. It's when all that life-producing stuff is over, then all the wisdom is in the root. That's when they [women] work with medicine the right way.' That was the understanding that he gave me. Timing, there's a time."

This powerful and poetic passage from Wounye' Waste' Win (Good Life Ways Woman), an Oglala Lakota, speaks directly to an important fact of life for any holy woman. Even if the dreams dictate that the woman will assume the role of a healer, she will not act upon those dreams until she has reached the time in her life when she is a winu'hcala (old woman), past her childbearing years.

Changes in attitudes toward the elderly have taken place in the native community that reflect the more Western attitude. Tribal governments have built old-age homes with federal dollars, creating a place to send the old folks, removing them from the family and often from their traditional community. The housing supply on most reservations is so short that this growth in homes for the elderly does free up space for others. Loneliness, isolation, and depression are affecting more elderly people on the reservation than ever before. Still, even with the recent changes, many families retain their old folks, and their impact on grandchildren remains profound. This passage from Mary Crow Dog, born in 1954, is a mirror of the lives of many Indian children and their ever-present grandparents.

Grandpa and Grandma Moore were good to us, raising us ever since we were small babies. Grandfather Noble Moore was the only father I knew. He took responsibility for us in his son's place. He gave us as good a home as he could. He worked as a janitor in the school and had little money to take care of a large family, his own and that of a son. I don't know how he managed, but somehow he did.

The old couple raised us way out on the prairie near He Dog [community], in a sort of homemade shack. We had no electricity, no heating system, no plumbing. We got our water from the river. Some of the things which even poor white or black ghetto people take for granted we did not even know existed. We knew little about the outside world, having no radio and no TV. Maybe that was a blessing.

Our biggest feast was Thanksgiving, because then we had hamburgers. They had a wonderful taste to them which I still remember. Grandpa raised us on rabbits, deer meat, ground squirrels, even porcupines. They never seemed to have money to buy much food. Grandpa Moore and two of his brothers were hunting all the time. It was the only way to put some fresh, red meat on the table, and we Sioux are real tigers when it comes to meat. . . .

Our cabin was small. It had only one room, which served as our kitchen, living room, dining room, parlor, or whatever. At night we slept there, too. That was our home—one room. Grandma was the kind of woman who, when visitors dropped in, immediately started to feed them. She always told me: "Even if there's not much left, they've got to eat."[8]

The following words by Darlene Young Bear, Minnecojou Elder, explains the difference between Lakota and Western women's attitudes toward aging.

When white women get near the time in life when they will no longer have their moon [menopause], they get depressed and frightened. Many of them feel that their lives are over. In our way, I looked forward to that time when I didn't have to worry about getting pregnant, about caring all the time for young children.

In our way, we look forward to it because it is the time when we can pursue other things full-time, become a medicine woman or [traditional] artist if it's our calling. Prior to that time, our powers of creation are too strong. Because we can make new people, our spiritual powers are greater than men's. After that time, we can hold the pipe, work with the sick, be a doctor if that is our calling.

A woman we will call Cathy Strikes has been having dreams for many years now. In the following dream she recalls meeting an older medicine woman, an ancestral spirit who taught her while she dreamed. Cathy is a full-blood Lakota woman, just now forty, with a husband, children still at home, and a full-time job to help support her family. She has a college education and is a well-respected woman who resides on the reservation of her birth.

That's her [a sacred grandmother] that I saw in a dream! Right beside me; it was like a round vision. In the vision I had a house, and it was out in the country. There was a sweat right there [near the house], and there was a little short woman, and she was taking care of that sweat for me now. You know how the sweat covers are [usually very wrinkled]? There were no wrinkles in this sweat. I knew whatever she did was right. It had to be done right, and she was standing there to make sure. I didn't know who she was.

And the grass was like it is out there [near Cathy's inherited tribal land] this time of year, and it was out on the flat. I was really surprised at this. Sometimes we lack confidence in ourselves, but the spirits will show us the way.

When asked how she first got the calling and how she picked her teacher, Cathy replied:

Not many women have that [the dreams indicating a calling]. I was young then, in my twenties. I even dreamed that I did ask him [to be my teacher]. I was sleeping, and I had a dream that I was to go to him. That's what I told him I wanted to do [to fast and learn his songs and ceremonies]. Here he looked at me, and it was like he knew it was going to be hard. He didn't say anything, but I knew it was going to be hard. He probably knew before I did. He was just such a good man that maybe I was drawn to him [in my dream]. Well, he taught all of us something, the things he said were good. I could feel it. I knew it was the truth.

In the traditional way, Cathy attached herself to the family of this man for four years. She fasted each year and learned his songs and ceremonies, just as a man would. She remains close to her teacher's family even though he has been dead for some time. When asked when or if she would use the years of dreams and formal training to fulfill her calling, she said simply, "I think I will. I just pray. I don't live out in the country yet [at the place in her vision], but maybe it's coming. I think it's getting closer. I'm not trying to rush it."

This very brief inside glimpse of how Lakota women are prepared for the walk on the path through life sketches a very different picture than a person from the outside world might have, based on racial and literary stereotypes. It is the image of a woman who is at the very core of her family and community. Women enjoyed their lives often at their own forms of recreation, like the stick game, a form of gambling, or more athletic games like shinny, a form of Indian field hockey. At its best we see an egalitarian society in which men and women are a team, one no less important than the other.

The ritual and family life presented here is also the foundation experienced by those special women whom people turn to for help with their daily problems, those physical, mental, and spiritual—it is also then the life path of holy women.

Transition

If we are fortunate we will live to see generations of our children come into this world, but there comes a time in old age when we must die. Death is an important ritual transition in most cultures. For American Indians, as for most peoples, the funeral service is a physical expression of beliefs about the fate of the soul. Among the Lakota it is the women who take care of the dead, conducting the funeral and all the practices that comprise a proper sendoff.

How the dead are treated during the funeral process and during the four annual memorial dinners is literally an expression of love and compassion for the health and the fate of the *Wanagi* (soul). It is for this reason that a "proper burial" be given. The Lakota way of death is a very powerful and effective celebration of the deceased person's life, an acknowledgment of family and community affection and of the idea that this is one of the last important things you can do for the spiritual health of your loved one.

When an elderly Lakota decides it is time to die, it is not uncommon for this person to begin to visit with the spirits of those who have gone on before. It is at this point that the women of the family may begin to plan for the wake and funeral.

When Lucy Swan was dying (in her own bed), she would say things seemingly to no one, carrying on conversations with people the rest of us near her could not see. At one point she called me close to her and said, *"Takoja* [grandson], I want you to do me a favor. If people are going to come in here crying around, keep them out. I am not sad about dying. I am glad. Soon I will see my husband, my sons. Soon I will see Jesus. I already see them; they are here after me. So tell people to be happy when they come in to see me."

Those who conduct funerals of parents are generally the oldest-born girls. Tilda added, however, that this might not always be true: "If it were my Dad who passed away, it would probably be my older sister who would make the decisions, because she's the oldest, and they were always close in this life. When Mom leaves us, I will probably make the decisions, because I have stayed closer to her."

Although subtle variations exist from family to family, the traditional rites of death are quite consistent regardless of the denominational ties. Catholics may have a funeral mass, and others may have a worship service, but the "Indian" parts remain consistent. According to Tilda this is how a woman should conduct a proper funeral:

If a funeral is to be done right, certain things must be done. Someone must prepare the body. Generally it is the close female relatives who do this. When they are bathing the dead and dressing him or her, they should try to be lighthearted, even joking, like the dead person could hear and enjoy the conversation.

The child closest to the deceased will be the one to go to the funeral home and pick out the casket and grave liner, unless the tribe provides it. The oldest brother might be involved in this, if costs are a question. All the children and many other relatives will donate to help with the expenses.

While the family waits for the body [embalmed, by state law] to be brought back, all those who consider themselves "part of the family" buy and prepare food, because all those who come to mourn will have to be fed, at least three times a day. There should always be food and drink available for those who want it.

It is the men of the family's job to be outside keeping a fire going under the [soup] cauldron. They may run errands; but fetching, splitting wood, and tending the fire for the four days and three nights of the wake is their job.

When the body is brought the women usually cover the lower half of casket with a star blanket and perhaps put moccasins on the feet. Special objects [such as a prayer pipe] previously asked for by the dead person may be placed in the foot of the casket as well.

When women come into a wake, there is a sound that they should make. They make themselves cry, and they hug the survivors. Usually a table is set up near the casket, and pictures of the dead person are displayed. Sympathy cards may be left on the table, and some people put money in their cards to help the family. During the four days each time people come into the wake they are expected to pass by this table and view the body.

In the evenings, but sometimes all day, people will get up and speak about the feelings they had for the deceased. It is a way for them to express their feelings in a good way. They may comment on childhood or life experiences with the deceased, or talk [eulogize] about the character of the person and what his or her life should mean to those left behind.

Gospel music groups from across the reservation, especially those loved by the dead person, perform. Each evening a clergy will conduct some sort of prayer service. When this is completed the family may feed the guests again. If the dead person loved Indian music, traditional drum groups may also come and sing; and of course food for hundreds of mourners will be prepared cooked and served all night.

The woman running the funeral coordinates the efforts of a dozen or more female relations. No book on Plains Indians and the role of women in the sacred would be complete without acknowledging this central and powerful female function.

> On the last morning a Christian clergy [generally Indian] will come to conduct the church and burial service. If the deceased was a soldier, there may be a color guard [twenty-one-gun salute]. If the family requests, Brave Heart songs may be sung over the body. Sometimes the mourners stop four times in a ritual manner as they carry the body to the grave, so that these songs can be sung. I have only seen this a few times.[9]
>
> After the casket has been lowered into the ground and the service concluded, it is the men in the family who actually pick up the shovels and quickly bury their dead relative. This is done quickly, with the men passing shovels, until all those who wish have helped to fill the grave.
>
> When the burial is over, all the mourners are invited back to the house of the family, and fed again. When the feast has been finished, all the belongings of the dead person are given away to the crowd.

In the oldest form, still practiced by some Lakota, the house is stripped to the bare walls. Nothing is to remain of the past that might cause the living to mourn too hard or lure the dead back to this familiar place.

Tilda explained why this is done in such a prescribed manner:

> I guess it is for the good of the soul of the person who has died. It is so that soul will have a good journey and be able to get to the other side. If things are not done right—the relatives are too stingy with the food or giveaway, or won't take the four days to run the wake and funeral—the person who died may not be able to leave or to make the journey because they are too angry or sad to leave the living and may be stuck between the worlds.
>
> If they come back to see us after they have completed that journey, it will be good. If they get trapped and are unable to make their journey it could be bad for those left behind. It is the woman's duty to do the best she can for the one who has died.

This idea that the dead can be encouraged, helped, and nourished by those still living is at the basis of the old "Keeping of the Soul" rite.

Mourning continues formally for a full year. Mourners male and female wear dark clothes, and they seldom go out except to go to work and take care of the needs of the family. It is expected that the close family members who are mourning won't go to public gatherings or Indian dances. In a real sense they are obliged to drop out of public life.

On the anniversary of the death an *Awa'spanyan,* or Memorial Feast, and *Wihpeya,* Giveaway, are held, in which special new things—quilts, blankets, and the like—are given away. These memorials are to be conducted until the fourth anniversary of the death. In this modern day, much of the essential meaning of the old "Soul-Keeping" ceremony remains in the four anniversary feasts and giveaways, which are conducted by the women of the family.

Understanding assistance in the proper transition from this temporary world to the "other-side camps" is critical to holy women. Where the spirits go, how they live, see us, speak to us, even warn us, and what they act like as spirits are important aspects of women's role in the sacred.

5

The Shadow World

We call the place you go at death the "Other-side Camps." That's the closest translation I could come to. I don't think there is a word for "hell" in our native language. There is no word for "devil." Some people call it the "Happy Hunting Grounds," but we Crow call it the "Other-side Camps." It is the next spiritual plane.

When our people are dying, the people from the Other-side come to get them. They take them to be with the loved ones who have gone on before. It is a loved one, a favorite grandma or perhaps grandpa, who comes to speak with them and tell them their time is near. We consider this to be a blessing.

—JACKIE YELLOW TAIL, Crow

If a child is raised from the time it can understand, being told there is no such things as ghosts, then that child has learned not to see the whole reality. If a child is never told that, it will see a very different world.

—MADONNA (BLUE HORSE) BEARD,
Lakota

Much of what goes on in the sacred and ceremonial life of the holy woman stems from her knowing how to breach the space separating the spirit world from that of the living. Because most Plains Indian religious beliefs are not dogmatic, ideas about death vary from individual to individual.

Understanding Plains Indian ideas about death requires insight into how the Indian sees the soul. Few see it as an integrated whole. Most, like the Lakota, see it in separate aspects that have different fates when the body dies.

The soul has at least four distinct attributes, although they may not be discussed as such. It must also be remembered that to translate anything in a Native American tongue into English tends to impose limits on it. The *Ni un* (life), or *Niyan,* is the "breath of life" that departs at the moment of death. In its visible aspect it is considered like the fog *Niya'sota,* which comes from our mouths on a cold winter day. This dissipates soon with the decomposition of the body. It may be seen as a life force that holds the corporeal body and the *Wanagi,* or intelligent ghost, together in life.

Some medicine people say that if this *Ni un,* this breath of life, is weakened or leaves the body, it causes certain kinds of illnesses. It then becomes the role of the holy woman or man to bring balance back to the patient by finding and retrieving or healing this aspect of the soul. As Mel Lone Hill, a Lakota man, says, "I had pneumonia four times as a child. Finally, my family asked a medicine woman for help. She had medicine with ghost people. She had to look for me for four days and found me in a different world. And she brought me back."

Some practitioners, often through the *Yuwi'pi* ceremony, or "tying them up," have a special talent for finding dead bodies or determining whether someone missing (in a blizzard, say) is alive or dead, or if the missing was killed or died of natural causes. Through the use of special clear, round stones (usually found on anthills) and the spirits they contain, which are called Yuwi'pi Wasi'cun, the holy man or woman may ask, through the stone spirit, the Wanagi (ghost) of the missing person where the relatives may find the body so that they need not suffer in doubt. As the Yuwipi person calls upon his or her helpers to heal the sick or do something mysterious, their powers are depleted and they become weaker, until one day they become used-up and the holy person dies. Holy people fast each year, constantly "collecting power" in the form of new spirit helpers, lest they become spiritually and physically used-up, perhaps dying younger than they would had they not been called to help.

This gradual dissipation may in part account for why working as a ghost communicator is a feared and respected calling. Not only are the demands on them great and unpredictable but the rewards are often little or nothing. Some old medicine people have actually felt abandoned in their last years because of some of these vague fears. One such fear is that over time the holy person has become altered, dangerous, or frightening. Another is the possibility that the holy person could use his or her powers for both good or evil. These two opposites may be highly subjective, depending on who commissions the holy person.

Another aspect of the soul is the *Sicun,* the Spirit Helper or Ally. Some believe the soul *(wana'gi)* is not born with this aspect—that it is acquired at the moment of birth. Others believe that the helper chooses a human before birth; whereas still others believe allies are acquired later in life. Humans may acquire more than one helper. At death these helpers return to live with the supernatural beings or are commissioned to help another human.

A third critical aspect of the soul is another's wana'gi, the shadow or shade of a living person, what non-Indians call a ghost. It is another's wana'gi that may become the holy woman's spirit helper, or Sicun. The wana'gi has been described as the ghost of the living person, the intelligent soul, and in its benevolent role it may watch over, communicate with, or warn the living. As Tilda says, "I remember one time we were outside, and we could hear women crying. They were not visible, but we could hear them. Shortly after that, within a few days, our grandmother died."

The wana'gi can make itself visible, so it has also been described as the "visible ghost" that resembles its living form. It may make itself visible to someone sleeping or while someone is awake. Our Western Christian notion that in heaven there is no disease, suffering, or unhappiness seems not to have a Lakota equivalent in the shadow world. The wana'gi can be malevolent and very dangerous as well as benevolent. According to Tilda, "The way someone was in life—angry, upset, or happy—the way they are when they die, if they are happy with those left behind and the world they left, is the way they will be in the otherworld. The same is true if they died unhappy."

The fourth aspect of the soul is sometimes called *Ton.* Ton is thought to be an innate spiritual quality or, in its animate state, a "power" that makes something *wakan* (holy). It is this property in certain objects like feathers, claws, and stones that makes these objects useful to the Indian doctor.

Even earth and rocks are part of the living Mother Earth (her "skeleton") and thus are the oldest part of creation. These things are used in helping the living, because they have power. This quality can be added or enhanced, as when a holy man or woman makes a *wasicun* (medicine, a talisman) that will protect or benefit the "patient." Along with her sacred songs and spirit helpers, these medicine objects are the literal tools of the holy woman's trade.

The Living and the Dead

It is believed that the behavior of the living may in fact affect those who are in the spirit world. Grieving too hard or too long may cause a soul to become trapped close to earth. Mitchell Zephier shared this with us:

> After my mother got killed, my grandmother really took it hard for a long time. I remember one day I came in the house, and my grandmother was crying. I said, "Grandma, what's wrong?"
>
> "Well I was sitting here sewing. I was thinking about your mom and feeling bad, and here I looked up and she was standing there, and she looked at me and said, 'Mom, why are you crying like this? I'm so happy, but you're making me feel bad. I want you to be happy, but you're making me feel bad. I want you to be happy—don't cry for me.'"
>
> Grandma said, "Grandson, I don't feel bad like I did. I feel good now. I'm not going to cry for your mom anymore."

Relatives and the ancestral ties that bind them exist even after death: according to an anonymous Lakota woman, "An old woman was visiting my mom one time, and she told us that she had a dream that the soul of a beloved aunt was stuck between this world and the next because she was so unhappy about how her family behaved after she died. We place great faith in our dreams, and this dream stood out, so she had told us to shape up."

In the ideal outcome, the spirit travels on a long path, taking it over the *Wana'gi Ta'canku,* which is literally "spirit road" but refers to the Milky Way. In one Lakota version, the soul is met by an old woman who looks to see if the soul has a blue dot, or tattoo, identifying it as one of The People. If not, the soul may be pushed off the road—sent back.

If the soul passes this inspection it is sent on an even longer journey, but how long that *Wana'giya',* or spirit journey, may take is unknown, because it is in spirit time. At the end of the journey the soul sees a tipi. In that tipi sits an old man (Wakan Tanka), who asks, "How was your journey?"—meaning the journey through life. It is he who first sent the spirit on its journey to this world. If the soul answers properly, it will receive safe passage and go on to stay forever in the happy mirror world of this one, the *Wana'gitomakoce* (world of the spirits). If not—if it grumbles or complains about its recent life, it may be sent back to live on earth again and learn more.

Still others believe that the two worlds exist side by side, that death means you enter a world that parallels this one, where the dead in the shadow world can see and communicate with the living and at times the living may be in contact with the dead. A variation of this idea is that the dead don't go anywhere but stay near their relations on this earth, where they are always present but only rarely make themselves seen.

Plains Indian ideas about death often include a reincarnative philosophy that allows souls to become "finished." There is, then, no one place where souls go, and the journey after death, like life on this earth, may be arduous and different for each soul.

The late Severt Young Bear gave the following explanation of how he believed this works. He drew a diagram of life that he called "Steps on the Red Road." When a child is born, he called the translation of it "slippery." In this step the child is a toddler. The next step on the sacred path through life is called "knee-deep in mud." This is the clumsy, awkward stage from about two through six or seven years of age. The next step he called "cold"; this refers to the child's "searching for identity." Next, the traveler must pass through adolescence, or "walk on thorns": this is when everything in life is difficult to understand.

The fifth step on the Red Road Severt Young Bear called "walks among swarming bees," and this is the stage where a true Lakota woman begins her own life, starts a family, and begins to express what she is thinking. If she lives properly, some people will be jealous and talk about her behind her back, hence the "swarming bees." The next part of the journey he called "walk over the body of relatives." This stage, he says, is hard and requires a "strong mind and body." It is at this stage that our relations begin to leave us behind on this earth. The seventh step completes the journey and in a sense completes the soul: he calls it "loneliness." This is when we are quite old, our spouse has left us for the other side, and our parents are long there.

If the soul does not become complete, dies too soon, or fails successfully to traverse a part of the path of life, then it will be sent back to live on this earth again until it completes the journey "in a good way."[1]

One can gain real insight into the core of Plains Indian belief and behavior by understanding their ideas about death and about what comes after 'ni un', the breath of life, leaves the body.

What follows is an account of a remarkable near-death, or out-of-body, experience from Madonna Swan. It also contains some of the universal themes seen in dream experiences of people who have returned from the world of the dead. Powerful and poetic, we believe it is unique in Native American literature and reveals a great deal about the Lakota worldview. The Levi she refers to in this passage was a childhood sweetheart, her first true love, who was killed in an accident while Madonna was still in a tuberculosis sanitarium in Rapid City. She had this experience in a hospital in Bismarck, North Dakota, about 1973:

During one of those times I lost consciousness, Levi In The Woods appeared to me. He was calling to me to go with him. Suddenly I saw a long log hall, so I came into the door. I was following Mom and Cousin Mary, but because I was having trouble breathing, I moved slow and fell behind. When I got inside I stood there looking for Mom or somebody I might know. I was looking around, and I saw them sitting in the northwest corner of the hall. Every person in the gathering was dead except Mom, Aunt Matilda, and Cousin Mary. They made room for me, and I sat down.

I kept looking around, some of the people I didn't know. The ones I recognized were all deceased! My relatives! It was a gathering, a dance, and they were all in their Indian clothes. There was my Cousin Marceline, and my Aunt Mary High Pine, and my Aunt Emma, Mary's first cousin, and my Grandma Julia High Pine! There was also some of my Lone Eagle relations, Grandmas [great aunts] on my grandmother's side, they were all there! I had a grandma named Medicine Boy—she was there, and her daughter. They are all dead and gone, I thought.

So there I sat watching; there was a man up front making announcements. He said, *"Naslo hon wacipelo wayun cipiktelo* (everybody, round dance)." Singers started hitting the drum and singing. Everybody got up and started making a circle. My Grandma High Pine didn't get up because she was lame, but she sat there smiling and tapping her toes to the music.

I was sitting there wondering at all of this, when Cousin Mary said, "Let's join in." And here my mom put a shawl over me and Mary. Even Aunt Matilda Chasing Hawk joined in; she was dancing too.

So we were dancing along, and here this man came up behind me, and said, "Somebody wants to see you out there," pointing to the back of the hall. So I asked him who it was. "I don't know," he said, "but there is a man out there, and he says he must see you right away."

I left the circle and started walking towards the door. I got to the door, opened it, and here it was Levi! And Gee! The hills were green, and covered with flowers all over the ground! There was every kind of tree, and it was so pretty there. Prettier than any place I had ever been. There were birds of every kind, and they were singing. The colors were so beautiful!

"Levi In The Woods was standing a short ways from me, and he said, "Come here. I want to tell you something." So I started walking towards him, and as I approached him he would move back away from me, but I kept following him.

Finally I stopped and asked, "What do you want?"

He said, "Come with me over here—I want to tell you something." So I walked towards him as I did; he kept moving away from me. So I just followed him.

Levi was down the path from me, and that path was such a beautiful place. There was every kind of tree you can think of, and flowers, along the edge of the path. So I'd stop and smell the flowers. The birds were singing; it was such a pretty sound they were making. I was just taking my time, listening and smelling the flowers as I went.

Levi would stop and smile when I would stop. Pretty soon Levi would call me, and I'd follow again. We had gotten quite a way from the dance hall, and I thought, If Levi chases me I can't run very fast, so I shouldn't get too far from the people in the hall.

So I just stopped and I said, "You come up here and tell me. I can't go anymore."

"No! You come over here," he pleaded. "I'm not going to take long."

So I started in again; I followed him. He went down a long hill. When he reached the bottom of the hill, I said, "I can't walk up hills very good, so I'm staying here—you tell me from there."

"Please," he said. "You come down here; it's important!" There was a stream down below the hill. It was a beautiful blue color, and it was so clear you could see every rock on the bottom. It was not like any stream I had ever seen at home.

I stood on the little hilltop looking down at the blue stream and said, "I can't come down, you tell me from there."

"No. Come on down here!" he insisted.

Well, I thought, if it's that important to him, I'll go down there. When I got down there, I thought to myself, You know, this man is dead, and I'm talking to him. Now he's trying to get me through that water. I'd better not go through that water, or I'll die. So I just stood there and Levi started through the water. He was up to his knees in the water, then his waist.

"Come and wade in the water with me; it's not cold," he said. "It's really warm. These rocks won't hurt your feet."

"But," I said, "oh! I can't wade in the water with my bare feet. I'm just going to leave my shoes on."

I started into the water, and it was warm, and so clear! He kept moving away from me, across the stream, smiling at me. I just kept going, and soon the water was up to my knees.

But he just kept going. Soon the water was up to his chest. So I said, "I'm not going any further; this is as far as I'm going!"

I thought, Well, I'm going to turn around and go back. So I did—I turned around and started coming back. "Come here," he asked again. "I'm going to tell you something important."

"No! I'm going to go back!" I told him. I reached the water's edge and started up the hill.

I stopped halfway to rest, but he was following, so I just kept going. I was so short of breath, but I just kept going, walking towards that beautiful path. Still he was following! Now I was breathing so hard it hurt my chest. If I make it back to that log hall I'll be all right, I thought. I just kept walking, and here somebody slapped my face, calling to me. "Donna? Donna? What's the matter? What's the matter, Donna?" the nurse was saying. I was just sweating! She asked, "Did you have a dream?"

"Yea," I finally said. "I guess it was a dream."

"Where did you go? Who did you go with?" she asked. "You were really talking when you came out of it [the coma]. We thought we had lost you," the nurse said, smiling. "I was with Levi," I tried to explain. "I think he wanted to take me!"

"And I think I was in the place where all my dead relatives are. That must be wherever I was." Saying this before I was awake enough to realize it wasn't making any sense, trying to tell this to the nurse.

It was such a different experience. It was so vivid. I remember Grandma High Pine so distinctly, sitting there tapping her toe to the drumbeat. She always wore a *Maza Wapeyaka* [concho belt]. She wore kind of a dark blue dress and a single-strand necklace. And my Cousin Marceline, when she was living, she always wore a long cotton dress and a wide leather belt. She had that belt on, and she had a blue scarf on her hair. I think she was buried in that. It was so real.

I have never had a dream like that! I believe I must have been close to death. It is a beautiful, wonderful place there. Since that time I haven't been afraid of death. I know what's on the other side. It's a beautiful place, and Levi wants me to join him there.[2]

The Lakota believe that the body can die and then the spirit can return once again, to reinhabit the body. Often upon returning from the land of the dead, a person seems to have been transformed into a better person for having "died." The following story, shared with us by Mitchell Zephier, actually comes from his maternal grandmother the late Mary Buck, also known as Woman Who Walks Holy, or Walks Holy Woman. Because it is very rare for this to happen, the stories are remembered and passed down. Upon returning, these people are at the very least consid-

ered Wakan (mysterious). The story also further illustrates how Lakota
people select and pass down spiritual, or Indian, names, usually picking
the name of a deceased relative or ancestor who had admirable qualities.

My daughter had a naming ceremony a couple of years before my
grandma passed away; she gave her the name *Wakan Mani' Win* [Walks
Holy Woman]. I guess Grandma wanted that name to be carried on. My
grandmother had two names. Her other name was Plenty Horse. Her father
had a lot of horses—that's probably how he came by the name. She was
very proud of that name, because her father had given it to her. She said it
was the proudest day of her life, when she received that name from her father. When I told her I was going to tell you her stories [for this book], she
said, "Make sure he uses both my names."

My grandmother told me the story about Woman Who Walks Holy. At
the time of her death she was a young woman, probably in her early teens.
Woman Who Walks Holy was Grandmother Mary's grandmother and took
care of her when she was a child.

They were part of Iron Nation Band of the *Sicangu* [Burnt Thigh Nation
of the Lakota] and were living up along the Missouri River.[3] She was kind
of a spoiled young woman and maybe a little conceited. Because she was a
very handsome young woman, tall and straight, the young men would try to
court her, but she would have nothing to do with them.

She had no time for children or old people. People had begun to notice
how she was and whispered about her. One day she got sick. They called in
a very wise medicine man, but over many days she got sicker and sicker until she died. When she died, her parents were really grief-stricken.

They dressed her up in the best outfit they could. In those times they
would put things they might need in the afterlife with them on the scaffold.
One of the things that she had was a knife with a beaded knife case. As my
grandmother said, "This was in the winter, and they buried her in a tree."

I asked her, "Grandma, how come they buried her in a tree?"

She said, "Well, the ground was frozen, so they couldn't put up a scaffold. In the summer weather, they could make a scaffold and put it in the
ground. Usually, if they were camped where there were trees, they would
put the burial scaffold in the trees."

After grieving for four days, her people moved to another campsite. She
was all alone near the abandoned village when she woke. It was like she
woke up from a dream. She felt very cold, and she was in the dark. She was
kind of disoriented and didn't know where she was.

Somehow she got her knife out. She was wrapped in a buffalo robe, tied
down on that scaffold. Slowly she cut herself free. It took her some time because she was weak. She had been without food and water for a number of
days now. I guess she'd been in a coma; they thought she was dead.

After she came back to life and cut herself loose, she fell from the scaffold. Woman Who Walks Holy followed the trail to the new camp. When they first caught sight of her they were afraid of her because they thought she was a wana'gi [spirit]. She got this name Woman Who Walks Holy because of the way she was walking—almost floating.

But what is perhaps more important is that she was given the name Woman Who Walks Holy also because when she returned, she had changed as a person. She was no longer a self-centered, spoiled child. People noticed a really profound change in her. They had a ceremony, and she related things that she had seen in that shadow world.

One of the things my grandmother told me is that Woman Who Walks Holy lived to be about one hundred and one years old. She told my grandmother that she saw herself as a very old woman in this dream world and that she had also seen my grandmother Mary as an old woman. "I saw you with white hair; you will live to be old—perhaps not as old as I am, but you will be old when you die" [my grandmother lived to be eighty years old].

For the rest of her life people who came into contact with her always felt they were in the presence of somebody who really was a spiritual person— she kind of emanated that. She was always telling people to take better care of the children. Woman Who Walks Holy always had time for the elderly. We believe it is the children, just coming from the spirit world, and the old people, soon to return, that are closest to the sacred. All her life she lived and walked as a holy woman.

I never knew my grandmother to drink, ever. She said, "I carry this name": "You know, you're going to have to tell your daughter that she can't take this name lightly, because the person that carries this name will have to live her life in a certain way, and that is that."

A *Wana'gi Wapiye'* (Ghost Conjuror) is by definition some man or woman whose function, by Wakon (sacred or mysterious) methods, is to call and speak with spirits. In this capacity the holy person serves to unite two communities or *Tiyo'spaye'*—that of the living relatives and that of the dead, and, in that sense, those people living in the present with those with knowledge of the past.

6

Dreams and the Spirit World

Dreams have always been an important part of my life. I think that is true for most people who are searching for spirituality and go out and fast. Dreams guide you; they show you the way that you should be living, or the direction, or give you signs to help someone else, and they are gifts.

—JACKIE YELLOW TAIL, Crow Woman

Dreams are central to the lives of Plains Indian people. Dreams—where direct communication with the spirit world takes place, whether experienced while awake or asleep—are access points for the shaman, the holy woman. They serve many purposes, from the initial "calling" through her spiritual indoctrination by the spirits themselves, until her death. This is made clear in the words of Good Lifeways Woman, an Oglala Lakota: "Pejuta Yuha Mani [Walks with Medicine], a spirit helper, came to me in a ceremony and told me, 'No one man will be your teacher. You will not have a human teacher; the spirits will teach you directly.'"

Ihan'bla: To Dream, to Have Visions

From earliest life, children are exposed to a whole set of beliefs and responses to all sorts of dreams. The Lakota have one core word for both, *ihan'bla*. There are special terms for certain specific dreams, such as *Tatanka wan ihan'ble*, Buffalo Dreamer, and *iwicawahan'ble*, the call to use the yuwi'pi stones and the yuwi'pi ceremony, but the root word remains the same. Children raised in traditional homes, in their early years before attending American-style schools, learn to remember, talk about, sort, interpret, catalog, and recall specific details of virtually hundreds of dreams. The most talented can recall vivid detail twenty, thirty, or forty years later.

Dreams form a large intellectual and spiritual complex and are looked to for important insights about oneself and other living people, often relatives. They are also seen as a source of contact and communication for those relatives now in the spirit world who may have help, advice, or warning to impart to the living. Dreams may then provide motivation for changing one's life.

"Special dreams" are the most common call to women to become involved with the sacred, to become what we are calling medicine women. Tilda recalls her childhood indoctrination into the world of dreams: "When I was living with my grandmother [Sadie Crazy Thunder], she used to discuss her dreams all the time. It seems that a lot of the old people liked to do this when they were visiting. It's not so much that way now with younger people. Sometimes I think about a dream for days and days."

Any dream that lingers upon waking is worth considering, pondering over, because to Indian people, that dream is a means of the most essential communication—that with the spirit world. One who is constantly communicating with spirits is considered to have very special gifts. It is these women who, later in life, have the potential to be healers. Dreams are often prophetic and may warn the dreamer of impending danger or changes in her life or that of a loved one. They may move the dreamer to action, or inaction. Interpretation is not always precise, but the dreamer will discuss the dream, or think about it until he or she is satisfied that its meaning has been revealed. Relatives who are known to be good at interpreting dreams are sought out to help in this process.

Ritual provides access to the otherworld. It is the songs, sacred objects, order, and detail of a holy woman's rituals of communication that are at the basis of her manifestation of power. Through these acts the spirits can understand and respond to human concerns. These "special dreams" are recognized as such and understood by the dreamer, because they are metaphors familiar to the living as well.

The following dream was related by Mitchell Zephier and comes from his grandmother's own experience. Her government name was Mary Buck; her Indian name was Walks Holy Woman.

When Grandma called me in, she was talking about the spirit food, *wasna* [dried pounded meat and pounded berries], that I had almost mistakenly eaten. She said, "You know, I'll tell you about the time I almost died. I almost froze, and this spirit saved my life.

"When your grandpa and I first got married, we rode horseback down the creek near our place to visit with the Roan Horse Family. I was getting impatient because it was getting kind of late, and Grandpa Bill was just sitting there, talking and talking. Him and old Pete Useful Heart, when they get together, they would just talk and talk about things they did in the old days like the rodeo in 1906. Since I was younger than Grandpa Bill by some years (not born yet), these things did not interest me.

"I went outside, it was wintertime then, and I was really getting mad at that old man. He would just drink some coffee, more coffee, and talk about things that everybody else already forgot about. So I went outside and I put my sweater on, and I said, 'Shoot, I'm just going to walk! I'll walk along the railroad tracks.' I thought, 'Well, maybe that old man will notice that I am gone, and he'll come back.' So I started walking down the railroad tracks. It was wintertime. It wasn't too cold yet. It was getting on toward evening and I was walking and walking.

"The more I walked the madder I was getting, because I kept looking back, and no Grandpa Bill. I thought, 'He's probably just sitting back there drinking more coffee and talking and talking.' I got to this railroad bridge over the creek, and I thought, 'Well, I'll go under this bridge, and I'll get out of the cold.' It was getting kind of windy and starting to snow. I was kind of pouting at your grandfather, so I didn't go back to that warm house. I went under that railroad bridge.

"One of the things that you will notice, if you ever come close to freezing to death, is that there is a point when you get real drowsy. When I was under that bridge I must have dozed off, because I felt somebody kind of touch me on the shoulder.

"When I came to, it was dark, but there was a man standing there. In Indian he called me 'Sister.' He said, 'Sister, you better walk with me, because it could get really cold here.'

"When I looked to see his face, it was wrapped in a blanket and dark, so I never got a good look at him. It was as if where his face should be there was just darkness. He said, 'I'm going to sing a song.' Then he said, 'Sing with me as we're walking. We'll both sing, and we'll get home.'

"At first I thought it was your Grandpa Bill, but he called me 'Sister.' I kind of felt a little scared, but his songs were so powerful—grandson, you have heard the song he sang that day. Whoever this man was, he had a beautiful voice, and he was just singing strong. I had my head down, and I was singing, and I was walking, and it was cold and it was dark by then. We were walking together down those railroad tracks a long ways when he just stopped singing.

"It was snowing hard then, and the wind was blowing. My legs were completely numb then. I couldn't walk any further. When I looked up to see him, even his tracks were gone! Covered by blowing snow. I heard a horse neigh, kind of whinny, and Grandpa Bill came up. He carried me back to the house. He had followed the creek with the two horses and gotten back before I did, so he already had a fire going. He sat me by the stove.

"When I was warm enough I started to talk. I told him that I almost froze but that some man came by and he woke me up, and I followed him. I told Grandpa about his singing. Grandpa got a real funny look on his face.

"He said, 'You know, there was an old man who used to walk along these tracks all the time. He used to go into town sometimes to get drinks. Sometimes he'd be singing Indian as he walked. That guy had a beautiful voice. One time he passed out on the tracks, and the train ran over him. It tore him apart pretty bad; that's why you couldn't see his face. If you live here long enough, you'll hear the dogs start barking, but there will be nothing there. Sometimes I have even heard him singing.'

"So you see, grandson, when you see certain types of food left out by Indians, *wasna* or *wojapi* [traditional fruit pudding], things like that, leave it. That is for the spirits, to thank them and let them know we still think of them."

Spirits, ghosts, and interaction with them are seen by Indian people as a normal part of life on this earth. All things, living or not, have a spirit that may manifest itself in the living, including insects, deer, eagles, even rock spirits. Helper spirits often manifest themselves in an object. To the Lakota, small, round rocks may be charged with great power and attach themselves to a living person, returning to them even when discarded. These rocks belong to a class of spirits known as the "rock nation." It is the little pebbles found on anthills that aid the Yuwi'pi practitioners in their ceremony. As an anonymous Lakota woman says,

> I was dreaming [asleep]. This girl and I were standing and talking. She started bragging about how she was going to be a holy woman. I told her that was good. I didn't want to discourage her.
>
> There was a little white rock [Wasicun or Tunkan] that was bouncing along in front of us. She tried to catch it and couldn't. I reached down, and I didn't even have to try. I caught it on the first bounce. Maybe it is the same rock my grandmother had.

Contact with spirits who reside in the spirit world is the basis of most Lakota ritual, and this is true for other Plains tribes as well. The thin veil between this temporary world and the lasting world of the spirits must be penetrated. Either the spirit of the holy woman must travel to that world, or the spirits must come forth and communicate with her at her altar.

Animal Spirit Helpers

The world is divided into various classes of animals, often referred to as the "Two Leggeds," "Four Leggeds," "Wingeds," and "Those that Live in the Water." Any one of these, if acquired by a human as an ally, imparts powers peculiar to its kind. Whether animal spirits are actually the spirits of deer, rabbits, butterflies, or owls is not always known or agreed upon. Some are thought to be the spirit of the animal; others are thought to be human spirits who call themselves by an animal name, as was the practice of the Plains Indian.

Like the humans they serve, spirits are specialists as well. Women who dreamed of specific animals were believed to have the kinds of powers generally associated with that "kind of helper." Bears, for instance, indicate a calling to doctor with herbal remedies. Dreams of a turtle might call a woman to help with menstrual concerns or possibly to make fertility charms. Spiders are common and powerful allies for spiritual doctoring.

In some sense, spiritual helpers and the principal influences they exert on humans may be divided into female and male. What follows is a short list of the most typical helpers, with emphasis on those associated with holy women.

Two Leggeds Only two nations belong to that of the two leggeds—the humans and the bear. Human spirits, or ancestral spirits, may attach themselves to a man or woman. These are often the most powerful of helpers.

In sacred language the bear is called *hu-nunpa,* the two legged. While the bear was considered an awesome animal in the flesh, its spirit is a powerful helper indeed. He is also the keeper of wisdom.

The bear is a very special animal, thought to resemble humans in many ways, including its ability to walk on two legs. It roots out herbs and thus has a knowledge, like the badger and skunk, of those plants that live both above and below the earth. The bear is the one animal who chooses to share his sacred wisdom directly with humanity, forming a unique alliance. Because the bear is ruler of the underworld creatures, it is closely aligned with the powers of Mother Earth and is also considered chief of all the animals when it comes to knowledge of herbal medicine. The female bear is said to represent Lakota attitudes toward bravery, especially in defending one's family.[1] Men and women who dreamed of the bear (bear dreamers) were often the ones who became physicians and pharmacists. A number of the women we have met have been *Mato Ihan'bla*, or bear dreamers.

Four Leggeds In the past, elaborate ceremonies were held to ask for permission for and help with an upcoming hunt. People who had spiritual contact with buffalo spirits were called buffalo dreamers. The buffalo is chief of all the animals that live on Mother Earth, and, because of its close relationship to Maka Ina (Mother Earth), is generally associated with female powers and things that influence human female behavior. The Lakota knew that in a herd it is the old cows that lead and that, once scattered by hunters, the herd re-forms by blood kin, around these matrons.

They also saw that the cows readily adopt orphans and displayed generosity in allowing the starling to nest in their woolly caps. These behaviors are thought to be closely tied to what is expected of humans.[2] It is they who have been called upon to speak to the Buffalo Grandfathers, honoring them with song and prayer and then asking that they might send their "children" closer to the village so that the human nation might live.

People who dreamed of elk were elk dreamers, and had their own society. As practitioners they made courting flutes and love charms, composed love songs, and in some cases perhaps acted as "psychologists" and "gynecologists," specialists in prescribing treatment for both male and female problems. The elk is spiritually associated with male powers invoked to dominate female powers, so the courting male may have some sacred help to win the heart of the woman he wishes for his wife. The elk is a manifestation of this power. Dream elk, however, do not closely resemble real elk.

Spiders The spider, although not a true four legged, has a sacred number of legs—eight—and is associated with things that crawl. It was the spider that led the first humans to the surface world, and it is the inspiration for human technology. Since the trap-door spider on the prairie was seen to borrow and seek the shelter of the rocks and earth, it is also closely associated with the powers of Mother Earth and is a particularly useful ally in doctoring the sick, and in various incarnations is a common helper of healers.

The Wingeds The Winged comprises all that have the mysterious powers of flight, including birds, insects, and bats. They have, among other things, control over the winds. Because they are associated with the sky they are also closely associated with the Thunder Beings. Dragonflies are respected for their association with water and thus with the Thunder Beings and, along with butterflies, are thought to have a connection with love in that their flight is said to be like the heart of a human in love.

Spotted eagles, black eagles, and lone eagles are all other names for various phases in the development of the golden eagle. When the eagle is young its tail feathers are white with black on the tip, but as the bird matures they become black with gray bars, thus giving the eagle many appearances and hence, for the Native American, many names. It is this eagle, and not the *wanbli peshla* (bald eagle), that Plains Indians feel is the most powerful of the winged creatures. Eagles can fly very high above the earth, seeing everything beneath them, and fly in a sacred circle.[3] They are seen as important messengers between man and the Sacred Mystery, partly because they can fly into the pure, rarefied air where the sacred can communicate with them away from the contaminating influences of earth.

Owls are also thought of as powerful spirit helpers. The owls—and their various physical forms, including its feathers—are actually feared and avoided by many Native Americans, the Plains people included. To see an owl, or to hear one repeatedly, is still very much thought of as a harbinger of death. The white owl is the most dreaded. Because they know who is going to die, they also know who is going to get well, making them auspicious spirit helpers. They are chief of the night creatures—chiefs of the second time.[4] Because they fly above the earth at night (when most healing ceremonies are held), they know all that goes on.

It is believed that owls are a particularly powerful spirit messenger, and are one of the most common helpers of holy women. All birds, however, like all living creatures, are thought to have sacred powers. According to Wounye' Waste Win, "One day I was coming out of work, and I thought, 'Now, who could I have lunch with?' As I stood there I noticed two crows on a electric wire above me. One of the crows looked at me and said, 'Go home and burn your tobacco ties.' I was absolutely amazed that they spoke, or made me feel their message, so clearly. I went home and did what they asked."

Animals of the Water Animals that live in the water—bugs, fish, frogs, and turtles—also were thought to have specific sacred knowledge and powers. The turtle is probably the most prominent of these. The Lakota believe that the earth was built on the back of a turtle. Therefore the turtle is synonymous with Mother Earth, the female procreative power. Beaded or quilled *Cekpapi* (charms) fashioned in the shape of a turtle are made for newborn girls. Lizard-shaped effigies are made for baby boys. In this umbilical bundle is placed the dried umbilical plug from the newborn child. The turtle symbolizes the care of Mother Earth and evokes the protection of the turtle's famous shell, just as the lizard symbolizes a sturdy constitution and good health: "The symbolic basis for the representation of the turtle . . . is found in the belief that the turtle has power over the functional diseases peculiar to woman, and also over conception, birth, and the period of infancy. The eating of the living heart of the turtle is regarded as a positive cure for menstrual disorders and barrenness."[5]

The following passage, from Belle Starboy, speaks about a "turtle woman":

I am from Oak Creek Community [Rosebud Reservation]. I remember when I was a little girl, maybe about nine, a woman came to my house. She asked me about how I was doing in school—just sort of visited. She took out a turtle to show me. It was green or dark on top, but I remember its underside was many colors of red and orange.

She visited with my mom and dad from time to time, because she was related to them, I guess. This woman's name was Elsie Flood, and she was an old full-blood woman. She was never married and didn't have any children. Grandma Flood always used to carry at least one live turtle with her. Sometimes she would give them to people. I remember that sometimes she would be sitting by the side of the road out in the middle of nowhere, and we'd stop to ask her if she needed a ride. She would usually say, "No, I must sit with my turtle friend a little longer."

Grandma Flood was well respected by the older people. She used to wear turtle things on her person, like a turtle-print dress or a little turtle pin. My older sister remembers that she came shortly before my younger sister was born; I wonder if that had something to do with it. I was born nine years after my sister.

Lakota women Sun Dancing. An older woman in muslin dress, perhaps serving in the capacity of the Buffalo Maiden, dances, representing the female side of creation. She leans on a sacred staff, the only aid she will use in four days with out food and water. Other women dressed in buckskin dance alongside men. *Photo courtesy of South Lakota State Archives.*

Heyoka ceremony (sometimes called a Kettle Dance), similar to the one described in chapter 2. In the background is the ridiculous lodge of the Thunder Dreamers. In the foreground the clowns prepare to pull the dog's head from the boiling kettle. One of the clowns is dressed as "warrior"; another is dressed in body paint representing rain or hail. This dance was held to bring health to the elderly and to fulfill the vow of the Thunder Dreamer, thus releasing him or her from fear of lightning striking. *Photo courtesy of South Dakota State Archives.*

Singular photograph of the White Buffalo Calf ceremony. The young lady stands, wrapped in a Navajo chiefs blanket. Above and behind her are some of the many items be given away after the ceremony. Before her stand boxes of crackers and kettles of soup, some of which contain sacred dog meat. *Photo taken before the end of the nineteenth century; courtesy of the South Dakota State Archives.*

Traditional Ituhan, or giveaway, which would follow the birth of a firstborn child, the White Buffalo Calf ceremony, or a modern Hunkapi. The woman being honored here stands to the rear, and the man standing beside her might be her husband or the *Eyapaha* (announcer) who is calling up those who will receive gifts and acting as master of ceremonies. Horses, beadwork, quillwork, Pendleton blankets, and shawls are still the favored items. *Photo taken at the turn of the century; courtesy of the South Dakota State Archives.*

Photo of Madonna Swan Abdalla. *Family photo.*

Lucy Swan in traditional Lakota attire: elk tooth dress, bone necklace, and dentallium shell earrings. *Photo courtesy of Scotland Studios.*

Photograph of the White Buffalo Calf ceremony. Note the young woman and her elder sponsor, sitting behind the buffalo skull altarpiece. Many "witnesses" line the fence, for they were an intergral part of the ceremony, increasing its positive effect on the community. *Photo taken at the turn of the century; courtesy of the South Dakota State Archives.*

Reminiscent of the story of Iron Woman, Lakota women sit outside in a typical turn-of-the-century setting, jerking beef to be sun- and wind-dried. Notice the Indian sausage on the far right. Very little that could nourish the people was wasted. This type of self-sufficiency transcended the free days into the reservation period but was ended once and for all with the advent of HUD cluster housing in the 1960s. *Photo courtesy of the South Dakota State Archives.*

Lakota women in shinny contest during tribal celebration. Shinny was an athletic, even rough, game not unlike modern field hockey. *Photo courtesy of the South Dakota State Archives.*

Just as men formed societies to keep the Omaha Dance (War Dance) alive, so women kept alive their own dances, including the Waktegli. This dance was a round dance that resembled the earlier scalp, or victory, dances. The dance celebrates the military accomplishments of their male relatives. Scalp poles, battle flags, and war bonnets are borrowed from the men for this dance. Perhaps this particular dance was performed after World War I. *Photo courtesy of the South Dakota State Archives.*

Photo of Isabel (Ten Fingers) Kills Enemy with Charles Kills Enemy, taken in 1971 with traditional sweat lodge stand beside them. *Photo by Herbert Hoover.*

Lakota grandmother dressed in finery for a parade. At these "show yourself" parades, often held on the Fourth of July, Lakota people allowed themselves a rare public display of their status and wealth. *Photo courtesy of the South Dakota State Archives.*

Photo of Brave Eagle Woman, or Julia Brave Eagle, taken in the 1940s. She wears a Pendleton shawl, ankle-length dress, and moccasins, as was common in her generation. She suffered from vitiligo. *Swan family photo.*

A photograph of Mrs. Bad Warrior taken about the time she received control of the Sacred Calf Pipe Bundle. The square-hewn, "sill and post"–style house was copied by Indian agents from military manuals and is typical of the period. *Photo courtesy of the Smithsonian Institute.*

Lakota woman ghost dancer who has "fallen" into the spirit world. This spiritual falling is the same one spoken of by Jackie Yellow Tail. *James Mooney Photo; courtesy of the South Dakota State Archives.*

Photo of Jackie Yellow Tail at the traditional-method Aaxua' Hide Tannery that she helped to found in Billings, Montana. *Photo from the collection of Tilda Long Soldier.*

Rare photograph of Lakota buffalo hide tipi village, where a hide robe airs out in the sun. Notice the toy tipi in the foreground, made from a blanket. Women owned the lodges and all the equipment associated with it, including the horses to move it. *Photo courtesy of the South Dakota State Archives.*

As in the story of Blue Earring Woman, a Lakota woman speaks or sings below what looks like the wrapping of a Sacred Bundle, perhaps at an induction into the quillworkers society. *Courtesy of the South Dakota State Archives.*

[RIGHT] Photo of Iron Woman taken in the 1920s. *Family photo.*

Martha Bad Warrior, keeper of the Sacred Calf Pipe Bundle, at the ceremony held in the 1930s to end the drought and the dust bowl. Family and friends surround her. Lucy Looking Horse stands behind her in the flowered dress, and beside her stands Stanley Looking Horse, father of the current keeper. (In Martha's lap lies the pipe that has been considered by some to be "another" pipe, not the Calf Pipe.) *Photo courtesy of the Smithsonian Institute.*

Mary Crow Dog, a Lakota writer from near Mission, on the Rosebud Reservation, remembered Mrs. Flood as well:

> I loved to visit Aunt Elsie Flood to listen to her stories. With her high cheekbones, she looked like Grandma. She had a voice like water bubbling, talking with a deep, throaty sound. And she talked fast, mixing Indian and English together. I had to pay strict attention if I wanted to understand what she told me. She always paid her bills, earning a living by her arts and crafts, her beautiful work with beads and porcupine quills. . . .
>
> She was also a medicine woman. She was an old-time woman, carrying her pack [medicine bundle] on her back. She would not let a man or a younger woman carry her burden. She carried it herself, being proud of her turtle medicine. She used turtles for her protection. Wherever she went, she always had some little live turtles with her, and all kinds of things made out of tortoiseshell, little charms and boxes. . . .
>
> The turtle woman was afraid of nothing. She was always hitchhiking, constantly on the road, thumbing her way from one place to the other. She was a mystery to some. The Indians held her in great respect, saying that she was "wakan," that she was some sort of holy person to whom turtles had given their powers.[6]

It is possible that these turtle women had power over infertility. Given the Lakota attitude toward "new generations," a turtle dreamer would have been held in high regard. It is in a beaded or quilled turtle amulet that the dried umbilical cord of a baby girl is placed.

Snakes   Snakes *(zuzeca)* fall into a category by themselves. Whereas all others in creation are seen as encompassing both good and bad, male and female in potential, the snake is universally disliked. It is possible, however, that the snake is closely related to Mother Earth and may in fact potentially help a medicine woman with the knowledge of herbs.

A woman, however, given the appellation *Zuzeca win,* or snake woman, has likely earned it by being mean to people, particularly to her relatives.

The Little People   There is one class of beings that has received very little attention by writers and researchers on the American Indian, and that is the "Little People." The Lakota call them *Can otipi* ("they dwell in the trees"); to the Crow they are the keepers of medicine and the Sun Dance itself. Some Lakota feel they are the teachers of the Sun Dance, as well.

There is little agreement on how big they are, although their general description is approximately the same. They are brown-skinned, have thick hair, and wear little clothing. Some say they have horns like the buffalo. All agree that they have magical qualities and can appear to humans or make themselves invisible. They are thought to have been around since the beginning of time and were created when everything else was.

Tilda heard stories about common sightings of little people by her grandmother. Sadie Crazy Thunder, the old medicine man's daughter and Tilda's grandmother told her, "You see that twisted old cottonwood tree down there in the thick forest along the creek? Well, that is where the little people lived when I was young. I don't see them anymore; perhaps things have changed [environmentally], and they don't live here anymore."

Some say they impart wisdom to humans, and others say they trick people to teach them important lessons; but generally when they are seen there is a reason. Tilda reminded me,

> I always remember the time when I first met Ted Wolf. He was telling us about that man who ran the sweat; it was Sidney Keith, I think. The people were in there [the sweat lodge] praying, and the curious people couldn't see anything, but [for those with faith] there were some little people in there. They told the holy man who ran it that they were in there looking around [at the people in the sweat]. There were two of them—one a trickster and the other a nice person. The trickster was going around and making fun of the people who were in there, imitating their expressions. To the little people it was just like daylight in the [darkness of the] sweat.

The little people were making fun of those who were just curious, those without faith in these ways—this is precisely their nature. As an anonymous Lakota woman says, "When my sister was a teenager, she used to live in my aunt's basement. She told me, 'In those days, when I was drinking a lot and smoking pot, I spent a lot of time down there. I would be down in that basement, hungover or whatever, and I'd see those little people standing around me, smiling and pointing at me."

Animals and the People

Animals are believed to be members of specific nations, such as the Buffalo Nation, the Deer Nation, the Mouse Nation, and the Ant Nation. All living and nonliving things belong to their own nation. Plants and animals are intelligent in the way of their kind, with all the native cunning and intelligence necessary to raise their young and perpetuate their nation. All animals have the means of communicating with one another as well as with humans: "if they have the ears to listen" is a common expression. All are also believed to have souls and thus also ancestral spirits. Animals may even communicate intelligently with and help humans while in their "living" form, as in the following, very old, story told by Oliver Brown Wolf, a Minnecojou Lakota elder.

THE WOMAN WHO LIVED WITH THE WOLVES

A Minnecojou camp which had settled down for the winter was raided by Crow Indians. The Crow stole many horses and took a Lakota woman back to their camp.

The woman was unhappy staying in the Crow camp. She missed her people. Some of the Crow women saw this and took pity on her. The gave her food and a blanket and told her to hide by a creek near the camp, that someone would be after her.

She hid herself in the bushes along the banks of the creek. A short time later some of the Crow men came looking for her. While the Lakota woman was hiding, two large wolves came upon her.

But the wolves treated her kindly and guided her along a path to the east. The wolves and the woman traveled together while the Crow were chasing them.

At night wolves would lie close to her to keep her warm; otherwise she might have been frozen. The wolves would speak fluent Lakota to her and told her they would take her to a safe place and that she should follow them.

A raging blizzard caught the woman and her wolf friends in the open prairie. Two more wolves joined them as they walked through the blowing snow. The small wolf pack and the woman struggled through the snowdrifts and the cold winds.

There is power to this story. The woman was able to get safely away from the Crow because of the blizzard. If one is traveling in a blizzard and remembers this story, one need not to be afraid.

She followed the tracks, and they came to a creekbed. They followed the creek for a long time when she noticed some huge rocky buttes off in the distance.

After many days of traveling, the small band reached Squaw Buttes near present-day Opal, South Dakota. They came to a cave in the rocks, and the wolves forced her inside. The cave had an awful smell. As her eyes adjusted to the darkness, she saw many wolves in the large den. She thought the wolves would tear her apart; she was very frightened. Instead the wolves dragged in a deer, tore it apart, and shared it with the woman.

The wolves advised her to go in where it is warm. She crawled inside, and it was warm. She sat down, and when her eyes got used to the little light she noticed many other wolves inside. Some were nursing their young ones. Some appeared to be old. They would sit up and lay down again. Not one even growled at her.

The wolves were one big family; many generations of wolves lived together in the cave. Each wolf had its own place in the family. The hunter wolves brought in the meat. The mother wolves nursed their young. The elder wolves taught the younger ones the skills of hunting. The other wolves kept watch over the den. In this way they all looked after each other.

If it got too warm in the den the woman would go out and walk around. Sometimes she would sit up on a hill, looking in all directions in case her people were by chance looking for her.

The woman made herself a home in the den. She learned to speak and understand the wolves' language. The woman would dry and store the meat for the winter. She got along well with the wolves, and they got along well with her. Soon she smelled just like the wolves she lived with.

The wolves knew their country well. They always knew whether the two legged ones passed through. The wolves usually stayed away from the two leggeds. The wolves did not like the way the two leggeds smelled.

At turnip-digging time of the year, the woman's mother was still in mourning. She thought that her daughter had been killed by the Crows. One day the hunter wolves saw the girl's mother near the den. The wolves went back and told their human friend.

The woman wanted to go back to her people. She was worried that they would not accept her back. The wolves told her to wave her blanket two times if her mother recognized her, and invited her back to live with her human family. If she waved once, the wolves would come and take her back to their den.

When the mother saw her daughter coming, she was so happy to see her that she cried. The young woman waved her blanket twice to the wolves, who were watching from the hills. The wolves saw this and went back to their cave.

The woman's name became *Iguga Oti Win*, or Woman Who Lived In The Rock. The rocky place where she lived is now considered a sacred area to the Lakota.

Be careful of this tale, because if it is told on a winter night, it might cause a blizzard.

This not just a story, it is a true story that happened in the early eighteenth century, and it happened seventy miles west of Eagle Butte near a little town called Opal, South Dakota.

While that woman lived, some evenings or nights—especially cold nights—you could hear the wolves howl for her. They missed her. But that's the way things go. Man and animal are closely related, and once in a while the animals show their affection this way: *Ihanke'*.

To show that this was a true story and not a fairy tale, Oliver added, "This is how the Brown Wolfs got their name. Philip Brown Wolf, Edward Owl King–Two Bears, Albert Owl King, and Inos Owl King were half-brothers. Also, Hard To Kill Woman, Albert Owl King's wife, was related to this Iguga Oti Win. Her mother is from Rosebud, South Dakota."[7]

Another remarkable story comes from Madonna Swan and gives wonderful insight into how, for Plains Indians, even the most seemingly insignificant part of creation is believed to have great power to help man. It is a story about her grandmother, Julia High Pine, and the time Madonna's mother, Lucy (High Pine) Swan, got a letter telling her to check up on her aging mother, who had been left to look after Lucy's infant niece, Rosie Iyotte:

> It was very cold when we started out for White River. We brought a four-horse team just in case we hit a storm and got stuck. We also brought a saddle horse. The trip took us two days. The first night we stopped near Stanford, South Dakota.
>
> We got to White river towards evening. No smoke was coming from Mom's cabin. Dad looked at me and told me to go see if anyone was home. I looked inside and found the house cold and dark. There was a window on the north side of the cabin. From the dim light, I could barely see what looked like a person with blankets over their head, lying on Grandma's cot.
>
> When I found Grandma, I yelled to your dad, "Come quick! Ina! Ina!" I called, yet no noise came out. Dad lit a lamp, and from the light I could see Grandma's eyes were glazed and she was very thin. There was the sound of a baby's cry from underneath Grandma's covers.
>
> "I'll get some wood and start a fire, you get some food cooked, and we'll see what we can do for your mom and Rosie," Dad yelled from the yard.
>
> We fed her and made the baby milk. Soon Grandma was able to talk. She said, "I was sitting here like this for four days. We were out of food and split wood, and nobody came by. I was getting cold, so I started to pray for help. Mice were crawling on me and sort of nibbling on us. I prayed to those mice: 'Grandmother Mouse, please send help, and please don't crawl on

us.' And I would sleep for a while, wake up, and sleep again. I got too weak to move, so I just stayed here and waited for help to come. Then you came! I believe a mouse whispered to you and told you."

Then Grandma went back to sleep. She woke the next morning; by then we had the house clean and warm. She smiled at me as she woke and said, "Tell your husband to take that check from the drawer over to the store in White River and buy some food for the baby and bring a bag of peanuts. I want to make an offering to the mice people." So that is what we did." [8]

Some details of this poignant story might escape the uninitiated. The four days she prayed to the mice people is the prescribed number for a sacred dream, such as in *Hanbleciyapi* (the Sacred Fasting rite). She prays to the Mouse Grandmother, spiritual grandmother of the *Itunkala Oyate'*, or Mouse Nation. Julia Brave Eagle then remembers to thank her new allies, knowing the essence of the peanuts will be "eaten" by the grandmother mouse spirit, expressing the necessary spiritual reciprocity. It also reminds us that Lakota people see themselves as only one of many animal nations, all of whom have spirits that are eternal and possess sacred knowledge and great wisdom.

The following passage comes from the Crow medicine woman Pretty Shield, as translated by Frank Linderman in the 1930s.

I had lost a little girl, a beautiful baby girl. . . . I had been mourning for more than two moons. I had slept little, sometimes lying down alone in the hills at night, and always on hard places. I ate only enough to keep me alive, hoping for a medicine dream, a vision, that would help me to live and to help others. One morning after a night spent on a high cliff, when I was returning to my lodge to pack things for a long move, I saw a woman ahead of me. She was walking fast, as though she hoped to reach my lodge before I could get there. But suddenly she stopped and stood still, looking down at the ground. I thought I knew her, thought that she was a woman that had died four years before. I felt afraid. I stopped, my heart beating fast. "Come here, daughter." Her words seemed to draw me toward her against my will.

Walking a few steps I saw that she was not a real woman, but that she was a person [apparition], and that she was standing beside an anthill.

"Come here, my daughter." Again I walked toward her when I did not wish to move. Stopping by her side, I did not try to look into her face. My heart was nearly choking me. "Rake up the edges of this anthill and ask for the things that you wish, daughter," the Person said; and then she was gone. Only an anthill was there, and a wind was blowing. I saw the grass tremble, as I was trembling, when I raked up the edges of the anthill as the person had told me. Then I made my wish: "Give me good luck and a good life," I said aloud to the hills.

I was weak. In my lodge there was no bed-robes for me, because I had long ago destroyed all my comfortable things. But now, in the medicine dream, I entered a beautiful white lodge, with a war eagle at the head. He did not speak to me, and yet I have often seen him since that day. And even now the ants help me. I listen to them always. They are my medicine, these busy, powerful little people, the ants.[9]

Dreams of Beckoning

Dreams in which someone visits a sick person many miles from home in a type of spirit travel, as in Tanya Ward's story in chapter 1, might be called "dreams of beckoning." Even common animals like dogs, as in this story by Tilda, can be powerful spirit helpers:

In my dream I saw my dog go into the spirit world. I love that dog very much, and it grieved me to see him just walk into that other world. I have always thought he was a spirit returned.

He went into that world, but he paced as dogs do when they are fretting, and he would look back at me as if he wanted me to follow. I knew that to follow him I must die or be killed. So I found a car and started to drive it very fast down the road, trying to find something to crash it into.

Soon I was flying above the road and saw a terrible head-on collision. I called down to the people near the car, or it came to me that no one had been killed. I saw my dog again, his white hind end going into the shadows of that other world. I just crossed into that other world. I was scared, but I did it. It was very strange there. In that world, the dog told me he was following someone named Mark and that we should bring him back with us. So we did. Then I woke.

Two days later my mother called and said, "Two nights ago your brother Pepsi was in a terrible car wreck. He was unconscious for a while, but he's all right now."

Pepsi's real name is Mark. Although we never call him that, my dog knew.

Dreams of Warning

Sometimes dreams provide warning about or insight into how others might wish the dreamer harm. Because the Lakota people believe that the medicine person's helpers are powerful yet neutral, and that evil is a relative matter, there are people known to practice *hgmuġa,* or casting of spells, with the use of a spirit helper, to cause harm to another person. This belief—that "what goes around comes around"—keeps most medicine people from practicing the negative aspects of shamanism, because they fear their own families might be hurt.

The following dream, related by an anonymous Lakota, is an excellent example of how this "intent to do harm" might be perceived in the dream state.

> I had a dream [asleep]; it was a terrible dream. In that dream my aunt was trying to take me away from my husband, whom I care for very much. She did everything to take me from him. Soon I was just touching him with my fingertips. I knew that if she broke this touch, one of us would die. I fought with all my mind: "You are not going to do this; I won't let you." Finally the dream was over. In about a week I got a call that my cousin had been killed in a terrible car wreck. I believe my aunt was trying to do something to me, and that was the result.

As in any *Ihanbla',* the message of warning may be heard or seen while one is either sleeping or awake. Mike Running Wolf, an old friend of Lakota and Blackfoot ancestry, is married to Florence Strange Owl, a Northern Cheyenne, and lives in the village of Birney on the Cheyenne Reservation. He told us of a famous Cheyenne medicine woman, North Woman: "There was this famous holy woman—she was called North Woman—and when the Cheyenne were fleeing north from Oklahoma, she found she could hear voices that told her where the soldiers were and in which direction they should travel to avoid the soldiers. She was always right, and those chiefs who listened to her made it up north safely. Those who didn't met a great hardship, and many of them died."

Another version of the same story comes from Rose Little Bear and was recorded in 1959 by Father Peter J. Powell:

> In the party was a medicine woman who had discovered her power during the flight north. One evening the Cheyennes had been ready to stop for their meal. The woman had gone apart from the others when she heard a voice. She stopped to listen. The voice said, "Don't stop and eat. Keep on

going. There are soldiers behind you." The woman hurried back to camp to relate this strange happening. When Little Wolf heard her story, he told the people to keep moving on.

After that, when the others were preparing to camp for the night, the woman moved apart from them to listen. If she did not hear the voice, the people would stop. Many of them had come to depend upon this woman, because she was guided by the powers above.

When this rift between Little Wolf and Morning Star was threatening, Little Wolf said, "Let us ask this woman for a sign or guidance. We will go by her decision." Morning Star answered: "We cannot listen to this woman. We are men-leaders. My mind is made up. Whoever wants to follow me can do so."[10]

Little Wolf was a Suhtai chief, part of an ancient sub-band of the Northern Cheyenne. With U.S. military forces in pursuit, the Northern Cheyenne people had fled Oklahoma to go back to the Tongue River country of Montana. One morning, when the chiefs argued about safety from the relentless army, Morning Star—also known as Dull Knife— wished to reach their old allies, Red Cloud's people, on the Pine Ridge Reservation by heading immediately north. Little Wolf did not want to stop; instead, he wanted to head northwest until they had reached the Tongue River country, their traditional homeland.

Later, with the guidance of North Woman, Little Wolf's band found a hidden valley and wintered safely, arriving in their sacred Yellowstone country that spring. Dull Knife's people were intercepted by the military and contained at Fort Robinson, Nebraska. Unarmed, they escaped from unheated barracks in the frigid night, only to see eighty of their people die at the hands of the cavalry.

Dreams of Human Spirits

Dreams in which returned spirits appear to the living generally fall into two groups. The first involves those spirits that have returned to help the living and become, perhaps at birth, an ally for life. Many spirits used in doctoring are actually ancient ancestral spirits and are called upon to serve humans as a communicator between the two worlds. Because the Lakota believe in reincarnation, some people believe that some of those currently alive may be sent back to live again or to help the people. According to an anonymous Lakota, "There was a girl in our community who was born with strange scars on her hands that resembled burns. She told people who asked about them, 'I am an old woman who has returned. I was badly burned in my prior life.'"

These spirits have made a happy journey to the other side and either have returned by their own will or were sent by the Great Spirit.

The following dreams are about "angry" spirits perhaps trapped on this plane or unable to complete the journey to the other side because they are unhappy about conditions they left in this life. Being trapped on this earth is the worst fate that can befall an angry Wana' gi.

In the following vivid dream, the recently dead appears to his own living daughter. He is seen exactly as he was in life and expresses concern for his most prized possession. This type of dream is not at all uncommon. The fact that this dream-vision takes place in broad daylight and continues through a whole series of events affords even greater insight into the nature and qualities of these dream experiences.

> When I was a young woman, my dad died from a heart attack. When he died, I was living in Denver, and we went to Rosebud, for the funeral, on a train. When we were coming back we were on the train again. I fell asleep on the train, and here I saw my dad sitting there in a blue suit, just like he was in life, and he spoke to me and said, "Why are you crying? Why are they doing that? My body isn't even cold yet, and they stole from me?"
>
> Later, when we got home, he was sitting there right in front of us in the apartment door. He opened it and went in, with his navy-blue suit and his white hat on, so we opened it and followed him in.
>
> He went upstairs and turned and went into the bedroom door, and we went in there and his favorite things, his dance outfit was gone, and that white hat and all his suits, they were gone. I was awake and following him.
>
> Soon his hat went down the stairs. When he opened the door we heard it close behind him. You know, I never dream about my father unless something is going to happen.
>
> So it is with my mother. Like I said, we were a close family. If something is going to happen, you dream, and they are all there for you. Sometimes you see them happy, or maybe they don't pay attention to you, or they are doing something that you notice. If you can read what they are trying to tell you, you will know what is going to happen. (Yellow Bird Woman, Sicangu holy woman)

Ghosts are not to be feared, then, but respected and treated as someone once living would be. Tilda's own experience provides a very clear example of how a visitor from the spirit world should be treated:

It was in the evening. My sister was still up, helping Grandma wash the dishes. Us younger ones were already tucked in.

She said, "Look, Grandma, someone is sitting on the couch." So I looked, too. From where I was lying, I could see this man, just behind the woodstove. He sat with his legs and arms crossed. He was very still. From what I could see, he was dressed in western clothes and wore a white hat.

My grandmother started talking to him like he was alive: "If you are hungry, help yourself. There is food on the table." She went on talking as she checked the windows and the door. They were all locked.

"If you're not hungry, I would like you to leave. You are scaring my *takoja* [grandchildren]." My sister was peeking from behind her. I stayed on the bed. I don't remember how the man left. Grandma prepared a dish for him and took it outside to feed the spirit.

The old people called the place where we lived *Oti wota* [an old traditional encampment]. People had camped and lived there for a very long time, and that is why there were so many spirits there. . . .

When I was living with my Grandma Sadie, and even after that with Grandma Dora, we would always put out bits of food for the spirits.

The Lakota believe that spirits or ghosts seen in daylight or at dusk can be dangerous as well as benevolent. Certain kinds of ghosts can cause those who see them to suffer *Wana'gi kteb*, or stroke. It is believed that seeing the wana gi literally surprises or "shocks" the person. Madonna Swan said, "I know it's not the way white doctors see it. We call it *Wana giktepi* and know that contact with ghosts of departed ones may in fact produce a stroke." This short passage from Mitchell Zephier, about an occurrence in 1992, shows these beliefs still persist: "I have a friend at Rosebud, a well-known medicine man, who told me of a relative of his who saw a ghost. He was collecting split wood for the cookstove at dusk, and he saw a ghost. You know, I thought about it, and the fellow he was referring to does have a twisted face, even though he is still fairly young."

Madonna Swan, herself a teacher and college-educated, nonetheless maintained a very traditional worldview. The following story is remarkable. Madonna clearly sees a recently deceased friend in broad daylight. Her affection for him is never affected by the tragic outcome of his visit.

In November of 1973 Jay and I had a good friend who had passed away. His name was Wally Knight. He was a good white man. He was married to Sarah In Amongst. They ranched for many years down in Red Scaffold Community. . . .

One day we were in Eagle Butte on a workshop. It was a strange day—kind of cloudy, windy, and cold. We were supposed to write some reports for college credit. . . .

So I was sitting there, helping a friend named Rose type her report, and I said, "I'm going to get up and walk around a little bit, and then I'll come back." Before I stood, I happened to look at that door, and Wally Knight was standing there, smiling, and he was pointing at me.

I said, "Yahhh!" and I looked away and then looked up again he just went out of sight into that room. Rose looked up at me, and I said, "Rose, I just saw a ghost!"

Eventually, I sat back down at the typewriter again and started to work on Rose's report. . . . I had typed for a couple more hours, and gee my back was really hurting me. . . .

I was just about to stand. I looked toward that door, and there was Wally Knight standing there, smiling just like he did in life. He was pointing and motioning for me to come talk to him!

Next thing I knew, I was in the hospital, in Bismarck, North Dakota. I'd had a slight stroke. I was kind of paralyzed on the right side. So I guess Wally Knight had come to take me with him, but I didn't go. He was a good man, and he wanted me to be in a good place.[11]

Little Warrior, Tilda's great-grandfather, successfully doctored the famous holy man Black Elk for a stroke he had suffered. Both men were in their eighties and had been teenagers at the Battle of the Greasy Grass (Little Big Horn).

The following was related to Michael Steltenkamp by Lucy Looks Twice, Black Elk's daughter.

I noticed that when everything was over that my father's mouth had straightened out, so he could eat. My father, after it was over, said to Little Warrior: "Yes, I'll admit you're good at it. But next time you come to doctor me, don't let those little spirits treat me so roughly. They were really treating me harsh. I'm really tired." Mind you, his mouth was straight, and he could eat after that ceremony. . . .

Little Warrior told me: "In my life there are good spirits and bad spirits. When you pray, the good spirit is always going to help you. In the morning, when you get up, stand in the doorway and pray that the day is a nice quiet day. Give thanks for the day—for coming through the night."[12]

For the shaman, knowledge of the spiritual world, including the lives and behavior of many spirits both good and bad, is the overwhelming pursuit of their lives. Working with something as powerful as spirits requires one to know exactly how to call them, communicate with them, and send them back. This requires countless experiences with the sacred, from which the student gradually develops her own rituals. It is through proper rituals and songs that the medicine woman accomplishes her healing.

7

The Calling

I never prayed to be a medicine woman. See, I learned from the first year that everybody gets enamored—they're so enthralled with the spiritual aspects of what happens. It's so real, and it manifests itself there in front of you! Everybody thinks that the highest is to be a medicine person. So then I read about it, everything I could. In my reading I learned that not everybody who fasts or prays becomes [a medicine woman]. So I knew early on, that is not what you pray for, that's not what you seek. I have always believed, "Whatever I would be, to be it fully."

—WOUNYE WASTE' WIN (GOOD
LIFEWAYS WOMAN), Oglala Lakota

Without question, dreams are not the exclusive property of one sex or the other. Both men and women can have powerful and sacred dreams that call them to a new role in the lives of their people.

When men are called to the sacred, there is often an established apprenticeship they must follow that will take at least four years; but for women the calling to serve the people may be much more spontaneous. During a conversation about his grandmother, Blue Earring Woman, Orville Mesteth made the following observation about how women get the calling: "I think for women it is different from how it is for men. A woman's calling is in her dreams; it is usually powerful, spontaneous. She does not always need to be trained in the way that a holy man would."

The most Sacred Relic that the Lakota have is the Sacred Calf Pipe Bundle. For hundreds of years the keeper had been a man. The bundle is held in such high regard that many people fear it, and perhaps with good reason. The following story, which took place in 1898, is still told on the

Cheyenne River Reservation. It shows that women's dreams are listened to, even under the most dire or profound circumstances.

> There were some five policeman involved in the theft of the Pipe Bundle, under the direction of the Indian agent couchman. Elk Head, ninth keeper of the Sacred Pipe Bundle, had possession. White Bull was a policeman at this time and was admired by the elders for his bravery and his fairmindedness. When the agent took the Pipe Bundle, a delegation of the Elk Head family went to see [Joseph] White Bull [Nephew to Sitting Bull]. He said he would go to see the agent and ask him to return the Bundle to the Indians.
>
> The agent agreed to do so, since his curiosity had been satisfied as to the contents of the Pipe Bundle. The five policeman who took the Bundle from Elk Head were ordered to return it. On the way back to the agency after depositing the sacred relic with its keeper, a cloud of mist, much like the one that appeared with the coming of the White Buffalo Calf Maiden, was seen. When it lifted, one of the policemen was dead. This happened twice more during the next few days until all five of the Indian policemen were dead.[1]

When Old Man Elk Head passed away the Pipe Bundle was to go to his son, Ernest. His daughter, Red Eagle Woman (Martha Bad Warrior), protested and took the Sacred Calf Pipe, saying that it had come to her in a dream that she was to be the next keeper. The tribal council met and ordered her to turn the Pipe over to her brother, but still she refused. According to Sidney (Uses The Knife) Keith, there was a meeting of elders associated with the Pipe in an attempt to resolve the crisis. The power of dreams in the Lakota intellectual landscape is made clear by what follows: "Well, what happened there that time is that Ernest [Elias Elk Head?] was supposed to have that [the Pipe], and she [Martha Bad Warrior] really objected to that. I don't know why, but she said, 'I should be the one to keep it.' So all of them [elders associated with the Pipe] got together and said, Okay, you can keep it. It will just break the tradition, but if she sees something different, then we're going to go with what she sees."

Some tribes have special medicine bundles so central to their origin as a people that the loss of these precious objects may threaten the very existence of their nation. These pounded rawhide bundles (in the shape of envelopes or cylinders) may contain any number of sacred objects, such as roots, herbs, bones, feathers, claws, fossils, stones, or relics, whose origins are traced back to culture heroes. The Northern Cheyenne (old allies of the Lakota) have two such bundles. *Is'siwun,* the Sacred Buffalo Hat, or Hat Bundle, refers to a sacred bonnet made from the scalp of a buffalo with the horns attached. It is as ancient as the people themselves and represents female Cheyenne fertility. If something should harm the Hat, or if it is not treated with proper daily ritual, it is be lieved that Cheyenne women will lose their ability to bring forth children. The care of this object falls to the Northern Cheyenne near Birney, Montana.

The other central Bundle, called *Mahuts,* is comprised of four arrows and represents the male side of Cheyenne continuity and is kept by the Southern Cheyenne in Oklahoma.

Mike Running Wolf told us of an exceptional woman of the Northern Cheyenne, Josie (Head Swift) Limpy, who, knowing the proper bundle rituals for *Is'siwun* better than anyone living at the time, was appointed keeper by her father: "Yes, there have been holy women among the Cheyenne. Back in the fifties there was a woman whose name was Josie Limpy. She was the keeper of the Sacred Hat Bundle. I think she was keeper for about five or six years [1952–1957]. You know, that Hat Bundle is just like the Sacred Calf Pipe that we Sioux have. It is everything to these people. It represents the woman's side of creation."

Josie Limpy told her own story to an Episcopal priest, Father Peter J. Powell, in 1959. Josephine was the daughter of Limpy, one of the old men who in his youth had made the devastating escape north from Oklahoma in 1878, and had survived until 1952. He was a Suhtai, an ancient sub-band of the Cheyenne. Suhtai custom dictates that a Suhtai man be keeper of Is'siwun, the most important religious position in the Northern Cheyenne tribe.

Head Swift, the keeper's, health was failing, and he was thinking about a successor. The men smoked together, and then Head Swift spoke to them about the Sacred Hat. When he had finished, the keeper sent for his daughter, Josie Head Swift Limpy, or Stands Near the Fire. When she arrived in the sacred tipi, the keeper again addressed the four men:

"The reason I sent for you to come is because I have had plans in my mind for some time. Now I want you to listen to me, to hear what I have to say to my daughter.

"Daughter, I want you to remember what I say. It is the law that a woman has the right to assist the keeper of the sacred tipi. You have been watching me. You see how I smoke the pipe in the morning and in the evening. This is not merely smoking. It is more important than anything else done in the tipi. It is a ceremony that includes prayer and the asking of blessings for the family, all the people.

"Someday I will die. You are not going to leave the tipi. Do not say anything to the soldier bands. They know that they may want a man to care for the tipi as I did; and they may decide to come over and take away the tipi.

"When they come, talk nicely to them. After they take the tipi away, a new man and his wife may not know exactly what to do. If they come and ask you, speak to them in a good way and tell them what needs to be done.

"Hineh ha! That's all!"

Throughout all this time Stands Near the Fire kept Is'siwun's home in order. When she rose each morning, she struck the four blows upon the poles to the southeast of the tipi door. On bright days, she carried the Hat Bundle outside and tied it above the doorway of the lodge. Then she went outside to care for the people and their needs. Next, she swept the floor with a buck brush, since a white man's broom is not allowed inside Is'siwun's lodge. At sundown, she carried the Hat Bundle back inside, fastening it to the tripod behind the keeper's willow back rest. Then she again offered the prayers. After sundown she struck the southeast lodge pole four times, closing Is'siwun's home for the night.[2]

Women who *ihan'bla* (dream) like men may be called to many different roles. A woman who has a dream that is to be acted out in public may perform the ritual only once and be done with it, or it may be a lifetime calling—the kind that might in the past have required her to join a dream society. These women are one class of dreamers.

A Winyan Wakon, or holy woman, receives in dreams or visions sacred knowledge, songs, and rituals, and these become the focus of her ritual life and her calling as a helper or healer. She is not generally called a holy woman, but is instead called after her helper—"she is a *Wanbli Wapiye* (Cures with Eagle Spirits)," for example. If the dreams and experiences that indicate a calling start when the woman is young, these women wait until menopause to fulfill their calling.

The woman receiving the dreams or "visions" may be the least suspecting of her future role as a healer. She may not see herself as having led a life that has prepared her in any way for this calling. If her personality and worldview are affected to a large extent by the traditional culture, her own ego may not allow her to accept or even recognize what is happening. There comes a time when these special dreams bring on or force a crisis. This may be a physical, spiritual, or emotional crisis, perhaps like the depression suffered by Good Lifeways Woman or, in the case of Yellow Bird Woman, health problems (cancer) that brought her near death.

Becoming Holy Women

In order to illustrate the process of transformation from uninitiated lay person to holy woman we have included the experiences of a number of women, but those of Wounye' Waste' Win (Good Lifeways Woman) are used extensively. It is not possible to give all the details of a holy person's dreams or visions, because the dreams are real and alive. It is believed that if certain jealous or vengeful people wished to cause this woman harm, they could do so by using details of her dreams.

Good Lifeways Woman is an Oglala Lakota mixed-blood who was raised in a Catholic boarding school and then received a bachelor's and later a master's degree. Attending college presents the native person with a scientific approach to reality. This acquired cynicism about the sacred may in fact become an obstacle when the spirit world is calling. Good Lifeways Woman is the mother of five children. She and her husband are still together. Because she was taken at an early age from her family and reservation and then sent away to Catholic boarding school, her use of the Lakota language is imperfect. This is something she suffers about, feeling that it has limited her in some ways. Her knowledge of Lakota, however, is sufficient for her to be a very effective singer. Knowing and using the correct songs in ceremony is critical to its effectiveness because it is through song that the spirits are called.

The dream world is considered the eternal and real world. For that reason this is only a generalized account; details and names have been changed at Good Lifeways Woman's request. She was willing to share this so that other women, particularly Lakota women, "might take nourishment, courage, and direction from their own dreams." Good Lifeways Woman is not her legal name but her spiritual name.

> The first experience I had with this was when we were still living out of state. I was lying in bed, and on the ceiling was a beautiful tipi. Around it were pine trees, and silhouetted against the poles and smoke hole was the moon. A sense of overwhelming peace came to me. It lasted for perhaps a minute, and then it left. I had never seen or felt anything like that before and didn't know what to make of it.

About a week later I had another strange dream. I dreamed that I could fly, and I was flying barely above the ground. I noticed that the landscape below me was made of money. Coins, thousands and thousands of coins, formed the mountains and valleys [perhaps representing the white world in which she was living]. I could see them so clearly that I could read the dates, and then that dream faded away—but it stayed with me.

In the summer of 1975 we were coming back to South Dakota for my sister's thirtieth wedding anniversary. It was shortly after Wounded Knee. It seemed that everyone was buzzing; there was a lot of excitement in the air, and it was for the ceremonies. [Many] people at home [on Pine Ridge Reservation] were going to [Lakota] ceremonies for the first time in their lives. Our relatives were talking like, "And you could see them come in! The spirits! . . . There were little blue lights everywhere."

When I was coming into South Dakota, coming home, it was in Nebraska that I first noticed the smell of the prairie. It was powerful. It told me I was home. The flowers were so beautiful, and the smell of sage, and the ground—the ground was speaking to me in whole thoughts. . . .

There comes a special point in a holy woman's life when she starts to have dreams that differ in quality from all the dreams that came before. No true Indian woman would want this calling or seek it without the right signs, because it might call for a lifetime of selfless service and, more than that, might place her in spiritual danger. Nobody can imitate this process, because the efficacy and power of the woman's dreams will be called into question by the community of the faithful every time she makes a prognosis or diagnosis or prescribes a treatment.

What follows is a recounting of just such a calling to a Lakota woman now in her early fifties. That she shared these remarkable dreams with us is a privilege Tilda and I greatly respect.

In her late thirties, upon a trip back to her native South Dakota, Good Lifeways Woman continued to have a series of spiritual experiences in the form of unusual dreams. Here is the continuation of this singular account.

I had bought a beaded staff and thought, "Well, if I'm going to leave South Dakota at least I'll take a few things to decorate the house." I was such a greenhorn then that I wanted to buy a pipe to hang on the wall with my staff. I told my sister that I wanted to buy a pipe, and she looked at me and her eyes got real big, and she said, "You don't just go out and buy a pipe, it's not like that." Well, I didn't believe her, because she was way older than me, a big sister and always so smart and all, so I ignored her comment.

One of the fellows at work was making pipes then, so I told him I wanted to buy a pipe. He got real quiet and didn't say anything. He was so quiet I noticed it. About a month later he came to me and brought me the pipe wrapped in cloth. When he gave it to me it was in two pieces. I thought, Geez, this poor old guy, he brings me a broken pipe! I was such a greenhorn I didn't know anything!

I had that pipe for quite a while, always thinking I would glue the two pieces together, bead it, and hang it on the wall. But every time I would go to look for it I couldn't find it. I would scold the kids and tell them not to play with that pipe and to put it back and leave it where they found it, things like that. They would just look at me blankly.

These experiences and dreams may go on for months or years. Sometimes they dissipate and don't return. Depending on the nature of the dreams and the particular calling, they may intensify and literally make the dreamer afraid or even crazy, as in dreams of Thunder Beings. These dreams may be a call to perform a specific ceremony or set of ceremonies such as the Sun Dance, Kettle Dance, or Horse Dance. At one time various dream societies like the *Heyoka* (Thunder Dreamers, or contraries) and Elk Dreamers also acted out visionary dreams in a public "dance."

The following dream of a Lakota elder, described to Tilda and me, led the dreamer to eventually act out the dream in public, which is the old way of purging oneself of the impulses associated with the dream. These dreams are not to be taken lightly. To ignore what the spirits want could be deadly to the dreamer or to a member of the family. This woman dismissed her dreams for some time, but they would not go away. She was what Lakota call *Wakiyan Ihan'bla* (a Thunder Dreamer), also called a *Heyoka*, or Clown Dreamer. These Thunder Dreams became so intense that she would run and hide when it rained to avoid being hit by lightning. Still, she put off the fulfillment of the dream, which was to conduct a very unusual set of four Sun Dances, for women only. When a couple of relatives died unexpectedly, she knew she could not put off her public ceremonies any longer. To fulfill her dreams she became a female Sun Dance *Itancan* (Leader or Dreamer).

I had a dream, a vision. I was wide awake when I had it; I saw this during the day. I was in the house, and I saw these *Heyokas* [Thunder Clowns] come in. In this dream I could see a Sun Dance ground. Behind it were four sweat lodges. There were only women dancing in this dream. At the time there was no Sun Dance for the women. You know, women participated in the Sun Dance; but up to this time there had been no dance where just women danced. In the dream these *Heyokas* [thunder spirits] came in the room and tied me up. I couldn't talk or holler. The drum was in the back room, and I could hear it. They danced before me.

The last one went out—his hair was all tied up with grass. The dream was all upside down and backward. When they were done they left. I was free to go.

I knew I had to do it [act it out in public], because that is the way it is with these dreams. For a long time I ignored that dream, pushed off until every time it thundered—I would huddle indoors, scared to death. I cried and tried to put it away. People around me got sick and died, but I was fine. Finally I performed it, the Sun Dance as I saw it. Four times I performed it, with other women. The dream is gone now, finished, and it doesn't bother me anymore.

It is not uncommon for others to be spiritually aware of a person's calling. These others, perhaps holy people in their own right, inform the man or woman of the content of their own related dreams to encourage and reinforce the "new dreamer's" calling.

It may also happen that jealousy comes into play, and other medicine people may seek to harm or retard the new dreamer's development. The holy woman quoted in the following is a Sicangu Lakota full-blood in her late sixties. She is a proud mother and grandmother.[3] She is revered, and her services are used by a great number of people. Her calling came late in life, but she told us, "my dreams are getting stronger all the time." We will call her by her Indian name, Zin-tkala Zin Win, or Yellow Bird Woman.

Today you can't find medicine men—you can't find one that's a true one. You ask one to come down here [Denver Lakota community], and you have to pay that medicine man. I can understand that they have to have some gas money to get here. Some want three, four, five, six hundred dollars right in their hands so they can come for one night and doctor just two people or maybe one. But there are a lot more people that needed help. The way I'm doing these things, it's not for my own self. It came from a medicine man.

I believe in 1985 or 1984 this medicine man came here, Joe Eagle Elk. He died since then. The first time he came here—and I knew Joe when he was a little boy, before he went into the service, before World War II. I didn't see him until he came here that time, and he said, "We came after you."

I said, "Who's we?" You know, I thought he came here with his wife and that was what he meant. [He meant the spirits.]

"No." he said, "We had a ceremony, and the spirits chose you."

So I said, "Now what did I do?" It was scary.

And he told me, he said . . . he had his hand out like this. "In this whole Denver area," he said in Indian, "there is no one, no woman, who would fit and sit in the altar. They looked and here they found you."

I started looking out the window, and "Oh!" I said, "What is it they want me to do?"

"They want you to work at the *Hocoka* [sacred altar]."

After a while I said, "Well I thought about it, and I can't refuse when I was asked to do something good for the people, something that is not bad for the people, but to pray for the people. I guess I'll do it," you know. So I said, "All right. I guess I'll do it, but you have to show me how to perform your Hocoka, your ceremony . . ."

We went to the ceremony, and here the whole room was just lighted up. The minister was the only one that saw the blue light inside the altar [besides me]. He said I was standing in the middle. Well, he told me what he saw. He said, "The sick were standing around you, around the altar; you stood in the middle." He told me, "Hold that pipe."

I said "Wow . . ."

In the ongoing development of a holy woman's powers, certain dreams begin to form the shape of the future. They may present the actual spirit helper and the essence of that helper's identity. Dreams may symbolically indicate the kinds of help the helper spirit or spirits will provide and eventually the rituals necessary to call upon them—the very basis of a personal ceremony. What follows is a powerful continuation of the dream experiences of Good Lifeways Woman:

Later that week we had the ceremony. Ted sat in the middle near his altar. I had never been to anything like this. He prepared and then filled my pipe and laid it on the altar on some sage. The ceremony was in Lakota Homes [Indian community just outside Rapid City], where we were living at the time.

The lights were put out, and the singers started. During the ceremony I noticed a large blue light above me. The light was like a cloud or a mist, and it stayed above me. I thought everyone could see it. I was in awe.

Soon it formed into the shape of an owl. Out of its eyes came little lights like penlights. It was a yellow light, and it was looking right at me. It spoke to me—not in words, but I could feel its message. It said that I would start to learn many things, but [told me] to be patient. It would start slow, and I would learn far into the future.

This owl has told me the same thing a few times. It told me not to look for a teacher but to look inside myself. It told me that the bigger miracle is the conception, not the birth. That you cannot know all that goes on underground before a flower pushes through the dirt.

I saw a lake and knew that you cannot know what goes on beneath the surface of a smooth lake . . . things like that.

Next, a huge buffalo was above me. I could see it very clearly, and its nose was wet, glistening. The buffalo was so big that its goatee hung down into the altar where Ted sat. All around Ted little lights were flashing and you could see him praying—his silhouette. I was truly left with a powerful feeling of awe.

Soon that vision faded, and I saw a man. He was wearing a mask over his face and a headdress, and there were little horns protruding from the sides of his head. He was naked from the waist up and wore a skirt like a Sun Dancer. Around his neck was a necklace of carved buffalo dewclaws, or eagle talons—I could not make it out.

When the lights were put on, I said out loud, "Wow! Did you see that owl? And that buffalo—its nose was wet, and . . ." Everybody was sitting there staring at me. After a moment I realized I was the only one who had seen it. I turned to Shirley, who was with me, and I asked her in a whisper, "Why can some people see it and not others?" She didn't answer, she just looked at me in a way that let me know I was a babe in the woods.

Later Ted asked me what I had seen, so I told him. He told me I should go find a teacher. I thought of two different men.

Before the ceremony was over Ted said, "The spirits are going to name you now." That is when I first heard my name. After that, things would happen to me. Where I saw nothing before it was as if a world had opened up to me, and now I saw things and heard things that I never had before.

More so with women than with men, dreams significant to the transformation from lay person to holy person may come at any time. Men who wish to enhance their abilities to "doctor," however, always *hanbleciya,* or fast, in a formal one-, two-, three-, or ideally four-day denial of food and water. These fasts, which women also undertake, place the seeker on a secluded hilltop or in a vision pit or sweat bath used as a hut of isolation, in an area where spirits are known to dwell. Although it is only a singular account from one woman, the following story from Jackie Yellow Tail, a Crow woman, shares many of the traditional attitudes about this *Hanbleciya,* or crying for a vision.

Recently we celebrated the fiftieth anniversary of the Sun Dance returning here to Crow. . . . In that Sun Dance I "fell," which is the greatest thing
that can happen. In the Sun Dance, when you go without food and water for
three or four days at a time, and you're praying almost constantly, you are
closer to the Creator than when your body is being nourished. Your senses
are keener, and that puts you in a state where you are closer to the Creator.
You're able to have that connection to hear better, to receive the messages
that the Creator has for you, whatever they are. It might be years and years
before someone has the opportunity [to fall at a Sun Dance], if ever. But the
thing a person hopes to do in our Sun Dance is to fall. Because when you
fall you go into a dreamlike state. You receive a vision that is the same as
that of a person who goes out into the mountains to fast.

Most often it comes in the form of a dream or seeing an animal that happens to talk to you. At that point you are close to the Creator and will be
able to receive those messages that he has, whatever medicine dream they
may bring to you.

From that dream at the Sun Dance I knew I had to go down to Wyoming,
near Fort Washakie, to fast; that is where my grandfather gets his special
medicine, a root he doctors with. It is also the home for the chief of the Little People, the keeper of the Sun Dance, who is also a medicine helper to
my grandfather in his role as Sun Dance leader. . . .

It was a wonderful experience. . . . it was like . . . I went home. I had
many questions about things that are happening right now, that my people
are going through, these and many other, more personal things. I was told
that things were going to be good, and I was given certain tasks to do. In
my prayers I say—and I truly believe this: "We are only human, pitiful; my
prayer is to the Creator." It also came to me that I need to look to the Creator for guidance in my daily life.

There are no guarantees that fasting will produce vision:

When you fast, you know you're not always going to receive help. There
were many times when I fasted and nothing happened other than thanking
God for the coming year. To say every person is going to get a vision the
first time they fast, is absurd. Usually it's not going to happen. That is the
way it was when I first went into the Sun Dance [fifteen years earlier]. I
thought, "Oh, wow, something great is going to happen to me." And it was
great after I got to know things and look back at things, but they come in
their own time.

When these visions come to a person, man or woman, it is often with
mixed emotions. Doubt, joy, and often dread are spoken of by people we
interviewed. As Wounye' Waste' Win told us,

Another time, I had a vision in a dream. In the dream I saw my family, and there was a thought, a voice or feeling, that said you must let them go. "Each one of them belongs to the *tunkasila's* [Grandfather spirits], and you must loosen your grip on them and let them go."

The spirit, I think, meant that I was too involved in the lives of those around me, and if I was going to continue on my journey, I had to let them go. It was an exciting time, and I carried around a sense of anxiety, a sense of joy, that I was learning these things.

Shortly after that, I was in a ceremony. I was sponsoring a *Wopila* [Thanksgiving ceremony], and we were praying for Ted Has Horses' daughter. She had kidney problems—cancer, I think—and they were going to pray for her. We had the ceremony in a house. Ted's daughter sat down beside me. After the ceremony started, a beautiful blue light appeared in the room. It was dense, almost like a blue rock that was glowing.

That light was *Pejuta Yuha Mani.* He had come to me, to help that girl. I thought, "Now what is this? Why would he come to me?" It stopped over me, and I thought, "No, not me! It's her that's sick." And I guess I was frightened of it.

Someone said, "Don't be afraid of it." The ball came down, and I held it in my hand.

Ted said, "You're holding him too tight, and he can't breathe." So I loosened my grip, and I could feel warmth in my hand. The light took my hands and guided them to the girl's back. They said for her to stand up, that they were going to doctor her—and then they sang this doctoring song. I could see Pejuta Yuha Mani come. You know, he looked like in that TV show— "beam me up" ["Star Trek"]—you know, like they turn into silver; that's how he came, and here he came to me, and I was sitting next to her. I was scared, so I resisted it, but the light took me and I let it.

The spirit took my hands, and I thought, "No! No! It's not me! They don't know me. Pejuta Yuha Mani is confused!"

But he had a stone about this big, and it glowed. He took my hands and put them like this. He put that stone under them, and the light came through. Then he went up my arms, like this, with the stone, and then he took my hand and he doctored her with my hand. My hands, with that warm blue light, went all over the girl's back.

Then, when the song was over, they told her to stand and tell what had happened to her. She said, "These small hands came and doctored me on my back." But he was holding my hands.

Ted said, "Okay, now tell what happened." He came over to me, and I told him, then I said, "He used my hands to doctor her."

He said, "Well, you know what that means." But I didn't. So afterward I asked him, and he said, "Now you can doctor with your hands." So I didn't really understand, even then. Of course, they don't give you instructions;

you know you have to pray about it. I was hoping they would say now is the time, and this is what you do, but it didn't happen like that at all.

It seemed to me that after that time, whenever I am in the presence of someone who is sick or has a problem, my hands get very warm.

It was at that ceremony—well, right before that, in a sweat lodge. I looked across from me and there was a bear—a white bear. I was watching and then it turned into a man, an old man with gray hair. Sitting across from me. And then at the ceremony, standing in the altar, was this huge bear [up on its hind legs, growling]! I kept having these images of bears, and so I asked my teacher's mother what that meant, that I kept seeing the bear.

She said, "It is because you have bear power." She said, "You're going to be a mean mother-in-law." She said, "You better never get that bear mad at you." After that I would see the bear quite a bit.

That summer I was at a powwow, and I was wearing a blue beaded buckskin dress. A man came up to me. He was a Chippewa from Minnesota. He came up to me and asked me my name. I told him. He looked at me, very surprised, and said, "I had a dream that soon I would meet a women, a special woman, and she would be wearing the same blue beaded dress that you are wearing. You are the woman I was told would come." He was a Chippewa medicine man, and he said, "There is a blue light around you. And I knew that I was supposed to see you."

Later that summer I met a friend, and she said, "René, this is my friend Wounye' Waste' Win, and the girl turned and told me, "Two months ago I went to a ceremony, and the spirit named Tall Grass told me that I was going to meet a woman with your name. She will be wearing a white buckskin dress and have blue beadwork." I had a dress on with blue beadwork. She told me she was glad to meet me, that she too was sure I had come to her in a dream.

All this was exciting but at the same time very strange.

The path to becoming a "doctor" is not always an easy one and can be fraught with dangers for the individual who is called to serve the people. Other medicine people may be jealous and use their own powers or position to prevent by spiritual means, or through malicious gossip, the fulfillment of the competing shaman's calling. Through the moccasin telegraph of gossip, they may deny the validity of the rival's dreams. This caused a spiritual crisis for Good Lifeways Woman that took years to overcome. During those years she did not practice her ceremonies or acknowledge her dreams. Good Lifeways Woman tells us of this very real and dangerous spiritual conflict with someone she trusted as a teacher.

During that time I was getting ready to fast. When it came time to fast, there were four of us who wanted to fast together, and we went about pledging a time and getting ready. I had wanted Ted Has Horses [pseudonym for a recently deceased holy man] for a teacher, but when I approached him he sent me to Francis No Heart. I approached Francis, and he said he would help.

When the time came we set up our camp at Bear Butte, where we were to fast. Then we got word that Francis had changed his mind and would not help us. I was pretty upset and thought, "Well, we are all ready and have everything we need, so maybe we should proceed without help."

I thought of Ted Has Horses, and I called him. He said, "It would not be a good idea for you folks to do this on your own." He said, "I will help, but it would be best if you came down here, where I am." So we went after him.

I noticed that when we finally did get on the hill to fast, even though each of us picked our own spot, the place that felt right, we had formed the four directions. I sat up almost all night praying. I was so tired I could not stay up, and I prayed that I could sleep for a while and that I would wake up when the time came.

I was facing north, and I fell asleep. In that state I saw a large shape approaching me. I assumed it was an eagle. It was so big it almost covered the sky. When it got closer I could see that it was an owl. It looked at me with those same yellow eyes. Soon that owl took on the shape of a man. From this I knew that this spirit had been around for a long time, and before he was an owl he was a man.

The man drew a circle in the dirt. In the dirt appeared an owl's face and an eagle's face. The blue light was present. It marched up my pipe stem. In my dream the blue light asked, "Are you ready? When you are ready I will help you"; and that blue light traveled all around me.

When I got off the hill, I spoke with Ted and asked him, "What did it mean when the spirit asked if I was ready?"

He smiled and said, "Well, are you? Are you ready?"

Shortly after that time I went down to check on my land on the reservation. As I stood at the fence I had a powerful vision. An old man named Martin High Bear appeared to me walking down the hill. He turned and looked at me.

Then I heard a voice in my head. It said, "The door is open, the door is open to you. You don't have to worry about what you will eat or what you'll drink, because those will be taken care of. You cannot even imagine what this road contains. It has nothing to do with human needs; it has nothing to do with those things. These things will all be provided, and this door is open."

Then I saw this mountain, like Bear Butte—it was covered with trees, and there was a fog over it, and I could see underneath there was a path. Again the voice spoke: "It's a difficult path, and you have to come up it. We are not going to carry you up—you are going to have to come."

Then I saw Martin High Bear again. He was walking away from me, off in the distance, but I could see that he didn't go by his own power. He looked like a puppet, as if there were lines to him like that, and he was walking away, and I could see that he was not going by his own power.

The discovery of previously unknown or new powers is part of the transition from uninitiated lay person to holy woman. These experiences teach and awaken the one to whom the spirits are calling.

I was going to graduate school in Minnesota, and I had a roommate named Eva. One evening when I came back I felt that she was not well, that she was hurting somewhere. I asked her if she was hurting, and she said, "Yes, my legs are hurting."

I asked her, "Do you want me to rub them?"

She said, "Yes." I was going to rub her feet.

"Your hands are hot!" she said. "Your hands are really, really hot, and there's energy coming into my legs." She said, "You're doctoring me!"

It's like I go into this comalike state, like watching it, and so it gives direction about where to put my hands. I just feel it, and then I got this message for her to turn over; I'm going to work on her back.

When she turned over I put my hands right on the back. When I put my hands on her back I saw her lungs. And what it looked like was like when someone has skinned herself and the wound is kind of weepy. Her lungs were real red and weepy. So after that, my hands would heat up and tremble, and I just leave them there until it stops. I sometimes I get direction on where to put it.

She was a psychic, and when I was done she said, "You have heat that radiates from your hands, and the whole time you rubbed my legs you were surrounded by kind of a blue glow." After that, I used my hands to help a number of people.

When I went back to South Dakota I went to talk to Francis No Heart [pseudonym] to tell him what I was learning, what I was feeling. He listened, and then he looked at me and told me that I was only hallucinating. I wasn't seeing anything, and that I wasn't hearing anything. [voice cracks] It was all hallucination. That I didn't hear anything; that I made it up. That everything I had experienced was a hallucination.

It hit me very hard, what he said, because I was sort of his student, and I trusted and respected him. I felt awful inside, like my soul was a wasteland. I felt abandoned, and worse. This feeling lasted until about four years ago.

I Sun Danced and fasted those years, but it was as if my helpers were gone and I was abandoned. It was an awful feeling—I had lost faith in myself in everything.

A lot of things had gone on for a long time when he told me that I was not having real experiences. And I believed him. . . . I believed him. It was like that was my greatest fear. My greatest fear was that it wasn't real. And I was always afraid . . . worthlessness; why me, why me? And so it's like he had done it again. Confirmed my worst fear. And I closed up.

So when I went to fast that year . . . once again, here they came, you know. All these things I started seeing in the clouds and the heavens. I said, "Go away! It's all in my imagination. Don't do this to me!" So I was shut down from that time until just lately.

It happened about 1981. I think it was a good thing, because now I think of this period like deprivation, like being in a wasteland. I thought—I thought they had gone.

I thought they had gone because I was bad. That they [the spirits] made a mistake. I didn't know then, I didn't realize, that I had shut down. I had lost faith. I had lost faith in myself. I no longer believed in myself. I had made "this man" my god.

In fact, soon after that, his helper died. My nephew Mitchell is going to be a medicine man, and so Mitchell talked to me one night and said, "The one that died came in a dream, and he told me, 'There is this man who is controlling you and that the thing he told you about your dreams is not true. You already are that holy woman. You are already that. He manipulates you in a subtle way so that he's holy and you're not. He manipulates you a lot and you're under that manipulation. You need to get out from that and believe in yourself again,'" but still it took a long time.

I did shut down, and I thought, "What's wrong? Why aren't they coming? I'm calling them." I was used to the spirits being around me, having this world, this otherworld, and then all of a sudden it was dead; they were gone—not totally gone, but it was significantly reduced.

These firsthand accounts provide the context for the beginnings of a true calling in the sacred. The crisis of faith, the jealousy of another "practitioner," and the scenes of spirits appearing in a Lowanpi ceremony are all well within the traditional Lakota, Cheyenne, and Crow religious worldview.

8

How Ritual Evolves

What follows are the firsthand accounts of how, through various channels, three women's personal rituals evolved and continue to do so. Good Lifeways Woman's experiences continue:

> I had a dream that I was fasting. I was in the Black Hills in this meadow with tall grass. It was surrounded by pine trees. On my altar there were only three flags instead of four. So I was sitting in the altar, and a close friend brought my pipe. She said, "Here! Are you ready?" And I thought, "She has a lot more faith in me than I do. I don't know what she thinks I can do." But I took it [the pipe]. It sounds like I was conquering myself in my dreams, saying, "All you have to do is pray. Just pray."
>
> So I took the pipe and I closed my eyes, and then I opened them and it was day. It was day, and the sky was baby-blue. Off in the distance there were pine trees. On the top of the pine trees, way off in the distance, was what looked like an eagle. And here came this big bird, a huge bird. I assumed it was an eagle. It was so big that it would just go down like this and up [moves her arms slowly, imitating the flight]. And then it came over me, right above me, and turned into a man.
>
> It was a man that came down, and for a long time that part of the dream frightened me so. It wasn't until I went to Minneapolis and was talking about the dream to a person and she said, "Before he was an owl, he was man." I just got this chill all up the back, you know. When he came down, his face was masked, his face was covered, and he had holes for his eyes and little owl ears, but the rest of him was covered, and he did something to my arms and made a circle in the dirt, he made a symbol, and then . . .
>
> I realized later that instead of an eagle's face he had an owl's face. The eyes were the sky. It had no eyes [pupils]; you could see right through to the sky—and this voice said, "Are you ready?" So later I went to see Ted Has Horses, and I told him about it and he turned to me like this and said, "Are you ready? Well, that's good."

These passages suggest how dreams are interpreted and used to develop ritual. In her dream Good Lifeways Woman is offered a pipe. In the traditional way, the *Canunpa Wakan,* or Holy Pipe, is at first refused. To the Lakota the pipe is synonymous with a calling to the sacred, a calling to doctor. She accepts this awesome responsibility to her vision by taking the pipe in her hands.

Next, Good Lifeways Woman describes seeing the construction of her *Hocoka,* her sacred center hearth or altar. What is to make up her altar, the central point of spiritual access, is critical. It is believed that her spirits guide her in the details, because it is they whom she is calling on for help, and it is they who must recognize who is calling them.

She has seen an altar in which there are three sticks protruding upright from the earthen mound. Because four is the standard spiritual number for the Lakota, this confuses and perhaps intrigues her, but the meaning of the three sticks remains yet unknown and to some extent unusable.

At this point in her spiritual indoctrination, Good Lifeways Woman does not know why she has seen this; she may not even know how what she has seen or experienced will "work for her" or what importance to place on it.

A spirit appears to her as an eagle. She immediately sees this as good, because Lakota believe the eagle to be one of the most powerful intercessors available. Later it is revealed to her that the bird she has seen is in fact an owl and, even more important, that the owl was previously a man. Owl spirits have specific knowledge related to life and death issues. Access to this Owl means that Wounye' Waste' Win will be able to tell her patients if they are to live or to die.

The owl draws some symbols in the dirt. These symbols may be used to make a small "sand painting" inside her altar whose sacred meaning is known only to the holy person.

The question repeated in this vignette—"Are you ready?"—implies a challenge and is meant to be rhetorical. The answer can come only from Good Lifeways Woman herself. Its answer is already known to the spirits.

So when I went to Minneapolis, this man came up to me. He was a Chippewa medicine man and he told me, "There is a blue light around you. I knew that I was supposed to see you."

I asked, "There's this blue light around me? What does that mean?"

He said, "It means you can travel [spirit travel]. It means that you can leave your body." Then he showed me how to use the bear claw to call the bear. He said, "Do you know how to call the bear?" So he showed me what to do. I tried it. I tried it and I called him, and I see him right now—he's here [indicates space beside her]! And when I called him I was sitting on his back. It kind of wobbled like that. At the time that he came there, I was meditating, and this big, fat bear came, and I was sitting there; he came and sat before me. He went like this, and when he sat like this he kind of rolled, and then I could hear him breathing all through my meditation [she imitates the sound].

Well, anyway, we had a pipe ceremony [near Minneapolis] with this Chippewa man—his name was Wood Hand. We put our pipes up there [adjacent to the altar], and here he said, "There is somebody in here that has a bear. There's a bear around one of these pipes." That was my friend. So that was validation from outside as well.

Another living shaman now revealed to Good Lifeways Woman that a blue light was clearly visible around her. This light signified the ability of the intelligent soul, or wana'gi, to travel outside the body. Soul travel is one way to access critical sacred information. If the shaman can travel over physical distance to witness or hear information important to herself or her patient, she has been given a powerful gift. She may also use this power to doctor someone distant from her or to fly into the spirit world if necessary.

The man also tells her that she has a close ally who is a bear spirit. Good Lifeways Woman does not know what the bear will help her with, but now she has heard about the bear helper spirit a number of times. The bear makes his personality and nature known to her so that she may know him in the future. At this point in her experience, the potential powers of the bear helper are unknown by her.

We're not often in a moment of quiet reflection. You know, they just come when they come. I reached up to turn off the light, and as I turned off the light, somebody started talking to me, and it was the man again: "You have been saying, 'Big deal, so you have bear medicine; so what do I do with it?'"

As I turned up the light he said, "Don't worry about it. When the time comes you will have it, so don't worry about it, let it go." So I didn't think about it any further, I let it go. And then about three or four years ago, after Sun Dance, my husband said, "I have something for you." He was very excited.

It was really funny, but things come to him—I mean, here he is, with all his big agnostic stuff, and he said, "I have something for you." He brought me a bear skull. He said somebody gave it to him. And so I got it, and I thought, Uh oh, now what, what does this mean? Is it time? What is that about?

Big Nose [her principal spiritual guide] said, "If you don't use it, it will go again," so I took the skull. I started to think, "What is this? What does it mean?" I started asking everyone.

Just a year ago I taught this class, and there were two people in there, but they really stood out because she was from Canada and he was from Fort Totten. What was outstanding about them was that he had a hat, and he had more medallions and feathers and plumes—I mean, it looked like a war bonnet with this stuff! And so the first thing you wanted to say to him was, Hi, Indian! He wears these big ribbon shirts, and this long, big belt with long fringes. I mean, he really dresses up.

So I noticed him, and the class wanted to sweat. I told them, "I can't tonight, but if you want to use my lodge, you could—I won't be home until nine."

So they said, "If it's only at nine we'll hold it, we'll wait for you." So they did. When I went in and this [Indian] guy prayed, there was a big bear in front of him.

So I told them, "Do you know that when you prayed I saw a bear in front of you?"

"Oh yeah," he said. "That's Big Bear. We have bear medicine."

I said, "You do! Come here [and explain what you know about it to me]!"

So he said, "Talk to my wife; she has bear power, and she'll talk to the grandmothers, and they'll help you."

So I talked to the woman, and what she said was, "When the grandmother spirit came into the ceremony, she said, 'We've been watching you for a long time, and it's good that you want to do this. And we've seen what happened to you. We know . . .'" So she showed me some medicine and told me some things, and then we had a little ceremony. And what they said was that I am not going to have a teacher. There was not going to be a medicine woman or man whom I would get my teaching with. I would learn direct [from the spirits].

This passage affords insight into how this woman's understanding of sacred meanings and metaphors, and thus her personal ritual, evolved. Good Lifeways Woman's altar includes the bear's skull and creates an access point for her bear helper to enter the ceremony.

She learned that her ritual teacher was not a single living human man or woman. Good Lifeways Woman's teachers were spirits of animals, humans, and departed ancestors. She was to learn from the living, those "who knew she was coming," and those that had something to give her or teach, such as songs. Even spirits of dead holy men could be her teachers. Out of all of this evolved a way of conducting her ceremonies that was uniquely suited to her and to what she was learning. In fact, her ritual evolves constantly because of this. According to Ray Dupris, "It is not enough to copy the songs and ceremonies of another holy man; this means nothing. If you truly have the calling, the spirits will teach you your ceremony, then you will have power—the kind of power that is so strong you could cure anything, even deadly disease, just by being there, praying for that person. This is the kind of power these people had."

Bits and pieces of ritual practice used by the medicine woman come to her and must be affirmed, generally by multiple dreams and then, later, by results.

> I had a dream—I came to a meadow, and I could see Pete Swift Bird, a *Heyoka*. It was his pasture, and I had a class with me, so we stopped at the fence, and I took a cigarette and wrapped a dollar bill around it and said to a student, "Take it to the man down there. I want to tell him that we want to go across." So he went down there, and when Pete got the cigarette he laughed and turned around and looked at me. He was so happy; and here he was, dead!
>
> He came up to the fence and said, "Come on, come on!" He was really tickled. Instead of taking us across the meadows he took me to a bluff, a huge bluff, and said, "You see those three stars? Three stars up there?" And then he said, "Now, you fix your altar with three sticks like that. Just like that! Do you understand?"
>
> I was going to pray, but I didn't have a pipe. I told him, "Wait, Pete, I don't have a pipe."
>
> "Oh, the pipe, bring the pipe," he said. They [spirits] brought out this pipe, and it was a really old-fashioned one; it looked like the one Ted Has Horses used. A big heavy bowl on it. He brought it to me. I took it, and then Pete walked off.
>
> I said, "It's not my pipe," but I took it, and I started to point. So that's why I do those three sticks. But when he showed them to me—I mean, they were just bent.

Now the student of the sacred begins to understand that her altar represents the sky, and the three sticks special stars. The ancient pipe represents her connection to the ways of a recently deceased and well-respected medicine man, known well by her. It may also indicate the need for her to adhere to the proper ways of doing things. Her songs and the order of her ritual's progression must in a sense fit within the expectations of these ancestor spirits. Achieving ecstasis, an out-of-body spiritual experience, can only happen if she uses her songs and ritual literally to work herself into this altered state of consciousness or spiritual receptivity.

So the first time I put them up, the bear came to me. And when he came he shook the lodge. Then he came right here. And that bear came in and stood up, like this, but he came in and he came again last night. This is the third time I used those sticks. The second time I used them, I hung that eagle feather on there, and the eagle came . . . oh, it was beautiful, it's like the end of that sweat opened up, and then it was the bear, and he was coming with this huge eagle, just soaring.

He said, "You made this altar, so I have come," and he sat with me. I wanted to tell the people in there, I wanted to say, "Look who's here!" But they couldn't see him, so they were praying.

I thought, "They're praying, and it's like they're in a veil, and they don't know he's here. But if they knew—what they could find out, what was available." They didn't know, so they were just sitting there. I wanted to know [about him], and he said, "Pray from your heart; let them know I am here." But they didn't know. I was thinking that if they could see him, they would certainly talk to him. I didn't see him sitting there, but I knew he was there.

Good Lifeways Woman relates a frustration at the fact that only she can see or, more accurately, hear or perceive the bear next to her.

From her initial calling, through a spiritual crisis brought on by a male teacher who puts doubt into her heart, Good Lifeways Woman traveled through numerous spiritual experiences and adventures. She rediscovered her calling, has walked the sacred Red Road, and has grown to the point where she has acquired a confidence in her spirit helper's powers that will not leave her.

Here, she encounters a spirit helper that used to "belong" to a medicine man who had passed away.

It's like I absolutely know that they are there; I hear them when they come, and I see the lights and sometimes I see who it is—Pejuta Yuha Mani [walks with Medicine] has come in. I see this man who stood before me with braids. As he stood there, he unraveled his braids, and what that meant to me is, See—that's how Pejuta Yuha Mani comes in, he has one braid wrapped and one braid unwrapped. I thought, Pejuta Yuha Mani has come! I'm almost scared to tell you this but one of the things that Ted Has Horses said when he was living was, "Why do you like that song 'Ate' wa u elo . . .'? Why do you like that song?" He said, "What do you know about it?"

I said, "That's the song they sing when the Sun Dancers come in."

He said, "One time when they sang that song, lightning came down, and a man walked down that lightning into the altar—and that's what the song is all about. His name is Pejuta Yuha Mani." And he said, "Sing that song and pray because Pejuta Yuha Mani has not chosen anyone's altar [to work with]. He has not chosen anyone, so you should pray."

Good Lifeways Woman's old friend and encourager, although passed from this earthly realm, appears to her and lets her know that the most powerful of his spirit helpers is now "unattached"—in fact, in search of someone in the physical world to work through. He tells her to think of him and sing his song, actually inviting her to call his old helper as an ally.

She decides to call him using his song: "Pejuta Yuha Mani . . . I prayed for him to come, sang his song, and he came to the altar and I saw him. God, that just hit me hard."

Lakota people have maintained more of their healing rites than many other tribal groups. The Yuwipi, Lowanpi, and Inipi [sweat lodge] ceremonies continue much as they have for the last two centuries and the coming of the female culture heroine, the sacred White Buffalo Calf Maiden.

Yellow Bird Woman, a Sicangu Lakota elder, now sixty-eight, came by her training relatively late in life. She tells us how certain aspects of her ritual came about.

"Okay!" Joe Eagle Elk says. "You be ready tonight!" He told me how to make my flags. You make this so big, he says; you make these so many inches, and you make so many flags, six flags, and you make them these colors, and these ninety-nine Canli Wapahta [tobacco ties], and you make that ninety-nine any way you want. So it came to my mind—seventeen red, seventeen yellow, seventeen white, sixteen black, sixteen blue and sixteen green. And so I said, "That's right," and I wrote it down, and it was ninety-nine of various colors. I fascinated myself, doing things like that.

Yellow Bird Woman feels she experiences a sacred insight creating precisely ninety-nine tobacco ties, without working out the math in her head. These small things reassure her and reinforce her belief that she has a calling and will receive the help she needs from the grandfathers. These ninety-nine tobacco ties will be incorporated into her emerging ritual. Knowing something without being told is also a sign that the messenger—in this case, Joe Eagle Elk—has received sacred information:

> So he told me, "I know you have a pipe."
> I wondered how he knew I had a pipe . . . but then I went back in my mind and I remembered, I do have a pipe! I just kept it.
> He says, "You bring that pipe," so I took that pipe over, and they blessed my pipe. They load the pipe, and that's what I have to use for the people, to pray for the people. My pipe was a chief's pipe, and I never knew what the handle looked like. I was cleaning the pipe when I noticed that my pipe had yellow, red, black, and white stripes on it. And I thought, "How in the world? I never knew this." All the main colors were on there. I said, "Gee!"

Again a minor incident acts as reinforcement. It is as if her eyes have now been opened to what is there. The sacred colors on her pipe were functionally "not there" until she looked with "new" eyes.

> We went to that ceremony, and he told me to load my pipe, and not to overload or underload it. I learned to do that the right way. I learned a lot of things from him. We talked Indian together, and he was younger than I am, and we exchanged a lot of things, words to remember. He told me a lot of things about the spiritual way of life. The spirits say things to him, and it's an experience for him. The herbs, the trees—you know, the names of the trees. We remember all those things. . . .
> I was praying as they were singing. He was over there on the other side, and he was praying, so all these people could know. I was praying, too. This minister [a full-blood Episcopal priest] said, "Did you see what I saw?"
> "What did you see?" I said.
> He said, "Where the people were standing on the outside is all women, and there were two women standing in the middle with you—spirits!"

Elements of how Yellow Bird Woman is to doctor the people, and that her helpers will be the spirits of women, have now been revealed in a vision. She is seen in the vision "standing in the middle," an allegorical reference to her own altar. The fact that her beloved Episcopal priest has also seen the vision and the spirits also reinforces the power of her vision experience.

> After it was over, I was still standing there, and the medicine man was blessing the water and the spirit food, and he heard the swishing of the water down there, and here it sprinkled me in the face. I was going to move back, but I just stood there, I was really praying.
>
> My heart was beating so hard and here he said, "He, he' con pisni yo [don't do that]. She's a pitiful woman, and you ask her to be here, and she's here trying to help you, so don't splash her." He says, "Whenever you ask them for something, they will try to help you."

The spirits get playful with her to remind her that they are there, they are real, and they have accepted her and will in turn help her to help others. With this experience Yellow Bird Woman, always a woman of strong faith, begins a new journey.

> They didn't talk; they were there praying for me. A lot of these things are happening today to me—it's sort of scary, you know, but I don't want to get scared, because whatever I have to do I will do it well. It's getting a little bit stronger and stronger every time I go into the sweat lodge. If I take somebody in there, there are spirits in there, and I see them. Little lights, little blue lights. There are two of them—one is red inside and white around the edge, the other one blue and white around the edge. They come on each side of me and sit there. And these lights—sometimes people see them and go across the sweat. And when I pray for someone they go across and sit beside them. And, well, I've been thinking—the sweat lodge has a light coming in from the outside, but it's pitch dark in there; it's always like that.
>
> There's a sweat lodge just close by here, and they ask me to run sweat Sunday. We have three of them, three sweat lodges. I doctor people for all sorts of things, mostly women for alcohol, spouse problems, even witchcraft.

The mention of the lights and a detailed description of how these two female spirits manifest themselves to those in the sweat is, within Lakota experience, entirely logical. Yellow Bird Woman's mention of witchcraft refers to a medicine man or woman who has *Hgmuga Chmuga* (cast a negative spell over physical distance) on one of her patients.

Not all that is done in the sacred is seen as positive. The spirits don't behave according to a specific moral code. If called upon to hurt or even kill someone, they will do it. The cost, however, to the holy person using the negative powers will be grave. The Lakota believe that a person who does this will shortly see a close relative die.

Like Good Lifeways Woman, Yellow Bird also experienced a severe spiritual and emotional crisis about the time of her calling and was treated for cancer. As in the case of Good Lifeways Woman, Yellow Bird's visions continue to unfold, pulling her into additional and new roles with the sacred.

Last June, before the Sun Dance, I had two dreams. It still bothers me, but I have to wait until it [meaning] comes to me. I'm always dreaming about eagles. In this dream I was at a Sun Dance and there were all women dancing, and I dressed in [a gray dress with red trim], and they all had gray dresses with old-fashioned red ribbons or binding on [the neck]—nothing else, just there. Like one of my grandmother's sisters used to wear.

Somehow, I never knew my grandmother Light In The Lodge, but I always feel that she dressed like that, with canvas moccasins, cloth leggings and gray hair like mine, but in braids, dressed like the women in my vision. And all these women, they dress like that—they're in a circle in the Sun Dance ground, and they all have an eagle on top of their heads. I was in the middle, but I had a dream about an eagle. It was still, sitting on my shoulder. It is supposed to give me long life. That's my interpretation. My hair used to be all gray [before her calling to the sacred], but now it is turning dark again. People tease me, "But you would never dye it like this!" My eyesight is getting better, too. The medicine man Joe Eagle Elk said so before he died; he interpreted a lot of things for me. . . .

Well, I'm sixty-eight. A lot of people don't believe that. They think I'm younger. "Where do you get all these answers?" they ask, but it comes. But anyway, I had a dream like that—I have an eagle on my head, too. And one that sits beside me, or on my shoulder. I don't know what the song was, but they sang—and I know all the Sun Dance songs, the prayer songs, but I never heard that one before. They were singing, and all these women were old-time dancing, weaving back and forth. And it seemed like the page was turned, and they were all dancing this way. Those eagles flew up above them, flying in a clockwise circle. They were all looking at me, and I was looking at them, and their eyes were yellow. They were scary, and I looked up and my eagle didn't even look at me; he was looking way over there. It woke me up, because that eagle's eye was yellow and big, and they were looking at me, flying in a circle, just low. I woke up and said, "Gee! What kind of a dream was this, anyway? What am I supposed to do? Am I going to do an Eagle Dance, or am I going to participate in a Sun Dance or something?"

Other plains tribes, like the Cheyenne, have maintained their Sun Dance and their Hat and Arrow Bundle rites essentially unchanged for a much longer time. For the Crow, the dance societies, Bundle rites, and functioning clan structure are remarkable testimony to systems that still work for the well-being of the People. An ancient and very central observance, the Tobacco Planting Ceremony, is still held by the Crow:

> I remember as a child watching my grandmother before she'd go to bed. I remember her reading from the Bible, or the Koran—she read both. But she would also go outside and offer tobacco with her prayers. She taught me how to pray in this way from the time I was a child. . . .
>
> Our pipe was important, but more important is the Sacred Tobacco Seed, which goes along with our prophecies. It is called the Sacred Seed—that is the usual translation—of the Tobacco Society or the Beaver Dance. My grandfather's oldest sister was in her nineties, and she was a member of that society. She passed away a year ago. She planted the seed. We are asked in the prophecy to harvest the tobacco. According to the prophecy it must be harvested, and when we stop doing that it will be the end of the Crow people. It is not done every year now, but it is still done. The Tobacco Ceremony, the sweat lodge, and the Sun Dance are our main three ceremonies today. (Jackie Yellow Tail)

It is easy to understand the importance of tobacco and prayer in Jackie's simple yet evolving ritual of healing. Lengthy and involved healing ceremonies like the *Yuwipi* have for some time been gone among the Crow, so in a sense there is no one from whom Jackie can learn detailed formal ritual, and she has no experience with it beyond what she has learned from her grandfather, the late Thomas Yellow Tail. When asked if in the old days there were medicine women in her family she said, "One of my great-grandmothers was that way. We called her Grandma Beans. Her name was Mary Takes The Gun. She was like a midwife and helped birth a lot of the babies; she delivered one of my aunts. She knew the herbs and the plants and the different things that are required to heal the sick. I think she was born in the early 1860s. She was gone before I was born, but the family has kept her memory alive."

Jackie realizes that she is young and only beginning to learn. She also realizes that she must learn from her visions and her tribal traditions how to go about these things: "I take a cigarette when I work on somebody—sometimes I take sweetgrass or cedar. If I don't smudge before I start doctoring, then I'll go back and smudge myself afterward. I don't have a set ritual, other than praying for that person right then and there. I take a cigarette and go pray; without that tobacco the prayer is not as good. It is to carry our prayers to the Creator; I still have great respect for that."

In Jackie Yellow Tail's ceremony, the cigarette replaces the pipe but the metaphor of prayers, physically manifest in smoke, remains. Her reference to smudging refers to an almost universal practice. Cedar, sweetgrass, and often sage are added to a burning ember to create a smoke that has spiritually purifying qualities.

Healers always smudge themselves, and if they are going to use any ritual equipment, such as a pipe, feathers, rattles, drums, or herbs, they pass those through the smudge as well. The house room, sweat lodge, or tipi that is used to doctor, as well as those in attendance, such as singers and family, are also smudged.

When asked how she actually doctors her patients, Jackie said,

Well, there are several things I do, from actual hands-on work with the patients to just listening. I've been able to sit and listen to people, and that is sometimes more helpful than actually putting my hands on them, if somebody is very upset. A lot of people are now starting to come and ask my advice in many different areas.

I think a lot of the experiences I've been through are helping me in that end of it, and always in the Sun Dance and throughout the year people bring me cigarettes, for prayer. That, I think, is the most important way. When they ask me to pray for them, that's an honor to me. My grandfather and grandmother both were the biggest influences in my spiritual life. Out of all other areas in which they taught me, that has been one of the most important things that they taught me—prayer. It's very important. . . .

I give all the credit [for the source of her healing success] to the Creator, because what I do when I touch somebody is to help them to heal their own body. I'm a go-between—between the Creator and the person I am working on. There's polarization, and there is working on people's pressure points. I use some reflexology I am learning, but the main thing is the prayer. You ask for the medicine father to come put his healing hand on that person, that the person would feel better and be well, not just physically but spiritually. They all work together—you can't have one without the other. . . .

[She has helped with] anything from arthritis to a bad back, to a bad knee, to people with lupus. People with many different ailments have asked me to work on them. I'm able to help everybody, but I don't take the credit to begin with, in the first place. It's not me. It's the Creator. I haven't really kept track of any success rates or know of anybody that's fallen by the wayside! If I've helped relieve some of the pain that they're feeling, then I believe that I've done something.

The issue of payment is critical to any understanding of medicine women. It is universally believed that to ask for payment is not right. The power to intercede in human suffering is seen as a gift from a power much greater than the shaman herself. If payment in some form is voluntarily made, the holy woman will offer it up to the Creator and then disperse the gift to someone else, sometimes a grandchild. As Jackie put it, "I don't ask for cash. That's not what I was taught. I believe that, in the Indian way, they pay me whatever they feel the treatment is worth, whether it is a cigarette, asking for a prayer, money, blankets, or whatever it is that they feel—but I don't ask. There've been many times that I haven't been paid, but that doesn't matter. That's not why I do it."

Faith has been such a universal theme with all the people we interviewed that we thought we'd also ask Jackie what position faith takes in her work.

> Faith is necessary in order to get something that you really desire. That you're going to be able to help that person is a matter of faith; likewise, the person that's being doctored must have it. It works both ways. The patient has to believe.
>
> I've also seen people come to my grandfather to be worked on, who say they want to stop drinking. Okay, that is good, but the question is actually for them—how bad do they want to stop drinking? It's just like putting them on their own. I'm just using that for an example. The person that is working on you must have the faith, or they wouldn't have the medicine; but also the person who's being worked on must believe he is being healed. Some might say it's just mind over matter, but that's not always a good explanation. The prayer and the faith are together! There's no separating them.
>
> It's just like the positive and the negative—they're really one. It's no different from a person going to a non-Indian doctor: they could be the healthiest person in the world, but if they believed that they were dying, then they have to die; it's been known to happen.

If the Creator permits, there will be a long and continuous education in the sacred. At some point the holy person may become so old, and her powers so dissipated, that she will remove herself from public life. Sometimes the period before death is one of loneliness and isolation.

The Lakota hope that the lives and careers of the holy women who shared with us here will continue in the service of people for some time. In conclusion here is a part of the last interview we conducted with Good Lifeways Woman, expressing ideas about her own fulfillment:

I have already done a few house ceremonies. I made my altar by re-creating my *Hanbleciya* altar. It was so powerful it frightened me. I know that someday I will be ready for this. More and more the people are being sent or are coming to me for help with their problems.

These are hard times. I have had to think a great deal about women who have experienced spouse abuse or who are considering an abortion. Through sacred understanding I have changed many of my ideas about these things and try to focus on the woman who is suffering.

9

Ritual

Friend, I will send a voice, so hear me.
Friend, I will send a voice, so hear me.
Friend, I will send a voice, so hear me.

In the west I call a black stone friend.
Friend, I will send a voice, so hear me.
Friend, I will send a voice, so hear me.

In the north I call a red stone friend.
Friend, I will send a voice, so hear me.
Friend, I will send a voice, so hear me.

In the east I call a yellow stone friend.
Friend, I will send a voice, so hear me
Friend, I will send a voice, so hear me.

In the south I call a white stone friend.
Friend, I will send a voice, so hear me.
Friend, I will send a voice, so hear me.

On earth, I will call a spider friend.
Friend, I will send a voice, so hear me.
Friend, I will send a voice, so hear me.

Above, I call a spotted eagle friend.
Friend, I will send a voice, so hear me.
Friend, I will send a voice, so hear me.

—Lakota Yuwipi song[1]

The old Lakota song that opens this chapter is believed to be very powerful. In this cryptic poem, spirits are called upon in order, by name, and
with great reverence. The rocks referred to are small, round rocks that
come to the holy person and aid him or her. Each of the four directions,
or winds, is separately called upon, invoking the powers and color of that
direction and the specific kinds of help associated with it. Mother Earth
is honored and called upon as well, the spider representing one of her
most powerful spirit helpers, the legendary Iktomi. The spotted eagle is
also called upon, to help communicate with Father Sky.

Ritual provides access to the Great Mystery and all the things that are
hidden. Songs, dance, hand gestures, movement, body stance, sacred objects, protocol, prayers, and more are all potentially part of the rituals of
healing.

These ritual acts are taught to new members precisely as they were
taught to their grandfathers and grandmothers. The Plains Indian holy
woman has oral traditions and shares in a collective tribal memory of
"how things were done," but there is very little concrete liturgy that tells
her how she is to access the sacred.

The sweat lodge ceremony, while it shares some universal elements,
such as fire, hot rocks, and steam, is as unique as the person who con-
ducts it. Other ceremonies, such as *Yuwipi* or *Lowanpi,* used in healing
the sick, are even more individualized.

In a general sense there is a pattern to the Lowanpi and Yuwipi
(shamanistic) rites of the Lakota. There is a purification rite (sweat lodge)
held, followed later in the evening by the preparation of an altar, the calling of spirits and their entry into the ceremony, the communication with
the spirits and then their departure from the ceremony, and finally the
announcement to the sick what the spirits have revealed for them. A
Wopila (Thanksgiving feast) always follows.

Although this general flow of Lakota ceremonies may be consistent,
tremendous individualization of spirit helpers, dreams, and beliefs en-
sures that details vary widely, and very personal ritual practices are the
norm. From the first offering of tobacco through the last sip of spiritual
water, each tiny gesture helps to create the spiritual inertia necessary for
the healers' shamanic act.

The Commission to Heal

Ceremony and ritual behavior start when the healer is first approached. The setting may be anything from the home of the holy person on the reservation to the parking lot of the Family Thrift Store in Rapid City. Quietly, with ancient and detailed ritual, a commission is made between the patient (or family member) and the healer. This is generally done with a cigarette or prayer pipe. Tobacco and sincerity are the key ingredients. The holy person listens and considers whether she wishes to perform the ceremony. After careful consideration, and after smoking the tobacco, the healer agrees to a prescribed time and place to create a sacred place, or cosmos, where spirits can be contacted. The healer may also decline.

Lowanpi (to sing) and *Yuwipi* (to work with stones) differ in that the holy person is not wrapped up in the Lowanpi ceremony but is wrapped up in the Yuwipi ceremony. Except for this major difference, both ceremonies create a place where human and spirit can interact for the good of the People. What follows is a generalized description of a spirit-calling rite and of how it might be conducted by a holy man or woman.

The ceremony generally begins with the holy person taking a sweat bath to purify herself and the prayers to be offered. Usually members of the family requesting the ceremony, and some of the holy person's assistants and singers may participate in the sweat. It is possible that the entire ceremony might be held in the sweat bath. It is very common for the person with the problem to be doctored in the sweat, in which case no lengthy indoor ceremony is required. The ceremony held in the sweat also follows the general pattern of the indoor ceremony.

Purification

A fire of split wood (a sacred pyre) and rocks is constructed in ritual fashion—a layer of rocks, a layer of wood, a layer of rock, and then more wood. A specific number of rocks is used, depending on the woman's dreams and the type of ceremony she is to conduct.

Once the sweat fire is lit, female relatives start cooking the meal to be served after the ceremony. What is to constitute the sacred feast is prescribed by tradition. Soup made from *papa* (dried buffalo, deer, or beef), *tin' psila* (wild turnips), *wagme'za* (dried corn), and *wagmu'* (dried squash) is prepared for the main course. At some ceremonies, dog meat may be prepared in a sacred manner. *Wojapi,* a simple pudding made from dried native berries, choke cherry, buffalo berry, june berry, or wild plum, is the most desirable. If eagle spirits are to be called upon, salmon might be added. Breads, both *Wigliun Gagapi* (fried) and *Gabubu* (with baking powder), are the favorites. *Ceyaka* (mint tea) and *Pejuta Sapa* (coffee) are generally prepared, and water is blessed to be used at the conclusion of the feast.

> The reason we use different foods is for the spirits; the human ancestors like the meat, bread, the coffee or tea, and the Wojapi, and the eagles and bears go for the fish. That's their favorite. The deer, buffalo, and horse spirits like the corn and grain [breads]. Each of these we include to let them know that they are welcome, that we remember them in a good way and are glad to see them. We never use metal pans for this [porcelain-coated cookware is most common]. And it should be served with a wooden or buffalo-horn spoon. We had no metal before the white man came, and the grandfathers don't like it. This is what my Grandmother Iron Woman told us. (Kenneth Young Bear)

Preparations for the Healing Ceremony

After the sweat is over, all the participants move indoors. Most of the furniture is moved outside to create an open floor space. People begin to come in and place folded quilts or blankets on the floor around the edge of the room. The windows and doors are covered to make the room pitch-dark and safe for the entrance of spirits. Any human images, pictures, or photographs are covered with cloth by the homeowners. The reason for this is that glass and steel are inventions of the white man and create a foreign environment for these ancient Indian spirits. Others say anything that reflects light, including rings and eyeglasses, must also be removed. The spirits manifest themselves as light and thus avoid things that are shiny or reflect light, and so may not come to the ceremony.

The mood at this time is light, even humorous. Comments and banter may be tossed back and forth, as is the norm at any Indian gathering. The time to be quiet and pensive is soon to come. Any obscene or sexual humor, however, would not be considered appropriate.

Creating the Sacred Center

While everyone moves indoors, the holy woman sits quietly, preparing her altar. The enclosure is approximately four feet square, if the ceremony is to be a Lowanpi. If the holy person is to be laid down, as in the Yuwipi, then the enclosure will be enlarged. The area where the holy woman is to sit is generally covered by a sage sprig of a type that produces soft, woolly leaves and grows from the earth on a single stock.

The altar generally comprises a sacred fence made out of four to six hundred tiny tobacco bundles. These *Canli Wapakta* are made from a one-inch square of cloth, into which a pinch of tobacco is offered to the six directions and then placed inside, along with whispered prayers for a successful ceremony. They are linked by a long cord of light string and are later arranged to form a sacred fence around the altar area. Although they existed before the coming of Catholic missionaries, tobacco bundles have been likened to an "Indian Rosary," requiring hours of contemplative prayer in the making. These little bags have been offered at the sweat for purification. The colors of cotton cloth used on the strings of "tobacco ties" are always the same: black, yellow, red, and white. Which color represents a certain direction is an individual interpretation, but blue, if used in addition to the other colors, always represents the sky element and green represents Mother Earth, the herbs, and healing.

The holy woman's altar may be configured in any number of ways, but generally its corners are demarcated by three-pound coffee cans filled with earth. Into this earth a slender staff of wood protrudes two or three feet. From each of these staffs hangs a colored direction flag. The tobacco ties are trailed around these cans, creating the corners of the sacred enclosure.

In front of the holy woman (facing west) will be her *Hocoka,* or center. The principal patient, or person who requested and is sponsoring the "sing," sits across from the healer, his or her back to the wall. The faithful sit along the walls, completely surrounding the room. A common arrangement of this central part of the altar might be a small earthen (sand) circle about one foot in diameter, surrounded by another small border of *Canli Wapakta.* Filled prayer pipes, brought and offered by the faithful (those asking for intercession or thanking the grandfathers for past help), are set on a bed of sage which rests on red cloth. Other articles, *Cangleska Wakan,* may be added to the holy woman's altar that reflect her personal visions, such as feathers, shells, deer tails, horse hair, medicine wheels, and so on. These may be attached to a staff in front of her. This too is supported by a can of earth. She may also use two more staffs, from which are suspended the sky and earth colors. The details of the ceremony may also vary depending on the help that has been requested and the requirements of the spirit, or spirits, who will be called.

The Central Ceremony Begins

When the people have all arrived and the chatter has died down, the doorman (a sergeant at arms) closes the door. If not already seated, the singers will take a seat. It is the doorman's responsibility to "guard" the door until the main ceremony has ended. Live coals are brought in from the old sweat fire by an assistant. The holy woman then adds sweetgrass, cedar, and perhaps sage to the coals. The purifying smoke is then fanned toward each quadrant of the room and toward the surrounding ring of the faithful—including the patient—who hold their hands out; some pull the smoke toward themselves and, with a washing motion, spread the smoke over their bodies.

When this is done, the holy woman smudges herself and her ritual equipment, item by item, cleansing them of anything that might weaken her ability to make contact with the sacred. The equipment she uses is chosen according to her dreams, but typical items might be her pipe bowl, stem, tamper, rawhide (*Wagmu'ha*) rattle, an eagle-bone whistle, a small hand drum, and a fan made up of one or more eagle feathers. A small bundle of sage may be passed around the room, each person taking a single stalk and placing it behind his right ear. All metal jewelry is also removed, so that the spirits may find everyone approachable.

When she has completed purification the holy woman draws a design into the sand using a small, sharpened stick and then smudges the painting using her fan. This design may represent her principal spirit helper, part of a dream, or even the face of the principal patient.

The last thing the holy woman does is fill her pipe. The hardwood (ash) pipe stem is moistened with saliva and joined with the stone bowl. She now sings the pipe song, which is picked up by the singers and any of the faithful who wish to join in:

Kola, le cel econ wo.   Friend, do it this way.
Kola, le cel econ wo.   Friend, do it this way.

Kola, le cel econ wo.

Friend, do it this way.

Leca nu kin taku ya cin kun iye ce
tu kte lo.

If you do it this way,
The things you want will happen.

Ho co kata ogna ilu ta keki
mi sku ya opage yo. He ca nu ki,
ni tunkasila wani yag ukte.

If you sit in the center,
Fill your pipe in remembrance of me,
If you do this, your grandfather
Will come to see you.

Canupa wanji yuha elu take ki,
ni tunkasila wani yag ukte'.

A pinch of tobacco, comprising commercial tobacco, red willow bark shavings, and other personalized ingredients, is taken from a small pouch and presented in the direction of the four winds, the Creator (and wingeds), skyward, and to Mother Earth. This presentation is repeated four or six times.

Once the pipe is filled, a small sprig of sage is placed in the bowl, which is placed in the pipe rack or beside the altar on the bed of sage. None of the equipment sits directly on the floor.

The woman now tells why she is conducting this ceremony and how she acquired her spirit helpers. She does this in a humble manner, asking to be pardoned for her human frailty, begging the grandfathers to be forgiving if she forgets something, emphasizing that she is nothing but a doorway for the spirits.

If this is to be the more common Lowanpi, the lights are turned out, leaving only a small kerosene lamp glowing near the altar. Now the kerosene lamp is extinguished by the holy woman.

If the ceremony is to be a Yuwipi, the room is darkened to determine if any light is coming in. Any light spots will be repaired and then the lights turned on to enable her assistants to tie up the holy woman. The holy woman stands in her altar, a "gate" is opened in the sacred fence of tobacco ties, and the attendants begin the lengthy task of binding her. First, her fingers are bound together behind her back using buckskin cord, then her wrists. Star quilts are draped over her head and then wrapped in place with more cordage, until she resembles a mummy. She is then laid facedown on a bed of sage within her sacred fence. At this point the attendants take their seats and the lights are put out, placing the room in blackness.

The singers now sing one or more *Tate' Opakiya olowan* (four wind) songs requested or taught to them by the medicine woman. These spirit songs, many of which the Lakota consider sacred in their own right, are sung in a minor key by men accompanied by a small drum, and at times the holy person or spirits may add a rattle. These songs are simple in structure but complex and all-encompassing in spiritual meaning. The words present broad philosophical and spiritual concepts in a tight, poetic form. The songs themselves help create the sacred access needed by the shaman and thus are critical to the success of the ceremony.

Kola houwayelo ayee

My friend, I am calling

Kola houwayelo ayee

My friend, I am calling

Wiyhpeyata

Toward the west, you told me

Sitomni, aye aye

I shall have relationship with horses

Tuka ya ni pi lo

This is why I am calling

He ha oi gou, yoyo

My friend, I am calling

Houwalo

Toward the north, you told me

Kola houwayelo ayee

I shall have relationship with buffalo

This is why I am calling

Waziyata tatanka oyate

My friend, I am calling

Sitomni, eye eye

Tuka ya ni pi lo

Toward the east you have told me

He ha pi fgou, yoyo

I shall have relationship with elk

Houwalo ayee

This is why I am calling

Kola houwayelo ayee

My friend, I am calling

Wiho ki pata hehaka oyate

Toward the south, you told me

Sitomni, aye aye

I shall have relationship with all

Tuka ya ni pilo

    creatures [winged, four legged, etc.]

He ha pi hou, yoyo

This is why I am calling

Kola, houwayelo ayee

My friend, I am calling[2]

Ketoka gata wamakaskan oyate

Sitomni, aye aye

Tuka ya ni pi lo

He ha pi gou, yoyo

Houwalo ayee

Kola, youwayelo ayee

This song calls upon the whole universe and invites the spirits. A more simply worded song of this kind comes down through Iron Woman:

Miye yelo, miye yelo, miye yelo.	It is I, it is I, it is I.
Tunkasila, ehaca ce wakiye	Grandfather, I prayed because
Na ma hu wo	you have said so.
Ni tunkasila ta wocekiye pilamayelo	Hear me
Tunkasila isnala ce wakiye	I pray only to the grandfather
Na ma hu wo.	Hear me.

At this point a *Wocekiye' olowan* (spirit-calling or prayer) song is sung. Here is a Lowanpi song directed toward the Great Spirit:

Tunwan maki lowanpo	Somebody I am singing to is coming
He wana uwelo, ayeew	Somebody I am singing to is coming
Tunwan maki lowanpo	I am singing to the grandfather above
He wana uwelo	Somebody I am singing to is now coming
He wana uwelo, ayee	Somebody I am singing to is now coming
Wanaton inyan tunkasila	He is coming
Maki lo wanpo	He is coming
He wana uwelo	
He wana uwelo	

Tunwan maki lowanpo	Somebody I am singing to is coming
He wana uwelo	I am singing to the grandfather above
He wana uwelo, ayee	He is coming now
Wanatan inyan tunkasila	He is coming now
He wana uwelo	He is coming now[3]
He wana uwelo	
He wana uwelo, ayeyee.	

At the conclusion of this song the spirits begin to manifest themselves. They generally appear as *Peta to* (small blue sparks), which begin to dance near the altar. They may move about the room, bouncing off the walls. Sounds of other helpers may be heard; these may include hooves, wings, or perhaps growls as other helpers enter and announce themselves.

The principal patient now prays out loud about the issue being addressed. The prayers must be earnest, humble, and tearful. While the patient prays, the holy woman communicates directly with the spirits using her voice. Small blue lights may dance around the patient. Some holy people invite each of those present to pray for the sick person and then add any personal prayers they might have. The prayers are passed counterclockwise. There is no set form or established length to these prayers, but those who pray well will include all of creation. Each person concludes his or her prayers with the phrase *Mitakuye' Oyasin* (all my relations).

At this point the singers set forth a *Wapiye' Olowan* (curing song). Again, this one comes down through Iron Woman:

Wakantanka tukahe ce wakeye'	I pray to the creator first
Wakantanka tukahe ce wakiye'	I pray to the creator first
Mitaku yepi cal lecal mu we lo	I want to be with my relatives
Wakantanka tukahe ce wakiye'	I pray to the creator first
Wakantanka tukahe ce wakiye'	I pray to the creator first
Mitakuyepi wani kta ca leca mu welo	That is why I am doing this

The spirits, seen as blue sparks, become hyperactive at this point and appear all over the room.

If dog soup is to be served after the ceremony, the singers sing a kettle song.[4] It is at this point that the singers give a Wicayujupi Olowan, and the spirits untie the holy woman (if a yuwipi), gathering up the cord and the Canli Wapakta into tight balls. Even the quilts are folded neatly or draped over someone the spirits have designated a "doubter."[5]

The ritual's crescendo takes place at the very moment that shamanic trance or contact with the spirit world comes, when the holy person is speaking directly to the spirits. Her speech becomes noticeably altered, and she becomes agitated. She appears to be carrying on an active conversation with no one. Good Lifeways Woman said of this moment, "I always cry at this point, when the spirits come in. I cry when I know they are there. I hear or feel them. It is not joy or sadness that make me cry. I cry because I know they [the spirits] are there."

At this point the holy woman reveals out loud what the spirits have told her about the prayers made, and she makes a prognosis as to the outcome of the problem. She may also make recommendations to the patient about additional spiritual help, changes in the patient's life, taking an herbal remedy, or all three.

The last song is a *Wanagi Kiglapi Olowan,* which politely thanks the spirits and allows them to leave.

O O tan inyan kinajin pelo
eyee
O O tan inyan kinajin pelo
eyee
Tunkasila tawokonzeca lena
cicu welo eeyo.

They stopped above, with their tracks showing
They stopped above, with their tracks showing
Through our grandfather's kingdom, I give [offer]
you this [in our ancestors'] way

The Ceremony Concludes

When the song is over the lights are put back on. The pipe or pipes are now lit and passed around the room in the same direction as the prayers were. Each of the faithful takes four puffs (children merely touch the pipe to their lips) and then says *Mitakuye' Oyasin* (all of creation are my relatives). Water, the source and sustainer of all life, is now passed. Again, "all my relations" is uttered in Lakota. When the pipe and water have been returned to the holy woman, her ceremony is over.

The time expired may be an hour or two, although time sense is often lost. After the main part of the ceremony is concluded, the altar is dismantled, and the holy woman takes a pinch of each of the specially prepared Thanksgiving foods, placing them on a small wooden or horn spoon. She takes these outside and offers them to the grandfathers in the four directions, then to Wakan Tonka and to Maka Ina (Mother Earth), and finally, facing southwest, she places them on the ground. At this point the food is passed out by the sponsor and his or her family. The feast should be large enough that everyone present takes home *wate'ca* (leftovers) to be shared for good health with those at home.

In the Inikagapi sweat ceremony and the Lowanpi or Yuwipi ceremony, the holy woman serves at least four distinct functions: 1) she has led her people through the entire set of rituals; 2) she has, through personal sacrifice—the sweat, fasting, and being wrapped up—put her reputation and her spiritual well-being on the line; 3) she has achieved a trancelike state; and 4) through that state she has become the instrument of healing and sacred communication. It is her desire, through this ritual, to return the patient back to spiritual balance and harmony.[6]

Using methods like these, Indian doctors have cured all manner of disease, from mental problems to cancer. The well-educated Jesuits who were missionaries on the Lakota reservations could not understand or explain it except by attributing what they saw to Satan. As Lucy (Black Elk) Looks Twice recalled,

In 1904 my father was called upon to doctor a little boy in Payabaya—seven miles north of Holy Rosary Mission. The boy's family wanted my father [Nick Black Elk] to doctor their son because they heard he was good at it. So my father walked over there carrying his medicine and everything he needed for the ceremony. . . .

When he got there, he found the sick boy lying in a tent. So right away he prepared to doctor him. My father took his shirt off, put tobacco offerings in the sacred place, and started pounding on his drum. He called on the spirits to heal the boy in a very strong action. Dogs were there, and they were barking [seeing the spirits]. My father was really singing away, beating his drum, and using his rattle when along came one of the Blackrobes—Father Lindebner [as we called him], Ate' Petecela [translated as Little Father]. At that time, the priests usually traveled by team and buggy throughout the reservation. That's what Ate' Petecela was driving.

So he went into the tent and saw what my father was doing. Father Lindebner had already baptized the boy and had come to give him the last rites. Anyway, he took whatever my father had prepared on the ground and threw it all into the stove. He took the drum and rattle and threw them outside the tent. Then he took my father by the neck and said, "Satan, get out!"[7]

10

Holy Women Who
Are Ancestors

The woman stood there with her arm raised, holding that knife; her hair was wild, and her hands were bleeding. My grandmother prayed in Assiniboine, asking for help, then she held up her hand like this [palm extended]. The woman took one step forward and then fell in a faint. It was as if the power in my grandmother's hand had knocked the wind out of her; she just fell [unconscious].

—The Late Kenneth Young Bear,
Hidatsa/Dakota

What follows is an account of revered holy women who have passed on, who are fondly remembered by their relatives. In each case, the people we interviewed took great pride in telling us of their great-grandmother, grandmother, or aunt.

There are common threads running through these women's lives: most were full-blood, and all spoke Lakota (Dakota or their own tribal language) as their first and principal language. Many were born in the period when the Plains Indians were still a free people (the late 1840s to the 1870s). They saw their people's anguished passage from freedom to confinement. These women saw many relatives die in the wars they fought for their way of life.

Often fleeing the poverty and despair of the agencies, these courageous women faced the complete destruction of their food source, the buffalo. They witnessed the Ghost Dance and heard of the tragedy of Wounded Knee. They lived to see the Bureau of Indian Affairs divide and parcel out Mother Earth and put their men on permanent relief. They survived the onslaught of hide hunters, miners, ranchers, and later the homesteaders from Eastern Europe. Because promised annuities and rations were often late or short, most of these people suffered starvation and survived often fatal diseases like measles, smallpox, tuberculosis, and typhoid.

Most of these women, despite the inconceivable trauma of the times, tried to fulfill the admonitions of the White Buffalo Calf Maiden, only to have their most prized possessions, their children and grandchildren, snatched away at young ages and sent to boarding and mission schools. They experienced the growing multitude of white missionaries, each of which advocated a different denomination, and witnessed the dividing up of reservations among these various churches, which ate away at tribal unity.

Many of these women joined and were dynamic leaders of those denominations. Most quickly became expert gardeners and seamstresses. They witnessed the development and spread of first railroads and later the motor car, electric lights, telephones, airplanes, and the radio. They saw World War I take their grandsons away over the great water. Many did not return alive. A few of these ancient women lived to see the boys leave for World War II.

If cultural stability characterizes the standard view of tribal peoples and change characterizes modern Western societies, then these women must be seen in all contexts as modern—in a sense, as our contemporaries. Change, and adapting to it while remaining Indian, has been and continues to be the life of Plains Indian men and women.

It was convenient for those who wrote of Black Elk to forget that he lived most of his life in the twentieth century. We must remember that the women in this chapter lived tumultuous lives considered threatening to the Indian way of life for the most part; whereas other aspects were seen as improvements.

Throughout their dramatic history, these women formed the central vertebrae of the very backbone of native survival. While "belonging" to and participating in a Christian church, these holy women were first and foremost keepers and practitioners of their tribal religions. They were all active in community life on a number of levels: all are remembered as compassionate and caring mothers and grandmothers, and all were pragmatic survivors, capable of great wisdom, insight, and adaptation.

What you will read here has never been recorded before. What follows should be a vibrant awakening for all people to the potential that is wasted by societies that block people from the fulfillment of their dreams. To appreciate their humanity fully, it is important also to see these women not as stereotypes but as people living in a specific context. Their spiritual accomplishments (manifested as miracles) and glimpses of their daily life were shared out of love and respect but also as an oral way of preserving historical testimony about the power of the Creator and these Indian ways.

This oral history is far from complete; these are the only women we were able to find through conducting relatively few interviews. We hope that what is written here will stimulate Indian households to discussion and that more of this legacy will surface, to be cherished by those families, their communities, and native women.

Blue Earring Woman

Blue Earring was probably born in the first half of the nineteenth century. She was a member of the Minnecojou Lakota band and spent her adult life on the west end of the Cheyenne River Reservation. She is remembered as a powerful medicine woman who cured the sick. Arlene (Mesteth) Marshall, her great-granddaughter, told us,

> I remember hearing stories about her. I guess she was a powerful medicine woman, but she died before I was born, so all I have are the stories. Now I wish I had listened more carefully. She used to use birds to doctor; but the way I understand it, she also used her powers to entertain people. She would unwrap her bird skins and then call on each of her birds to sing the song it had in life. Because she could call her helpers day or night, she would do it during the day, and sometimes she would "show her powers." I guess that would entertain and encourage people.

Arlene suggested we ask her brother about Blue Earring. Orville Mesteth, now almost sixty, proved to be a fountain of information. Although he never met his great-grandmother, he visited with and listened to old women, including his own grandmother, Blue Earring's daughter, and recalled for us what he could:

> My grandma had an older woman friend whose name was Mrs. Crow. I knew her well, even up until my midteens. She knew my great-grandmother, Blue Earring Woman, quite well. I remember her and my grandmother speaking of Blue Earring Woman often. I was in high school then

and already interested in history and oral tradition. Mrs. Crow was not a close relative, but she was related to us through the Landrys and very close friends with my grandmother. She told us of the time my great-grandmother was dying of smallpox. I think that was in 1909, and my grandmother was only fourteen. All the people were really frightened of smallpox at that time, so nobody would go near her. It was up to my grandmother to stay with her. She was taking care of her mother.

The old woman was going to die, and she knew it. My great-grandmother was one of those who had strong powers to influence the weather. When she was in a camp people were never afraid of storms, because they knew she could turn them. She had power over storms. Blue Earring would go out into that storm and [pray] cry and point her pipe, and the storm would change its path.

Well she could do this because—unlike a *Heyoka,* who gets power from the thunders—she had four little water spirits as helpers. When she realized she was dying, she called my grandmother to her and asked her to get a bowl of water from Cherry Creek. They used a wooden bowl. My grandmother went down and got her that bowl of water. Blue Earring held that bowl near her mouth. She coughed, and four small objects went into that bowl. One was a small fish, and it appeared to be lifeless. One looked like a little worm. Another was like a water bug—the kind that move around real fast. Still another was a water spider—the kind that walk around on top of the water.

She told my grandmother, "This is where I get my power from. Take them down and put them back into Cherry Creek. Watch them and tell me what happens." When Grandma did that, the fish floated and the others scurried off. Grandma went back and told her mother what happened. She said, "Since the little fish spirit is dead, I will die soon. Daughter, everybody is afraid of me, won't come near me because I am dying of this smallpox. But you don't have to be afraid. Because you are helping me, you will never catch smallpox."

Back in the late 1930s, the superintendent put out a call that everyone was to be vaccinated for smallpox. Grandmother went to be vaccinated, and it wouldn't take. They scratch your arm and put serum on it. There is supposed to be a reaction, but there wasn't: she was already immune. The words of my great-grandmother proved true, even years after her death.

I think it's kind of interesting that sometimes medicine men say that the power to doctor came down to them through their dad or grandpa, but is has been my observation that women are selected by the spirits at random. Great-Grandma had learned a lot of things. She doctored all sorts of things. One case I remember hearing about was a man who came to her with a swollen head and black eye. He didn't know how he got that way. This was in 1889, shortly before Wounded Knee. Great-Grandma doctored him, and while she was singing over him she pulled a horse hair out from his eye. She said, "The reason you are this way is that you have been beating your horse. You have been beating your horses, haven't you?" The man was amazed that she knew this. "Yes . . . ," he said.

"Well, I'll doctor you this time, and ask the horse grandfathers to heal you, but if you ever beat that horse again, it will be the last time."

It got back to Blue Earring that he didn't follow what was told to him and kept beating his horses. Well, that man was one of those who went to Wounded Knee, and he was killed there. That story stayed with me, because we had a great-uncle, Owns His Saber, who was also killed at Wounded Knee.

There are so many stories about Blue Earring Woman! Mrs. Crow told me that Blue Earring used humor laughter, to doctor. She had a little buckskin doll, about a foot tall. She would make this doll walk around in a little circle after her, and when Great-Grandmother would laugh, the little doll would laugh and skip around—kind of dance behind her. The people would gather close to look at this and they would be laughing too. I guess maybe this distracted the patient from his illness and let Blue Earring's power go to work.

Another thing I was told is that she had a number of dried bird skins. She would take these out of her bundle. Now remember, all these things were done in broad daylight. She did not need a long ceremony to doctor. She could do it spontaneously. She would sing a medicine song, and pretty soon one of those birds would pick up that song in its own voice. It would chirp, sing, and dance around. Each bird took its turn singing a medicine song and "dancing." She also did this to doctor and entertain. These birds were singing healing songs.

One time they had this ceremony to doctor a young lady. Perhaps she was having headaches or bad dreams. My grandmother asked for a buckskin. In English, I guess you would say it was two feet square. She took a whole bunch of quills, some dyed ones too, and she placed these in the middle of that hide. Then she rolled it up very tightly. Next, she sang a song [probably a Double Woman song] and told that woman to take the hide and hold it tight. She told her, "No matter what distracts you, pulls on you, or bothers you while I sing, do not let go of that hide. If one of those quills falls out, you will be a loose woman."

Well, the woman was young, and she certainly didn't want that, so she hung on tight. Even when Great-Grandma was finished with her song, she asked for the hide back. The young lady was reluctant, thinking a quill might fall out. Blue Earring reassured her, and she handed the hide back. Then Blue Earring unfolded the hide, and it was all quilled, finished. She told that woman she would go on to be a great quillworker. Grandmother took that quilled piece and gave it to someone else present, who was also cured.[1]

Wanyeca Win: Lightning Bug Woman

Blue Earring's daughter (Orville's and Arlene's grandmother) was also a Pipe Carrier. She married an Englishman named Bridwell, who had come to ranch in South Dakota on the Cheyenne River Reservation. Her nurturing and maternal character and the Lakota sense of extended family is wonderfully illustrated in the following recollection of Madonna Swan.

The day before I was to leave for the [tuberculosis] sanitarium, Grandma Bridwell came down from her place, on the Dupree mail truck. Dad was looking out the window and said, "Grandma Bridwell is coming from the store." Dad went out into the yard to greet his aunt.

"Nephew," she said, "why do you have these signs on your house?"

"Madonna is sick with TB. She has to go to the Sioux San. They wanted her to leave before Christmas, but I refused, so they put these red tags on our house. That's why," he told her.

I was sitting inside, but I could hear them. "We'll see about that!" Grandma said. She walked over and tore that red tag off the house. "They don't need to be here," she said angrily. "She's not bad; she's going to get well!" Then she tore off the other one.

To have TB was a big disgrace in those days. They treated those that got TB, and their families, like lepers. Those that didn't have it told their children to stay away from the kids who had TB in their home.

I had never heard much about *canhu sica* [bad lungs], as it was called in Indian. Some people said it was the same as syphilis, some kind of social disease. Mom and Grandma Bridwell were talking about it. Mom said, "They say *wikoska* [venereal disease] when they talk about people with tuberculosis. It cannot be true; it is a lie!"

"Yes, it is a lie," Grandma Bridwell said. "My mother, Blue Earring Woman, was a strong Indian doctor, and she told me they have nothing to do with each other, except that they are white man's diseases."

On December 28,1944, I left for Sioux Sanitarium in Rapid City. Dad had promised Dr. Fleishman that he would have me at Dr. Kremer's office by eight o'clock, and we kept our promise. I started out with Dad and Uncle Dick Swan at six o'clock to meet the hospital car in Dupree. Since we had left so early we were not in a hurry, and Dad said, "We have some time; let's go over to Grandma Bridwell's place."

Grandma Bridwell was already up, building a fire in her wood cook stove, when we got there. She heard the car pull up into her yard and came out to greet us. She said, "You come into the house, and I'll make you breakfast and coffee. You must be on your way to Dupree."

I started to cry, and Dad told her, "Madonna is frightened. Today is the day she has to go to the sanitarium. We have to take her to Dupree to meet the hospital car, and then they take her to the Sioux San."

"Oh, my little Donna," she said, turning toward me; her eyes were suddenly sad. She put her arms out, and I ran to her. She hugged me and told me not to cry.

She took me into the little room where she had her bed. "Tell me what has you so frightened, Donna?" she asked softly. We sat down on her bed, and she took my hand.

"Because I have tuberculosis, and I'm going away from Mom for a long time, maybe forever. I'll probably die over there. I'm such a disgrace to my family. I feel so dirty and ashamed," I told her between sobs.

"Now Donna, you're not going to die; and for being a disgrace, if you're a disgrace, then there must be a lot of them around here. Nearly every family in Cherry Creek and Red Scaffold—perhaps all of Cheyenne River Reservation—has had to send relatives to the sanitarium. Your mom and dad love you. We all love you! You are no disgrace. You will get well and come home!" she said, looking into my eyes.

"I feel like such a bother—and now I feel like a baby, crying in front of you," I told her.

Then she preached to me saying, "Donna! You go there and be brave. When you come back, you can stay with your mom and dad and never leave. You do what the doctors tell you, and pray every day. You'll come home! I'll come and visit you in the San," she said quietly, as she rubbed my back and tried to blot my tears with a cloth.

We went back into the main room, and Grandma finished making breakfast. I wasn't very hungry, but Dad and Uncle Dick ate everything. When they had finished, Dad said, "Thanks for the breakfast and for helping Madonna."

"Oh, can I ride down there with you?" Grandma asked, stepping toward Dad. She waited for his answer.

"Sure, if you want to. You're certainly welcome to," was his reply.

When we got to Dr. Kremer's office, the hospital car wasn't there yet. Grandma said, "While we wait, I'm going to pray." She took out a small pipe. She sang softly, put tobacco in it, then lit it. She took a puff and handed it to Dad and Uncle Dick, and then to me. Then she prayed, "Grandfathers, please let the medicines of the white doctors help Madonna. Grandfathers, help her to get well. Grandfathers, help her to be brave.

Grandfathers, let the older people in the hospital watch over her and teach her well."

Then the hospital car came from the agency. Mr. Lewis was driving the car. He noticed the little pipe Grandma was putting back in her bag. He smiled in approval. Mr. Lewis was also an Indian, from Oklahoma, so he didn't say anything.

So we left Dad, Uncle Dick, and Wanyeca Win standing in the road, waving. I waved back, trying to smile, as I fought back tears that blurred my sight. . . .

Grandma Bridwell was a traditional full-blooded Indian woman, married to a white man. She was a very good person and well liked by everyone. Grandma Bridwell—Wanyeca Win, Lightning Bug Woman—was killed in a car wreck. She never got to visit me, but I'll never forget her![2]

Martha Bad Warrior

Martha Bad Warrior, also known as Red Eagle Woman, was born in 1854 to Red Hair, also know as Old Man Elk Head, who was the eighth keeper of the Sacred Calf Pipe Bundle. When he died in 1916, Martha, who had taken care of her father and lived on his place, claimed that her father had entrusted her with care of the Bundle. She took possession of the Pipe and assumed the duties of keeper. In the 1930s, a dust bowl had swallowed the land of the Lakota. Martha Bad Warrior was approached by a number of Itazipco elders and asked to pray for an end to the dust bowl and the terrible drought. Sidney Keith, now seventy-four, who is a Sun Dance leader, Lakota philosopher, and educator, fondly remembers the times during his own adolescence he spent with Martha and her family.

We used to go over there and visit them. Mrs. Bad Warrior still does that [honor the pipe]—every morning before sunrise she goes over to that log house. She smudges the place, then sings an honor song over there.

She sang [an honoring song] for me one time. That was something. My name is Little Chief, *Naca Cikala,* and she put that in the song. My Dad is related to them. I liked her, and I stayed there as often as I could. She was a good woman, generous and kind. She was a really nice person, just like my grandma. I go there pretty often, so I knew her. When school was out, or when we got a weekend pass from the boarding school, I usually went there instead of home.

The people did not treat her any different than any other woman, except that they would bring gifts to the Pipe, not to her. She really praised them for that, for bringing a gift for the Pipe. Like tobacco or tobacco ties—she says the Pipe lives on that, those special gifts, just like eating. So when they did that, she was really thrilled. And you know, the family gives stuff away in her honor, always giving stuff away. Inside her house were hides hanging everywhere. Some were tanned soft, some not finished—and you know, that's hard work. She was always making moccasins. When someone would come to visit, she would give them moccasins or a hide. That's the way she was, always working. When people would come from a long way away she would greet them, and they would hug and cry.

She stayed near that Calf Pipe all the time. She had a little tent she patched up, and we stayed in that tent, too, with her grandson, Oscar. He was my same age. We'd talk about work—that Martha, she was always back in her garden; all you'd see was the top of her head, picking garlics, or in her stand of corn. She'd go to the barn and clean the chickens, and then she'd go back to the log house and start scraping hide, always working.

She was not too old at that time, maybe seventy-eight or seventy-nine. I've got it written down someplace, what year she died. She was eighty or eighty-something. . . .

Martha would take care of that Pipe, smudging it [with smoke sage mixed with flat ceder and sweetgrass]—that's what she did, and praying. As soon as that sun comes up, she starts singing, and then that's it. They never lock the doors [on the enclosure of the Pipe]; nobody goes there at night. It's so sacred they're scared of it.

As the first woman to be the Pipe Keeper, Martha remembered the basic promise of the White Buffalo Calf Maiden: that so long as the People kept and respected the Pipe, she would help them. The dust bowl had killed plants, animals, and humans. The People were suffering, and Martha decided to ask, through the Pipe, for the help promised so long ago. Sidney Keith went as a teenager with his parents to witness Martha's prayers with the Pipe. Here is a rare and insightful firsthand account of that event.

At the time I witnessed this ceremony I was about eleven or twelve. I remember, because earlier that fall my grandpa made me smoke a pipe with him. He said, "You're twelve; you're now a man." So I remember when I was twelve years old.

I remember a lot of things at that age—places we went, horses I rode, I know their names yet. My mother and them used to go to the town Lantry; it was twenty miles to Lantry from where we lived. One day they went to town. They used to stop at Bad Warriors. That's where Martha lives; she was the keeper, my dad was related to them. So they stopped there for dinner and then came back.

When they got home my mother said, while we were eating, "Next Saturday we are going to Green Grass. Martha's going to be there to open that Pipe, so people can see it." That was during those dust bowl years, during the Depression. It was really bad—dark all day long because of the dust in the air. Sometimes you couldn't even see the sun. Cars, the Model As and the Ts, always had their headlights on, and they looked red. The people and animals got sore eyes, and after a while the horses and cattle that were weak, were dying. Down by the rivers and the creeks you could smell the fish; everything was dying.

So they said, "She's going to open that Pipe, so that everybody can view it." It took them twenty days to prepare and get the word out. By then, everybody should have gotten a notice. Soon, it was that Saturday. Most of the people who came were from the north—Mandan and Dakotas. Nobody came from the south—Oglalas or Sicangu; it was all Cheyenne River and north. One morning, the folks said, "We're ready to go." I think it was a Friday morning. So we took off on horseback. There was a whole bunch of us.

That day they were going to open that Sacred Calf Pipe Bundle in Green Grass; they came from the Bad Warrior place. Martha [Bad Warrior] rode in a buggy. The Pipe Bundle was tied to a travois. It had a little spotted pony dragging it, and we went there. Martha was wondering who could lead that little horse and travois.

There was a young man that seemed to come out of nowhere. Nobody knew him or had seen him before. This young guy had long hair. I saw him, so I asked him if he could lead the horse with the Bundle on it. He said, "Yeah, sure." He took his shirt off and was left with just his pants. Martha's family gave him some moccasins and tied an eagle feather in his hair. It hung down his back, and he looked real traditional.

He led that pinto with that travois. He went halfway, and they stopped at a creek to rest, but that young man walked all that way in one walk. It was probably thirty miles straight. That buggy that Mrs. Bad Warrior rode in, and two wagons besides that—a small one and a big one—were stacked with all those giveaways [offerings to be distributed to those in attendance] stacked on them. They also had a large number of horses, and they gave them all away.

My folks were coming in a wagon. It wasn't very far, probably eight miles.

When we got to the Looking Horse place [Martha Bad Warrior's daughter]—you know, where that hill is [above where the Pipe is now kept]—I was on a horse, and we were sitting up there. It was windy up there where we were sitting, but down below it wasn't that bad—you could see clear for about a half-mile, at least.

We were watching, and people were coming in from that side, from the road. There were wagons and people on horseback and Model Ts, and they were camping all in a circle. A big circle.

That night, when my folks came, I took the horses across to where there was pasture. I was sitting up there on that hill looking down at the camps there, and I noticed that right below us was a sweat lodge.

By the time it was getting dark, an *eyapaha* [announcer] came around and said they were going to sweat. They were going to have a meeting at the Looking Horses. There was a shade there, near a frame building, and that was where the meeting was to be. We were sitting up there, listening and watching. When it got dark I came down and went to bed. Early next morning, as usual—my dad always gets me up—I kind of looked out, and everybody was standing at where they cook, waiting for coffee. I noticed that it was still dark [from the dust in the air]. I got up, and my mom already had soup and stuff, so I ate.

When I had eaten I headed for my horse. The horse was way over near where the gate was, so I brought him back and watered him. The water was all muddy in the Moreau River, so I hobbled him again and came back to my folks' tent. I was sitting up there and the eyapaha came around and said, "At noon today Martha is going to be at the log house. Near the log house is a little squaw cooler—it isn't finished. That is where she will be." There wasn't any covering there. "She's going to sit there, and you're supposed to go by." So that was announced, and after that he said, "There is going to be a giveaway and feast."

When we got ready, one of my cousins and my brother, Raymond, and I looked at it, and it was just an ordinary pipe. But I found out later that wasn't the Pipe, the sacred Pipe, because she didn't want to show it. I don't know why. I saw the [real] Pipe at Bad Warrior's, and I'm not going to tell it, because it was different; this was not the Pipe. That was the only pipe she had out there on her lap like that, and everybody thought that was the Sacred Calf Pipe and looked at it, but she was smart and kept it hidden for some reason.

Anyway, we went by and looked at it. Later that day they had a giveaway and a feed, a big feast. After the ceremony they gave all that away. That night they had that dance, too, and they still gave away all that stuff, everything in that house! All the stuff they gave away was handmade. Lucy and Suzy and Hanpola and Martha made all that stuff, brand-new moccasins and all kinds of things like hides that you could cut up for moccasins.

Then they announced that there would be a powwow at Looking Horse's. We were sitting up on the hill, and they were starting to "cry" again, so we heard them—they were starting to sing. It wasn't a powwow, it was a Rabbit Dance and Honor Dance, and people talking [giving speeches]. You know how those old people talked! So we were sitting up there on our horses again, and they were getting ready to have a sweat. I remember that it was about ten or eleven o'clock because I usually get tired then and want to go to bed.

At that time I heard some coyotes howling, and that was unusual, because we never hear them—in fact, there were no coyotes near there at that time. I think they all died or were trapped out or something. These coyotes were calling up on that hill. The horses were neighing, and the cows were noisy. I thought, "Something is going on here." Where they were dancing, everybody stopped. After a while the wind died down and we could see the stars, and it got kind of quiet.

I heard somebody pray out there at the shade, and you could see that they all had quit dancing. I could see the lanterns and gaslights were going back toward camp. Early the next morning, again my dad came and woke me. I looked out, and the sun was shining, and man, that was good! The sun was up, and it was clear out. I thought, "That was something!" My dad said, "You should bring back the horses, because we're going back today." So I brought them back and tied them.

We ate breakfast there. My folks said they were going to go over and visit Martha. I told them I would like to go home with the boys. So they said I could. Later I rode over to the house and talked to my mom, because I was going to ask her for the house key. She was sitting there in Lucy Looking Horse's house. There were no chairs or anything. They'd given everything away. That's the way they do it. My mom used to do that too—if some relative dies, everything in the house goes. It all comes back to them eventually.

We headed back, and they came after us. It was almost midafternoon when my folks came back. We went ahead and got some big catfish and put them on the table. So when they got back, we cooked them, fried them. All the neighbors came. They were very social, and we fed everybody. We had fresh corn, a big feast, and they were talking about what happened. They said, "It was a miracle!" That was the way they talked. It just quit, and now sunshine. From then on, the wind just stopped.

That was something. It broke the weather. Just her appearing there. She cried [humbled herself to tears], and she sang, and she prayed. She sang for that Sacred Maiden. It was the first time I heard her sing that. She said, "Thank you for the Pipe!" She says this all in Indian, so I knew what she was saying.

It is said that the strain and suffering of sitting outdoors—she refused shade, saying it would not be a sacrifice—led to Martha's death some three months later. She died October 25, 1936. At her death the care of the Bundle went to her son Ehli Bad Warrior, born in 1882. It is alleged by some that he had only a minimal knowledge of the ceremonies that were the duty of the keeper and that much was lost during his term. When he died in 1959, the Pipe went to his sister, Lucy Looking Horse, who was born in 1891.

Lucy Looking Horse

No account of the keepers of the Sacred Calf Pipe would be complete without acknowledging Lucy (Bad Warrior) Looking Horse, who was born in 1891. When Martha died she left the Pipe to her son, Ehli. It is said that Ehli did not want the responsibility and did not always fulfill his obligations. The daily duties were performed by his sister, Lucy (Bad Warrior) Looking Horse.

From 1959 when Ehli died, Lucy took sole care of the Bundle, continuing to perform the daily duties of singing and smudging the Bundle. In those days the Bundle was moved from near Bear Creek, where Martha had lived, to Green Grass, another Sans Arc community, where Lucy resided with her husband, Thomas Looking Horse. Sidney Keith, who grew up in Bear Creek community, shares some of his memories of this remarkable woman:

> When I first knew her, Lucy watched over her mother, Martha. Lucy took care of her, told her not to work too hard in the garden. Martha thought it was her job, tending to the garden all day long, besides her job as keeper of the Sacred Calf Pipe. So that was Lucy's job, while her mother was still living, to make sure Martha ate well and had clean clothes. She always took good care of her. Lucy learned what to do with the Pipe from her mother.
>
> Lucy had three sons, but the oldest one died of tuberculosis. The youngest one was Stanley. The only one who wasn't very good at taking care of the Pipe was Oscar. He was really a good kid, quiet and all that, but when he was older he began to ride broncs and loved rodeos. He got pretty good at it and became a bareback rider. Then he got to be a macho man and started drinking.
>
> The older folks didn't like him to be doing that, because of the Pipe. But he died drinking. Froze to death. He had a Model T Ford, and he passed out from drinking. They found the Ford parked with the motor running, so maybe he died of asphyxiation. They found him south of Eagle Butte.

All those years [after Martha died] Lucy was the one who looked after the Pipe. The people all knew the Pipe is sacred and treated Lucy like they'd treat anyone else. I don't think they idolized her. They respected her because of what she did every day; they all knew that she took good care of the Pipe. She was herself. She was not sacred, but she really knew her stuff; the wisdom that she had was incredible, and it seemed like she knew everything [about sacred ways]. You could go to her and ask her anything, and she would have the answer. People would go there and take her tobacco ties and tobacco, even tanned hides, things that she could use. She in turn used those things to give away, to honor her obligation as keeper of the Pipe. She was a good beadworker and was always making things as gifts for people who went over there to visit her place.

She didn't show the pipe to people. They didn't even go over there to pray. They just went to talk with her because of what she did and who she was, what she knew—you know, sort of like a sacred woman. They didn't treat her like that though, because she wouldn't let them. She loved to visit and laugh. She always joked with us kids. She told me one time, "You ride like a woman, all slouched over." Things like that! She loved to make us laugh.

Lucy chose to skip over her own son, Stanley, and shortly before her death on April 12, 1966, she named Orval, her eight-year-old grandson, as the keeper. He has been the keeper up to the present time.

Brave Eagle Woman

Not all the spiritual events in family histories happened to women who were thought of as holy women. Many stories told late at night, during casual conversation, recall the accomplishments of everyday women, mothers and grandmothers who used their faith to call upon the Great Mystery.

An Oglala Lakota, Brave Eagle Woman, known later as Julia Brave Eagle, was born in 1860. She married High Pine, later known as Thomas, two weeks before the Custer Battle in the big Lakota camp on the Greasy Grass (Little Big Horn River) in 1876. She lived to be ancient, finally passing to the spirit world in 1943. The following story was told by Lucy (High Pine) Swan before her death in 1983. This is an account of using a pipe and earnest prayer to turn away a terrible storm—a story of how the sacred can be called upon to effect change in the weather.

A man rode by the house and said, "A tornado is coming, and it's coming right this way! You better leave, it's already killed animals and destroyed houses!"

"No, I'll stay here!" *Unci* [Grandmother] said.

So then she went into the house and got her little pipe. When she was ready she came outside. By then the storm was close, the wind was blowing things around, and the dust made the air brown.

Grandma just pointed her pipe stem at that storm and prayed, "Grandfathers above and in the four directions, please hear me. Grandfathers above, spare this house, I'm praying! Grandfathers!" She prayed, and that storm split and went on either side, close by the house, but she was safe.

Isabel Ten Fingers

Isabel Ten Fingers was born to John and Ella Ten Fingers on April 18, 1906. She was an Oglala Lakota. As her daughter, Valentina Janis, pointed out, "Mom was born the same day as the San Francisco earthquake." They gave her the Indian name Rising Wind. They lived in a small Indian camp called Can Sa Sa, Red Willow, northeast of the village of Oglala. She went to school at Oglala Community School Number 7, then she went to school in Rapid City, until the eighth grade. That was the most education a girl could get without being sent far away. According to Valentina,

Mom always knew about Indian medicine from her father. He was an elderly man, but she was very close to both her parents. She spent a lot of time with him, learning about plants and the sacred songs that went with their use.

When she was a little girl she kept having this dream of a man dressed all in black coming down the hill to take her. Soon after she was baptized in the Episcopal church she stopped having those dreams.

After finishing eighth grade she stayed home with her folks, caring for her father until his death in 1927 at seventy-two years. That would place his birthdate at 1855, back in the days before the reservations, when Indian doctors were all there was.

When Mom was young she had her future foretold: she was told that she would live until her first great-grandchild was born, and she did. Up to that time [menopause] she doctored but it was just family. She had a little trunk that had been her dad's, I think. In there she kept all her remedies. She always doctored—that I remember—mostly her cousins and their families. She had herbs for lots of things, like fever and diarrhea. She told me that when God gave [the whites] Jesus, he gave the Indian the Pipe.

When my great-grandmother Mary Pretty Face died, Mom heard voices coming, and when they left, her grandmother was gone. Mom was like that; she would hear and interpret [spirit voices]. My great-grandmother told her never to use her medicine for anything bad, that it would come back on her.

When I was a little girl I had TB, so Mom made her own remedy. She boiled herbs every day and gave me the potion to drink. I was cured. She told me, "Maybe someday you could get a good education and take this medicine and have it made [by a pharmaceutical company], so that all people can use it."

Sometimes she would make medicine that was burned, and she would blow the smoke on us. She would use a lizard to doctor arthritis, letting it walk on the patient's legs.

She was always a very good horsewoman. Mom's older sister remembered when the dogs would bark that she would ride off at night in the dark and come back with a bunch of rabbits or whatever the dogs had treed. I also remember Mom telling me that one time, at a celebration in Pine Ridge, it grew very strange outside. The grass was waving and the dogs were barking. She looked out from under the tent to see if it was a ghost. The wagon tongue broke on Dad's wagon, the next day as they travelled home. She said that happened because she was trying to see a wanagi, and he was hurt. Mom doctored him that time, and then she got real sick. After that she wasn't so interested in ghosts.

In the early 1930s Mom met and married my father, George White Magpie. He died in 1968. It was around then that she met Charley Kills Enemy through the Red Bears. She married him in Yankton and moved her things to St. Francis on the Rosebud Reservation. Together, Charley and Mom used the Eagle and Spider spirits. I think they learned from each other. Charles had his ceremonies; Mom had her knowledge of herbs, and her helpers. That's where Charles got his power—from my mom and what she taught him.

I was gone then and only came home once in a while; we lived in Scott's Bluff from 1951 until 1972. So I didn't get to go to many of her ceremonies.

I remember one time, though. She doctored a woman from White River who couldn't walk. The doctors told her her legs would have to be amputated [from diabetes]. They had a ceremony for her, and she walked again. Another time my mother doctored a little boy named Lebeuff. He couldn't talk, so they doctored him. He spoke soon after that.

Mom was a quiet person; she prayed all the time. She was also a strong Episcopalian. After she married Charles, she went to a Catholic church. I can remember that before a ceremony she would sit for hours tying *Canli Wapakta* [tobacco ties], touching each one to her pipe as she prayed. She thought highly of her pipe. I remember one time she took it to Green Grass and prayed with it and put it near the Sacred Calf Pipe Bundle.

At one time I had a little dog, who somehow got split open [from a gunshot wound]. I was sure the dog would die. We were living together by then, and she took that dog into her room. A week later the little dog was cured.

Charley and she traveled all over, doctoring people as far away as California. I was living in Lawrence, Kansas, when I heard they were having [marital] trouble. Charley had been asked to doctor someone in Colorado. He dropped Mom off with relatives in Wanblee. She went to stay in Rapid City. About that time, they sent for her with the police, because Charles had been burned in a house fire in St. Francis. It was soon after that I moved to Wanblee with her. By then she was getting forgetful. In my mind [I believed] Charles was working [casting spells] on her.

She was really old-fashioned. Like other ladies her age, she would tie up all her possessions each night, as if, like the old days, they might have to move in the middle of the night. Each night she would pack all her clothes and blankets in a big bundle. She said, "Your father is coming in a wagon to get me." On another occasion she told me that her mother and father were coming to get her.

When she died I was home. By then, she was what today people call senile. We couldn't find her. Time went by, and we knew she must be dead. It was very hard for me. We had to have services without her body. Sometime later her body was found in the badlands. She had wandered out there to die, or perhaps she was lost.

Mom was not the only woman of her generation to doctor. My Uncle, Narcisse Ten Fingers, told me of a woman from over toward Pine Ridge. She made an altar with sand [Lowanpi ceremony]. Then she would spread her bundle out near that altar. In her ceremonies, little deer would walk about.

Millie (Seven Rabbit) Lays Hard

Mrs. Lays Hard was an Oglala from Kyle. She was born in the early 1860s and died in 1938. She used a type of ceremony called a *Yuwipi,* which means "to doctor with stones" or, more currently, "to tie one up many times." It is a type of ritual that involves tying up the medicine person, using buckskin cordage. The woman's fingers, wrists, knees, and ankles are bound, then multiple layers of cloth, usually blankets or quilts, are draped over the "doctor" and then secured, mummy-style, with more cordage. The shaman is then placed facedown on a bed of sage within her *Hocoka* [sacred center, or altar], with the lights turned off. This ceremony is considered to be the highest calling of a medicine person. To accomplish this in the daylight is, we are told, the very pinnacle of power.

In a public display of this power, the shaman is unwrapped by the intercession of her spirit helpers. This "escape" may occur almost instantly. In preparation for a Yuwipi or Lowanpi, windows are covered with quilts and blankets, and the ceremonial chamber (a house emptied of its furnishings) is generally made pitch-black. During the ceremony spirits manifest themselves visually, often as bursts of energy or sparks flying all over the room. The faithful may also feel and hear the presence of the spirit helpers, in the form of wind from a bird helper's wings or the sound of hooves of a deer helper.

Stella Janis, who humorously admits to being "almost sixty-five," spent a great deal of time with her grandmother. She was kind enough to share some of her memories with us. Tilda spoke with her first in Lakota, as was our general practice, explaining briefly what we were looking for. Sitting in her home near Kyle, on the Pine Ridge Reservation, this is what she told us over coffee.

She was my Dad's mom. Her maiden name was Millie Seven Rabbit. She married my grandfather, Frank Lays Hard. She died, I believe, in 1938, when she was seventy-eight or seventy-nine years old. I was about ten years old when she passed away. She had three brothers. I remember her saying often, "It's not me, it's [the power] from God. That's how I do things."

I remember going out on the prairie to collect medicines with her. She would always take a sack of Bull Durham with her. When she found a plant she was after, she would place tobacco around it. I remember that we would take an old lard bucket with us, and that was what she put the medicine in.

I never did see her go in a sweat lodge. They had one on their old place, but I never saw her use it. Whether she did or not I don't know, but I don't think so. Grandpa drove a little pickup truck by the time I came along. I remember that Grandma was not particularly shy and would visit with whoever came by. She was not strict with us, but Grandpa could be mean. I was his only little granddaughter, so he wasn't mean to me. He would always bring me something—candy, shoes, or a dress—when he went into town. He was mean to the boys, though, and gave them a hard time.

The boys would always joke about his nice sleigh or his pickup, saying, "We'll sure have fun with this, just wait 'til Grandpa dies."

I remember that in the spring Grandma would cut herself and let it bleed. A lot of the old-time people did this; they believed it made their blood stronger and would make them stronger as well.

Our family was always close to your Grandpa Little Warrior, Tilda. I remember going over there with my grandparents. Your grandpa would put on a little powwow at his place. They would sing Indian songs and dance almost all night. They would serve tea, coffee, or fry bread about midnight.

I remember when Grandma died. She had a close friend in Wakpala [Standing Rock Reservation], and she was beading a pair of leggings and a vest for him and wanted to take them to him during their celebrations [community powwow]. I remember her staying up at night to finish them [by lamplight]. She said, "I know I might not live long; I might die and I want to finish them."

A bunch of folks from Kyle were going up to that powwow in Wakpala, so they hired Johnny Ferguson. He had a truck with a big box on it. They put straw in there and piled in their tents and bedding and satchels. On the way up there it started to really pour. Even though they tried to cover themselves with the tents and bedding, Grandma got soaked. That night she got very sick with a fever.

They took her to the hospital in Pierre because it was the closest, but they couldn't help her there because she was an Indian.[3] I remember them telling her she was sick from gallstones. They took her to the Indian hospital in Pine Ridge. Soon she called for Mom and Dad to come after her, because she wanted to get ready to die. She was prepared, and put on all her burial clothes—her slips and stocking and moccasins, things like that.

On the Fourth of July 1938, they brought her body back. She had a tipi, so they waked her in a tipi. I remember that they put ice around the body.

The family got a cow and butchered it. People came and kept coming, until there was quite a camp. She was well respected and had no enemies.

Grandma Millie believed in the schools. She taught beadwork and quillwork. The principal told Grandma how to help the other [white] teacher, so she did. The school superintendent thought a lot of her and said they could use a school bus for a hearse, so they did. They held the service and buried her at St. Barnabas Church. We went to the funeral in a wagon. Lots of wagons followed that yellow school bus to the cemetery.

After the burial they fed the visitors. I remember that lots of old people came, so Mom served them kidney, liver, and *tani'ga* [tripe]. That is what I remember.

Another granddaughter, Delia Two Crow, told us:

I was just a little girl when Grandma died, but there are a few things I remember. . . . Anytime, day or night, that someone would come by needing help, Grandma would go. In those days, people traveled about by horse or team and wagon.

If she didn't have the medicine she needed, Grandma would send us out to look for it with a lantern. She said that when we found the right medicine we would hear an owl hoot and that we should not be afraid of this. She doctored with owl medicine and with ghost helpers. People said she *Wanagi Wapiye'* [doctors with ghosts or spirits]. I remember that she would be wrapped head to foot [in a yuwipi-type ceremony].

When her ceremony began, you could hear the owl make noises from one end of the house to another.

Grandma would conduct her ceremonies in the daytime; I remember them covering up all the windows. People would pay her with whatever they wanted, but all she asked of them was some Bull Durham.

She was a kind grandma and always had us grandchildren with her. She was active in the school and worked as a teacher's aide. She believed strongly that children should have a good education. I remember when she died—I think that was in 1939. They used a yellow school bus to take her body to the wake and the cemetery.

Maza Win: Iron Woman

Kenneth Young Bear was Mark's teacher, his introduction into traditional Sioux religion and ceremony.[4] It is to him that Mark must acknowledge his first exposure to ceremony, song, and philosophy. From 1973–77 he taught Mark. The setting was usually his home on the Cheyenne River Reservation where Mark lived. Sometimes they would drink black coffee, speaking until the sun came up. During some autumn visits he would stress the importance of the creation stories, breaking them down, explaining what they meant below the surface. At other times of the year he might explain the origin and meaning behind a ceremony like the sweat bath, reminding us of the significance of each detail of the ceremony. Mark was not the only one Kenneth taught. Carol Little Wounded, Mitchell Zephier, Jim Marshall, Glen Good Thunder, Jimmy Good Tracks, and Kathy Smith all fasted under and learned from this man. We call one another brother and sister.

Our songs, learned from Kenneth, were, like much of his knowledge, passed from Iron Woman to his uncle Victor to Kenneth and then to us. We are heirs of Iron Woman's spiritual legacy.

Kenneth would always remind us that all his teachings had come from a woman, his grandmother. Kenneth would tell us stories from his own experiences with this barrel-shaped, forceful woman. He carried one of her necklaces in his medicine bundle. It was his most prized possession.

Because Kenneth passed away in 1983, it was his wife, Darlene, who shared what she could remember. Born Darlene Knife, she is a Howojou (sub-band of Minnecojou) Lakota from a ranch near the Red Scaffold community, on the Cheyenne River Reservation. At over fifty years old, she is now completing college and has undertaken years of study to become a Catholic lay minister. She sees no conflict between the two paths. "I want to use my training in the church, to reach out to the reservation youth, because our children are the future."

You might think that because Kenneth grew up in Fort Berthold that his grandmother is Hidatsa. He was born in 1937. She was an Assiniboine.[5] Her relations live near Wolf Point and Frazier, Montana. I remember Kenneth telling me that she was short, around four foot something. Kenneth stayed with her from the time he was ten years old.

Kenneth told me that she doctored him one time, that he had become blind once, so she spoke with Kenneth and asked him what hurt, so that she could doctor him. They lived out in the country then, so they weren't close to anything but a little substation. When she doctored Kenneth's vision, he got it back. He had the mumps. That's how he went blind. Kenneth really didn't know if it was something that comes on and goes away fast, or whether he healed because she doctored him, but he got well.

I will tell you what Kenneth told me about how Iron Woman first got her medicine. I guess her mother died during the night. They thought she [Iron Woman's mother] was sleeping, but she was gone. That next morning they couldn't wake her up. So they looked all over for Iron Woman. It was the fall of the year, already cold.

Later that day they found her lying by her mom in the wagon box [used for a casket] where they had put the body. Iron Woman got out and she was very happy. She said, "I'm going to a land where my mom is." Everybody was scared [that she would join her mother], but she lived. As she was lying there in the wagon box, her mother's spirit was talking to her. She told her to come back to this world—that she was going to be with her, that she was going to tell her what to do. She got happy after that. This was when she was twelve or so. She was very young when her mom died.

It was long after that [when she was past menopause]—I don't know how she got that way, but she was able to travel between this land and the spirit world.

Her youngest son, Victor, told us about a time when Iron Woman was sitting at the table and a dog came and sat. It had very weird eyes, and it came and sat and looked at her, and a weird light was coming from the dog's eyes. The light was going up and down. Iron Woman was trying not to be scared of it. The door wasn't open, but [the spirit dog] came through into the room.

You know, if these [Indian] cowboys were in a rodeo and broke a bone, they'd have her come and doctor them and then go right back to riding again. And she didn't use a cast. She would put medicine on it, and that would kind of set it. One of the things that Kenneth used from her teachings is that she was strict in everything she did. She lived by it, and then more things came to her, so she got to be that powerful.

The same guy [that she had doctored for a serious injury] came over to us one time and said, "Your grandma is the one that cured me. But I asked for it, and if I died I wouldn't be here having a hard time now. I went to her and she doctored me. Nobody could help me, and you know what? She didn't go through all this thing about locking the windows up; she doctored in broad daylight. She put her flags up, and she doctored me in that way. So like that, she doctored me right away." When they do that, that's when the special song is sung.

Kenneth Young Bear told Mark the story of an event that happened while he lived with Iron Woman.

When I was a boy, ten or twelve I think, I was living with my grandmother. Her name was Iron Woman. She was well known for her powers and had helped many people. She used to doctor through the use of bird spirits. In her medicine bundle she carried a number of dried bird skins, and in her ceremonies she could make each one sing its song as it had in life.

I didn't know what to make of this, because I was young and she was my grandma. I guess I didn't think too much of it.

We lived out in the country, and even though the white people had many cars by then, few of us Indians did. So we used to travel by team and wagon.

One day a man came by. He looked very frightened. He said his neighbor's wife had become crazy and tried to kill her husband with a knife, and that she had torn the house apart and would let no one in there. He asked my grandmother if she could help, because he was frightened for the woman's husband and children.

Pretty soon Grandma Iron Woman had her things [her medicine bundle] ready, and I had hitched the team for her. Because there was no one home I went with her. When we got to that place, where the crazy woman was, you could hear things being smashed around inside. You could see the little windows on the front of the sod-covered cabin were broken out, and she was screaming. The husband was bleeding, and neighbors were tending to him. Their children were crying.

Grandma climbed off the wagon. I don't remember if she did anything first, but pretty soon she was walking toward the house. I was scared and didn't want her to leave me alone, so I jumped off and ran up behind her. When she opened the door the woman was standing in what was her kitchen.

The inside of the house was destroyed. What furniture she had was all smashed, and even the curtains were torn off. There were clothes and broken things everywhere. I had never seen anything like it, and I was really scared.

The woman stood there with her arm raised, holding that knife, her hair wild and her hands bleeding. My grandmother prayed in Assiniboine asking for help, and then she held up her hand [palm extended]. The woman took one step forward and then fell in a faint. It was as if the power in my grandmother's hand had knocked the wind out of her; she just fell [unconscious].

Later Grandma told me to go outside and fetch her things [medicine bundle]. She said, "Send the woman's husband in." Soon I could hear the sounds of birds coming from the house. It seems that today a lot of cures are performed in the dark, but in the old days they cured in the daylight.

Well, it must have worked because after that the woman was herself again. She rested for quite a while, but eventually she went on with her life, and those things did not happen to her again.

It is from her [Iron Woman] that my uncle Victor learned the things he knew about our ways, and it is from Victor that I acquired my teaching. That is why to this day I carry her medicine necklace in my bundle and remember her often.

We are fortunate to have interviewed two of Kenneth's sisters. They now live in a comfortable home in Bismarck. According to Vivian, "We decided on Bismarck because it is in the middle, between Fort Yates and home [Fort Berthold]. My husband was from Fort Yates, and so my kids have close relations there." Both Cissy Young Bear, the younger sister, and Vivian Bull Head were quite animated and mirthful during the interview. Thanks to them, we have an additional, very intimate "portrait" of this remarkable woman. This shared recollection is wonderful in its detail. Through it we can experience much of what reservation life was like for this holy woman's family in the 1930s and 1940s.

Kenneth was born September 22, 1927. I was born in 1929; Clifford in 1932; and Cissy in 1940. Iron Woman was the only name I ever knew Grandma by. I don't think she had another [government enrollment] name, like we do today. One of the things I remember is that Iron Woman was also a midwife. She spoke many languages—Dakota, Arikara, Hidatsa, Assiniboine, and Mandan. At home with us, she spoke Hidatsa. She never had to do anything to get her power, that I know of. She was born that way. I remember her being a stern woman, sometimes too strict, but she did love to laugh.

Grandma had a certain way of doing everything, and you'd better do it that way, too! We had to leave our shoes at the door. You can see that she is still with me. I still take my shoes off at the door, even though I don't ask other people to do that. And you'd better not be caught putting your feet on the pillow! We lived in two rooms. She had it arranged pretty well, though.

She always wore plain moccasins, no beadwork or anything. She wore a long calico dress. And she always wore an old-fashioned belt. It was what you'd call a studded belt, because it was covered with brass studs on thick leather. It went around her waist and had a part that dropped to the ground. Grandma wore her hair in braids and joined the braids together.

My grandfather's name was Paul Young Bear known in Hidatsa as Beaver Head. He was a little older than she was and died when my mom was still young. She was a widow for a long time. So I don't really know how they were together [as a couple]. They had about ten children together—Walter, Catherine, Blanche, Frank, Joe, George, and Victor are the ones that lived. Victor was the one that learned from her and taught her ways to Kenneth. Blanche is the grandmother, so to speak, of all those Mandaree Singers.

I think Iron Woman was from a tribe of Assiniboine from Canada. Her folks were from up there, but I think she was actually born and raised stateside.

I remember people coming over to ask for help. They came all the time. She used many different things to doctor. She used herbs and also spirit helpers. She did all kinds of ceremonies, some in the dark and some in broad daylight. Most of the time she doctored in broad daylight. She doctored animals, too.

One time, some men were cutting horses, and they were cutting a colt from its mother. That little horse was a good one, and he was fast. He ran and ran, and they couldn't get a rope on him. He ran until his hooves fell off. I remember when they brought that little colt to Grandma. She prayed over those little hooves. Then she put right to right and left to left and put those hooves back on. She put something on those hooves and tied them on with a scrap of cloth. Those hooves grew back on, and that horse was fine. I think one time she even doctored somebody's pet coyote, and she doctored people's sick dogs.

When she prayed, I think she usually prayed in Assiniboine/Sioux. Some of the things I remember her doctoring were pneumonia, measles, that sort of thing. Most of the time they brought the patient to her because she was getting up there [in age]. People really respected her power. I never remember her not being able to cure anyone. Sometimes people would give something for doctoring, but sometimes they had nothing to give.

This was in the horse-and-buggy days. She had a really nice buggy. It had high, narrow wheels. She had lots of horses and sheep. People had given her these for her help. She gave those to her children and grandchildren.

I remember that she would pray with her pipe every day. It was a little one, with a small bowl and a short stem. She had a longer pipe that she used only for ceremonies. I guess she was Catholic, because she would say Rosary every night.

Grandma was always doing something. She had a big garden, maybe what today would make up four or five city blocks. She had corn, beans and squash, and she kept the garden very clean. She was always out there, bent over, pulling weeds. It never had any weeds!

In her garden, just like everything else, everything had to be just so. She had three cellars, one in the house and two outside. She filled them each with different crops. These cellars were very deep and narrow at the top. Logs were used to prop up the roof of the cellar. She used a long ladder to climb down. It was dark down there. I remember going down in one only once. She had built little walls or fences to separate the different kinds of squash and pumpkins. I remember looking up, and it seemed very deep, and I could see the stars up there. Isn't that strange?

When the cellars were full, she would cover them up with cardboard and straw and manure, to seal them up. She would tell us we should do this, put things up for hard times.

Grandma always had a big scaffold to dry her food on. She made lots of jerked meat, and she would dry it up there. She had a big stick with two leather straps that she used to frighten the birds off.

When the corn was ripe she would pick it and put it in big piles on the ground. She would invite people over there to help her put it up. They would peel the husk back and then braid the husks together into long, thick braids of corn and then hang these over the scaffold to dry. This was always a good time. The one that braided the most would get a gift of clothes, blankets, or cloth.

She never did use those things in the cellars. They were for other people. In the spring the people would have no money and would run out of groceries. They'd come by to see her, and Grandma would open her cellars and feed the people. A lot of people would come by.

My mother was a lower Sioux, from Morton, Minnesota. Her maiden name was Courselle. She was part French. They were Mdewakonton Dakota. Grandma liked my mom, even though she gave her a hard time. My mom was the only one who could live with her, because she put up with my grandmother! I think my grandma really did like my mom, though. They respected each other. That's why we lived there all together.

I remember when the plums, cherries, and berries would get ripe. Grandma would take that one-horse, high-wheel cart of hers and back it up under the bush. She would spread a canvas in the back of the little box and hit those bushes. The little cart would soon be full. Because of her, I know how to preserve fruits, from watching and helping her.

She'd take out her [grinding and pounding] stones. She had really nice ones—a nice, big, flat, kind of dish-shaped one for the bottom, and one shaped like an old telephone receiver to pound with. They were granite. She would pound the cherries and make them into patties with her hands. A big canvas would be spread on the scaffold, and we would place those patties in perfect rows to dry. If I didn't put them in straight rows, Grandma would get after me. She'd cover them at night. During the day she had a big whip made from a pole, with two thick pieces of leather attached to it. She would scare away the birds with that.

June berries she wouldn't pound like that, because they don't have seeds. She would scatter these on the canvas to dry. The plums she would split with a little knife she always carried. One at a time she would split them open, and squeeze the seed out. Then she would dry them.

She would harvest the wild beans and potatoes that grew along the creek. To this day I don't know how she knew [where to dig], but she would push her digging stick in a certain place, and there would be beans. I guess the mice gathered them. The potatoes she would pull up; they would have a long root. She would pull off the little potatoes and then rebury the root and pray, so there would be potatoes the next year.

At the right time of the summer Grandma would make a little lunch, and we would go to dig prairie turnips. She had a certain stick shaped just perfectly for that. She would push that stick into the ground and pry out a turnip. She seemed to know how deep to push it. When we got home she would slice those turnips into little pieces and dry them as well.

Grandma made coffee from parched corn. She would burn the corn on the top of the wood stove, then grind it. She would put it in boiling water. I suppose it tasted like coffee, although we were kids, and so I never tried it. She didn't drink that much coffee; instead, she picked all sorts of things for tea, which she would dry. She dug lots of different roots, and some of those she made into tea. We never went to a white doctor whenever we got sick; she had whatever we needed right there.

I remember Grandma doing all the traditional arts. She did quillwork and beadwork and tanned her own hides. She never sat us down and said, "Now you are going to learn this." We learned by doing. You know, you have to go through a certain ceremony [double woman] to do quillwork, and we never went through it, so even though I guess I know how quillwork is done, I have never done it myself. I guess my sister and I are afraid something might happen to us!

She told us all the sacred stories, creation stories, and Ohukankan and Iktomi stories. Fall is the time, in the Hidatsa way, to tell stories of ancestors and spiritual matters. It is October [now], and it is all right to talk about these things. For Grandma, the sweat was her hospital. She took her patients in there. She even took babies in there.

Mrs. Blue Hair

Mrs. Blue Hair was from Cherry Creek, on the Cheyenne River Reservation. She had a son who had followed her calling; his name was Robert Blue Hair. He was a practicing herbalist in the early 1970s, when Mark first lived on the reservation. Her name came up many times in conversations with Lucy and Madonna Swan. At that time they also lived in Cherry Creek.

Mrs. Blue Hair's methods as a Pejuta Win would seem to fall within the third category of doctoring used by medicine women. It is more generalized in use, more spontaneous, and often utilizes a physical medicine, applied or taken internally, with minimal ritual. This form is often alluded to when describing the acts of medicine women but never, in my experience, those of modern medicine men. Today, the Lowanpi, Yuwipi, or Inipi (sweat lodge) ceremonies are used by medicine men, although male herbalists were certainly known historically. We believe these references to "spontaneous doctoring" may be similar to an older practice used by *Mato Wapiye'* (Bear Doctors), because Mrs. Blue Hair was a *Mato Ihan'bla* (Bear Dreamer).

Darlene Young Bear told the following story about Mrs. Blue Hair.

Mrs. Blue Hair doctored my great-grandmother. I heard this story from my grandmother [great-aunt], Louise Montley. Remember, she was the one who lived with us. She tied tobacco offerings and prayed for us until she died in 1979, at age ninety-six. My great-grandmother's Indian name is Elk-Face Woman. Louise was Elk-Face Woman's daughter and my dad's sister. In those days she probably had been given a white [first] name, but she never used it; she is enrolled by the name Elk-Face Woman.

There was a time when Elk-Face Woman's knee swelled up, and that was when she went to Mrs. Blue Hair. Mrs. Blue Hair stopped there to visit. Mrs. Blue Hair saw her kind of limping around and said, "I'm going to doctor your leg before you go to bed tonight."

So just before they went to bed, Mrs. Blue Hair got into her [medicine] bag and told somebody to get her a basin of water. When she was digging around in her bag, she was kind of making *sss-sss-sss* sounds. She was singing a little [medicine] song to herself. They went and got the water. At that time they didn't have chairs, so they sat on the floor. She put that basin underneath her knee and mixed some medicine. Louise didn't tell me how she mixed it.

At that time they used buffalo fat to put that medicine in; they would always grind the medicine and mix it with that. She put it on the side of Grandma's knee that was swollen, and then she probably prayed, and I guess she was blowing on it from the top. Mrs. Blue Hair was blowing on it, and when she was doing that she told Elk-Face Woman to take her leg away. So Grandma did. Mrs. Blue Hair took that basin and looked in there, and she said, "My daughter-in-law, you have been *hġmuġa* [stricken] by the use of insects." It was something like that—ants or insects—and she mentioned different ones, the name of the person [who bewitched her].

I didn't question Louise about what they were in English, but that's what she said was in there. And that was all. After that, Mrs. Blue Hair said, "Take that salve I made and rub your knee with it, all the way around." Elk-Face Woman didn't have to take any pills, medicine, or anything. The next day that swelling started to come down.

Chauncey Dupris, then seventy-five years old and himself a Sun Dance Leader, holy man, and herbalist from the same village, Cherry Creek, knew Mrs. Blue Hair well. He had fond memories and, despite his own frail health, gladly shared what he could:

I was born in 1918. I remember Mrs. Blue Hair well. She was not my teacher in these ways. My grandmother, Sophie In The Woods, came from a long line of medicine people, and she taught me when I was only twelve or thirteen. She came through her dad's side on that. They were Bear Dreamers. But people can doctor with many different kinds of spirits—coyotes, bears, wolves, ghosts.

One day she told me she was not going to live long. She gave me a pipe and taught me many things. She said, "You will have to work for what you get in these ways. You are going to learn about the good and the bad in all things." And that's what I have been doing for fifty-eight years. She said I should do that and keep it going. She died soon after that.

I think Mrs. Blue Hair's first name was Marsha. She lived to be in her nineties. She was a powerful medicine woman. She doctored anything that came along. As far as I know, she never failed anybody. That's how powerful she was.

She would doctor in the daylight or at night. It depended, I think, on what kind of ceremony they wanted. She never went anyplace; she stayed right there at home. I never remember her using the sweat lodge. She doctored in her home. So mostly, I think, the patients came to her. She was a friendly woman. I never saw her get mad; she was always happy about something.

She had one son that she trained in her ways. That was Robert, but he's been dead about fifteen years. She was born a long time ago. I think that when she was born Pine Ridge was the only agency [late 1860s]. I think probably she was a Minnecojou.

I remember going once or twice to her ceremonies. She used herbs and ceremonies, and I remember that she used an altar.

All those who doctored—Mrs. Blue Hair, my grandmother—had a vision that they went through. They all have some kind of vision that they follow. Sometimes they pay her; sometimes not. When people come to you, you just take care of them, that's all. People worry too much about money. They think money is the only thing we can live on today. But you have to doctor the people that come. There is no retiring, until you go back to Mother Earth.[6]

Mrs. Thin Elk

One important group of healers, not encountered on our journey, are those who use sucking, or what today might be called "psychic surgery."

Mrs. Thin Elk, a Sicangu Lakota, was also known as Holy Horse Road Woman. Her grandson, Ted Thin Elk, now an elder in his seventies, said "You know, I only knew her as Grandma, and what she did was more on the woman's side, so I heard very little about it. I just thought of her as Grandma."[7]

What follows is the most complete and singular description of this ceremony that we have heard, and we were told about it by the patient herself, Lucy Swan. The ceremony took place in the late summer of 1910.

Let me tell you why I couldn't go to school when I was little. . . .

When I was a little girl I would sometimes die.[8] When I was dead and then came back to life, I could not remember anything. Some of the other girls were going to school. I couldn't, because of these times when I would die, or faint, or whatever it would be called now.

When I was ten years old, I wished very much that I could go to school and learn like the other girls. I talked to my mom about it, and she talked to Dad.

One summer day, not long after that, we were swimming and splashing in the creek and playing move-the-village games. I heard Dad calling, so we raced back toward the log house. I was ahead because I was the fastest runner, even though I was younger. Before I reached the house, my heart felt like it stopped, and I fell dead. My sister Mary told me later what happened next.

My dad picked me up and carried me to a spot beside the house, then he sent my older brother to bring Mrs. Thin Elk, dad's sister-in-law. We were kind of afraid of her because she was said to have a lot of power. [She was] the kind the Catholic priest warned us to stay away from. My parents used to tell us not to be afraid of her, because she was a good old woman who could cure the sick and had never hurt anyone. Still, we would make up witch stories about her and run when she came.

Mrs. Thin Elk came quickly, and she told my dad to spread white muslin on the floor of his summer tipi and then to lay me down on top of it. She said she would try to find the problem.

All the children were sent away; just the adults came into the lodge. Mary, my sister, was peeking under the tipi cover. The old woman told my father to sing and fill his pipe. When he was finished, she had him stand near me and point the pipe at me. Mrs. Thin Elk took her little parfleche [pounded rawhide] satchel and opened it. She took out a piece of red flannel and laid a buffalo horn and a bundle of sage on it. Then the old woman began to pray. As she prayed, she brushed my head and neck, and then my body, with the bunch of sage. Next, she stood up and sang to the east. When she sang, her chest made a noise like a bird singing. Then she picked up a handful of gray dust, and when she blew it out of her hand, it was yellow. Next, she sang to the south, and again the bird noise came from her chest, and she picked up the earth and this time when she blew, black dust came out of her hand. Then, to the west she sang and blew the dust. This time red dust came out. Finally, to the north she sang, that bird noise coming from nowhere and the gray dust came out as white dust.[9]

Mary told me later that she was really scared, but she was too amazed to leave. As she watched, the old lady bent down over me and turned me on my side. Making a loud noise like a buffalo, she put the buffalo horn on my neck and sucked. Very soon she asked for a white piece of buckskin. When Mom brought it, Mrs. Thin Elk tipped the horn onto the buckskin and a red blood clot came out. She told my dad that this was causing all the problems and that I would never "die" like that again. Then she said to get a frog. My dad had seen Mary peeking around, so he sent her to get a big frog from the creek. Mary ran to our swimming place and was soon back with a frog. Mary didn't exactly see what Mrs. Thin Elk did with the frog, but she wrapped it and the blood clot up in that buckskin and told Dad to place it on a high hill. Then they smoked Dad's pipe.

When I woke up, Dad gave Mrs. Thin Elk a horse to take home. Mom gave her a pretty shawl with flowers embroidered on it.[10] Mrs. Thin Elk thanked them and said, "That is more than enough for curing my own granddaughter." You see, old Mrs. Thin Elk was married to my Dad's brother![11]

Lucille Kills Enemy

Sidney Keith was Madonna's brother-in-law. Lucille Kills Enemy was his great-aunt, and he shared these memories with us when we asked him if he knew any medicine women in his lifetime.

Well, there are some herb doctors, but they don't do any ceremonies; they just tell you what to take. . . . They usually have a whole suitcase full of stuff. You go to them, and you get a little medicine in a sack. They are good ones, but they don't perform ceremonies. The only one I know of [who performs ceremonies] was my aunt, Lucille Kills Enemy. She lived in Kyle. I remember one little spirit—it was a deer, because the deer ran around in there [during her ceremony].

Lucille was the only one who could do that, and she was successful. She don't kid around; she tells you what is wrong. Her husband sang for her, and he used a great big drum in there. And that deer ran around and sounded like he was going to slip in there. I think she was playing with that deer spirit, but then they got serious. This rattle comes in there, and she tells the patient what's wrong. Sometimes it's something very simple.

I went to her ceremonies when I was young. We didn't go for ourselves, but we went over there, traveling in a team and wagon. It was a long way. Later, we went there in a Model A. We used to go to Kyle and Oglala to visit relatives, then come back. Later, we had a new pickup we used to go back down there. Those people are all dead now. The roads were all dirt then; just the good ones were gravel. In spring, when it was rainy, you'd really have a hard time. A Model T could go anyplace in the mud with those little small tires. They never get stuck. Yeah, those were the days. . . .

Madonna Swan shared the following with us. It is also part of the last interview we had before she started out on the spirit road to join her ancestors.

When we went to be doctored by Mrs. Kills Enemy, she put a young man on the hill [to fast for a vision]. That man's wife was staying there, and there was a boy and girl. I remember that after Mrs. Kills Enemy put that man on the hill we were staying at her house. She told us, "If you go outside, cover your head; it could be dangerous. There are lots of spirits roaming around during this time [of fasting], so cover your head."

That young man was up four days and four nights [the maximum, and most ideal, number of days]. When he was to come down, we went up there with her. She performed a ritual and then had him step outside the fence [of string and tobacco ties].

They had the fair in Kyle at that time and we went to it with her. I remember that we saw some *Heyoka* [Thunder Clowns] there [dancing]. That was the first time I had ever seen them.

Neither of us had ever heard of a woman putting up men to fast. This was a remarkable revelation that added both to our own understanding of the status this holy woman had achieved and to our insight into the apparent reverence for holy women in the days before the reservations. To fast under someone is also to be that person's student, usually for four years. A person compelled by his or her own dreams to follow a path in the sacred, to fast for a vision or spirit helper, would not choose a teacher lightly.

Mel Lone Hill, vice chairman of the Oglala Sioux tribe (1993), was a patient of Lucille's in the early 1950s and also knew her as an elder whom his parents and grandparents respected and visited.

They used to live north of Kyle. I don't know what her maiden name was. She was married to a man named Frank Kills Enemy. They had only one son, Matthew, but he's gone now. She lived with her husband, but she had her own room. He was the spokesperson for her. Nobody could go near her. She was pretty strict. It was probably in the early fifties when she doctored me. She was a Wana'gi Wapiye'. I remember going to visit her, and I remember her, but not the time she doctored me. We used to go to her place, and she used to come to our house.

She doctored me at our house. Four years in a row I'd had pneumonia, and the last one killed me. I was gone [dead]. She had to go find me on the other side. She was probably the only one I knew of who was that powerful. I think she was in her mideighties when she doctored me. She died in the early part of the 1960s somewhere. So she must have been close to ninety when she died.

Lucille Kills Enemy was a full Lowanpi priest. She had to travel into the spirit world and retrieve the wana'gi of this boy, to bring him back to life. This is a classic function of the shaman.

Mr. Lone Hill mentions that her husband was her spokesperson and that he protected her privacy and was her "agent." He also remembered her having her own room. It is typical of powerful medicine men, who have acquired tremendous "power," to live in a small house separate from their wives, where they also keep their ritual equipment. Mel's mentioning this separate room further adds to our picture of this spiritually potent woman, who, it would seem, behaved in virtually every way just as a man with her powers would.

This image and those of the other women in this chapter may defy what many experts had previously thought a woman might attain in Lakota sacred life, but they are in fact clear records of the truth. Women who had real power were encouraged to follow their visions for the good of the people.

11

A Healing of the People

*I was told by an interpreter, "As long as you pray from the heart, all
the pipes that have ever been will back you. If you have the honesty to
pray for real, from the heart, you will be heard."*

—Wounye' Waste' Win

For two years we investigated an area of human experience, a well of collective wisdom, one until now largely ignored and often denied. In some
sense we felt we were being "watched over" on our journey—that perhaps Wakan Tanka never intended half of the human race to suffer feelings of spiritual inferiority and was, perhaps, blessing our attempt to set
things a little straighter.

We have learned that, at least in these tribal cultures, women did not
have to relinquish their roles as females to obtain spiritual power and social respect. In fact, we continually had our eyes opened as to how "ordinary" these women were.

Changing Attitudes Toward Women

We met women with well-developed powers to speak with ghosts, em-
bark on soul travel, heal the sick, predict the future, and lead public ceremonies like the Sun Dance. So male-biased has the history of Native
American ethnography been, that records of women's roles in the sacred
life of the tribe has largely been abbreviated, or simply overlooked.

In his recent book, *Animals of the Soul: Sacred Animals of the Oglala
Sioux,* Joseph Epes Brown comments briefly on the role of women:
"What is remarkable about the rites of the vision quest among the Plains

peoples is that it is accomplished not just by special people . . . but that every man or woman after the age of puberty is expected to participate either once or even continually throughout his life."[1]

We believe that the Judeo-Christian patriarchal bias in most "Native American literature" has, over time, actually served to reduce the spiritual role and social status of Indian women at a most crucial level. For some tribal members, both male and female, ideas about the proper "place" and abilities of native women have changed, limiting their potential for contributing in this sacred way to their own people. Worse yet, these changes have seriously distorted the actual relationships between men and women in Indian life.

Oppressed and Oppressors

As buffalo herds were systematically destroyed and the occasional dependency of the early reservation settlement became a permanent reality, wholesale unemployment for Indian males began to take its toll. Along with this loss of status came a change in the way some Indian men view women. One Lakota male, himself a Pipe Carrier, responded to my question "Did you ever know of anyone who was a holy woman?" by answering, "Holy women? There was no such thing!"

While both sexes have suffered emotionally, spiritually, and physically, women, at least, continued to have a central role in their tribal world, performing virtually all the tasks they did in the free days. With fixed log homes and gardening, the types of work changed, but women were needed and were very busy. For men, there was little "worthwhile" work to do.

There is no doubt that men tried to adjust to physical imprisonment, but the two most important family and community roles—those of soldier and hunter-provider—had vanished. Some men made a successful transition and found work as farmers or cowboys for the large ranches that had moved into the vast prairies of former Indian country, while others literally joined the circus, the wild-west shows that traveled to Europe and beyond.

The army employed some as scouts to guide the containment patrols sent out from military posts to keep fellow Indians on the reservations. The Bureau of Indian Affairs hired former warriors as policemen to enforce government edicts. All this, however, provided work for only a few.

The soldier and dream societies withered like the herds of buffalo and eventually died. Priests, ministers, and doctors purposefully and aggressively attacked the reputation of holy men, sending those who wouldn't conform to prison and to special Indian mental hospitals.[2] Even the Sun Dance was forbidden.

The early twentieth century saw the growth of the Bureau of Indian Affairs, with its colonialist schools, hospitals, and shops. Many of the jobs created were for women. Schools were built far from Indian communities. Boys could go to high school; girls could not. In 1913, after the Wanamaker Expedition, War Dancing and the giveaway tradition were outlawed or severely restricted.

All that was Indian—especially old ways of nomadism, warfare, and hunting—was denigrated. Old people were said to be blanket Indians who were entirely ignorant and irrelevant. At school tribal languages and religion were strictly forbidden, and all that was white was presented as a prize to be sought.

From the age of six years to age eighteen, only summers were spent at home, and that was for the fortunate. Some children stayed at schools or were placed with white families for entire years at a stretch. Separated from family for most of their childhood, these children were raised in military-style boarding schools. This educational system systematically destroyed Indian parenting patterns, slowly squeezing the life out of the traditional Indian attitude toward extended family. Through the efforts of assimilationist policy proponents, each generation lost a little more of the old ways, from the 1880s until the official government policy changed in the 1930s.

There are still, however, many Indian children who attend boarding schools. Some are operated by the Bureau of Indian Affairs, but most are run by religious denominations.[3]

Most young men joined the United States Armed Services. Many fought in the Spanish-American War, and, later, in World Wars I and II. Those who came home alive had lived, fought beside, and gotten drunk with white soldiers as equals. They returned home, however, to a very different social climate and little opportunity.

World War II is credited, or blamed, for much of what damaged the fabric of Indian life. A country that wanted Indians to fight in its wars welcomed them home to discrimination and poverty. Many returning Indian veterans tried, at the encouragement of the Bureau, to leave the reservations, often finding the white world strange and inhospitable.[4] Perhaps, as the racial oppression of America bore down on proud veterans, alcohol became the vent for social and personal frustrations. Of course, women were often the easy target for the violence that alcohol nourishes.

As the twentieth century progressed and the traditional culture diminished in influence, the loss of traditional respect and the physical abuse of women became a growing problem. This is what Ted Thin Elk, a Sicangu Lakota and pioneer in the Native American alcohol treatment movement, said:

> I don't remember spouse abuse being common. When I was a boy in the thirties, I remember a man who lived farther up the White River from us. He was known to be a wife beater. The community knew about it, and he was never invited to serve on committees or take part in any community activity. That was how they dealt with him. He had no respect from anyone. He was the only one I remember.
>
> It wasn't until after World War II that it began to change. Men got used to drinking in the army and kept it up when they got home, even though it was still illegal for Indians to drink. Now it seems that some men feel it is their right to beat their wives, but it was never that way in the past.[5]

During the "dirty thirties," successful Indian farmers and ranchers with their now dry allotments lost their livelihood, throwing even the strongest families into deeper poverty. Strangely, the Depression and various government work programs like the Works Progress Administration (WPA) provided work for men. The wages were very low and the work was hard, but it provided a boost for the difficult socioeconomic status of men. And the fact that much of the labor lived in temporary tent villages actually preserved many of the community traditions. The thirties are often remembered fondly by elderly Lakota.

In the years of Johnson's war on poverty, through Nixon's Indian self-determination policies, and afterward, tribal government and bureaucracy have grown. While creating some well-paying jobs for men, they have still created more permanent work for women than for men. Recently developed Indian community colleges, Indian-controlled schools, and contract medical clinics have created employment in greater numbers for women as well. Although Indian gaming has created employment on some reservations, because of isolation and small rural populations it has not developed on most of the sprawling western Plains Indian reservations.

This loss of power to participate fully in the family economy, augmented by superimposed ideas about masculine roles, has altered the way some men see themselves, and that obviously affects how they see the women in their lives.

As children in more families were exposed to the destabilizing influences of chronic alcohol abuse, some of them, in turn, perpetuated it in their own adult years, with the result that in those families it has become "normal," and the status and self-respect of women, who became objects of abuse, has suffered. The culture was losing one of its most valuable assets, the power of its women. This is how Mary Crow Dog put it:

> Some warriors come home drunk and beat up their old ladies in order to work off their frustrations. I know where they are coming from. I feel sorry for them, but I feel even sorrier for their women. . . .[6]
>
> There is a curious contradiction in Sioux Society. The men pay great lip service to the status women hold in the tribe. Their rhetoric on the subject is beautiful. They speak of Grandmother Earth and how they honor her. Our greatest culture hero—or heroine—is the White Buffalo Calf Woman, sent to us by the Buffalo nation, who brought us the sacred pipe and taught us how to use it. . . .

Notions of female inferiority have permeated and done great social damage to a system that was very different from the dominant culture of America, a system in which women were once so highly regarded as to be called upon to cure the sick. There is no doubt that as time went by, fewer women encountered encouragement of their sacred activities outside the churches. Although it is certainly damaging for a boy to see his mother beaten, it is likely worse for the self-esteem of his sister. Perhaps it is true that when people feel oppressed long enough, they look for someone to oppress in turn.

The Christian missionaries' wholesale dismissal of the value of virtually every aspect of Indian culture has reaped a grim harvest of disorientation, dislocation, and violence. There is a common saying in Indian country: "The white man came, and all he had was the Bible; now the white man has everything, and all the Indian has is the Bible."

The American Indian had, and continues to have, a very adequate Bible—albeit an oral one. The Native American religion was one that eloquently spoke to all aspects of life, including the proper behavior of men and women, children, plants, and animals.

Indian readers have come to rely on the accuracy of largely non-Indian writers, who have often unintentionally filtered back through their own cultural perceptions what they thought they saw in the tribes they studied. In most nineteenth-century writing, Indian women come out looking like prostitutes, packhorses, wrinkled hags, or slaves. In twentieth-century writing they are all but invisible, and this has only recently begun to change.

New Age Genre and Native Women

Not all distortions, however, have been written by white male missionaries, historians, and ethnographers. New Age books have only added to and perpetuated many stereotypes that hurt Indian women and obscure the actual strength of the cultures they purport to describe. In contrast to what we found on our journeys, these writers give us some strange images, including their fabricated version of the Indian battle of the sexes.

The New Age genre often presents only a small portion of the truth and can thus misrepresent the culture and ceremony it is intended to explain. The genre denies the role of the community in ritual life. Here is what Mitchell Zephier says of the New Age genre:

> If you think about the Sun Dance or the Buffalo Calf ceremony, they were all performed for the good of the people. You might have only one young lady going through the ceremony, but all the people witness that, and they all absorb the transmission of values from the elderly people.
>
> I remember going to Bishop Hare, an Episcopal boarding school, and to talks given by Father Noah Broken Leg, a full-blood Lakota. In one of his Sunday talks, he said, "You know, these old Indian people, the traditional people had high moral values that a lot of people can't live up even to today. They were honest people, they lived by a certain code, and they practiced their beliefs and lived these beliefs in how they related to one another."
>
> What it reminds me of is that there is a right way to live, a right way to do things. A lot of these New Age people, because they are so spiritually hungry, are like people starved for food—they'll grab anything and eat it without question. Today there is a lot of controversy about whether to let New Age people participate in ceremonies, but like the lies in these books it's sad, because for many years now the dominant society has tried to eradicate native beliefs. Now people think they can make them up, create history and culture, and play with our beliefs.

Obviously these distortions do not go unnoticed by Indian people, but because Indian religious systems do not have political and legal arms, and because their methods of disseminating information are through oral tradition and ceremony, they go largely unchallenged.

The Earth Goddess and Sexual Politics

What Pte' San, the White Buffalo Maiden, presented to the Lakota, including instructions about family, motherhood, the proper role of women in the sacred realm, and an orderly Lakota society, is generally lost in the literary stretch and political manipulation of some feminist writers.

No one has the corner on sacred truth. The religious genocide perpetrated on Indian America in the name of Christ has sadly cost all mankind precious pieces of its collective experience and wisdom. The fact that all peoples of the globe have a valid share in this great collective spiritual wisdom has been brushed aside by those with a politico-religious agenda.

Indian religions are complete systems that must be seen and understood in the context of the culture they came from, and borrowing isolated parts like the sweat bath or the image of the White Buffalo Maiden can lead to confusion and misunderstanding.

We have made a long spiritual and intellectual journey, both in our hearts and in actual miles, and have often found it difficult to connect Native American theories of disease with Western European man's. It is almost impossible for wealthy Americans to understand Indian spirituality as an everyday tool for basic survival, when for many the search for truth comes out of a lack of personal spiritual fulfillment in a sexist and materialistic world—or even out of a sense of boredom in which spirituality is a topic of fashionable discussion, a momentary, trendy fad. Perhaps their desire is also for a belief that technology will heal their estrangement from the earth itself.

The belief that there is faith in something beyond science and money is at the core of what each of our teachers shared with us. They have shared the heart of these ways, not just the shell. These personal memories, beliefs, and feelings are the past and present of real women not hindered by the sexist prejudices of the dominant world religions. Good Lifeways Woman, when asked to summarize what she wanted to communicate, said, "One of the largest things I'm learning is that nobody is going to tell you exactly what is ahead in your spiritual journey. I thought, when I set out to follow my vision, that these things would be clear. But all you get is a little bit at a time. When you have fully understood that new thing, they will give you a little bit more."

Much, in fact, has survived in their oral history and traditions useful both to Native Americans and to all mankind. What we found was a rich legacy and an ongoing set of vibrant ceremonies.

The unfortunate persistence of the "vanishing red man" image in history and literature affects Indians more profoundly than it does anyone else. There has grown for over one hundred years a tendency to protect one's own culture in response to constantly being told it will vanish. There is, however, a purposeful passing on of information through social practices like the powwow and the ceremonies of modern Plains Indian life.

What we found was a living and self-renewing belief system and a group of women who continue to serve a vital role in constantly changing tribal societies. There was, in all our interviews, a constant sense that the importance and respect once common among Plains women is making a slow but steady return. All the native people we spoke to said they hoped this book would give Indian women more confidence to follow their spiritual dreams.

There is no doubt, though, that Native American women continue to respond to the needs of the People, to dream powerful dreams. The creation in 1979 of a new dream society, the *Sina Wakan Win Oklakiciye'*, or Sacred Shawl Women's Society, is the physical manifestation of a much larger dream—to restore the status and perpetuate the wisdom of Indian ideas about the importance and role of women in Lakota society. The words of Bernice Stone, an American Indian woman and visionary, have a haunting resonance for a larger society that seems to be degenerating into family violence and gun-toting social madness.

Today we have fallen away from a lot of traditional values and beliefs. A man can beat his wife to near death and not receive punishment. Almost every day, women whose husbands or boyfriends beat them up are brought into the hospital in Pine Ridge. These men are rarely prosecuted in a court of law. We feel that the problem of wife beating is of vast importance to the Oglala Lakota people, as it affects our prime natural resource—our children. The violence that they see and experience is not forgotten and is often repeated when they have families of their own. It is necessary to stop this cycle of violence and teach new ways of dealing with their problems. For if our children do not grow up healthy in mind as well as in body, there is no hope for the Oglala Lakota people. Our children are our future. Sacred Shawl Women's Society believes in strengthening the family and in working to eliminate domestic violence.[7]

While sacred visions continue to be acted out by women for the good of the people in the modern setting, many questions still remain for future searchers. Is the sacred calling of medicine women among Plains Indian tribes dying, or is it actually still vital?

We asked Wounye' Waste' Win what it was that she wanted to leave people with, what central thoughts had occurred to her during the time that we worked together on this book:

It would be something like don't judge or compare your spiritual experience with somebody else's. Don't compare yourself with books; you'll always come up short. The more you follow the inner voice, that quiet voice, the more you will learn and grow in your own way.

Sometimes you hear a voice, sometimes you feel or understand something. Different people will teach you—sometimes a woman, sometimes a man. Maybe it will be a new song. When you hear it, feel it, there will be a deep knowingness that you can trust. When you're true to that, your understanding [of sacred things] will grow stronger.

You must follow this inner voice even though it contradicts what others are expecting, even though it is contrary to what others are doing and saying.

Just recently a man approached me and told me to keep doing my women's ceremony: "Keep doing that, because I will send people to you, there are many people who need and want your help." He is the second person who has told me recently that he has "seen" my ceremonies and the people coming to them.

When we asked Good Lifeways Woman why she was so enthusiastic about this book she said, "Because it will nourish the People, help the men and women see themselves in a better way. Women will once again be encouraged to follow their visions for the good of the people."

We hope she is right. *Mitakuye' Oyasin.*

Notes

INTRODUCTION

1. Michael F. Steltenkamp, *Black Elk: Holy Man of the Oglala* (Norman: University of Oklahoma Press, 1993), pp. 124, 125.
2. Dora Little Warrior Rooks was the youngest daughter of Johnson Little Warrior (an Oglala holy man) and Ella (Cloud Horse) Little Warrior. When Tilda was ten years old, her Grandmother Sadie grew sick and, within months, died. Within a year of Sadie's death, Dora began to take care of Tilda, her two sisters, and two of her brothers. Tilda remained under Grandma Dora's care until she finished high school.

    It is to Dora that Tilda attributes her knowledge of the traditional arts of her people and her first exposure to the traditional ceremonies. Even though it was thought that Sadie had inherited her father's powers, she remained a devout Episcopalian all her life. This is a clear example of how the Lakota extended family works and of the practice of calling all one's grandparents, brothers, and sisters "Grandpa" and "Grandma," even though the dominant society designates them great-aunts and great-uncles. It is a sad comment on our nomadic/urban life that these even fairly close relatives are generally only casual acquaintances.
3. Most Lakota people, particularly the full-bloods, live in two spiritual worlds simultaneously. While they may be Catholic and attend Catholic rituals, their dream world, social system, behavioral ideals, and, for many, ritual world revolves around the old beliefs that predated the coming of missionaries. Even families that don't actively attend or participate in Lakota ritual are fully aware of the meaning and implications of these rituals.
4. Mark knew Madonna Swan Abdalla for over twenty years. In this book she will be referred to as Madonna Swan although she was in fact married to Jay Abdalla, of Yankton Sioux and Syrian ancestry, and was therefore Madonna Abdalla. Madonna and Mark collaborated on a book, *Madonna Swan: A Lakota Woman's Story* (Norman: University of Oklahoma Press, 1991). She was a remarkable woman in all respects and someone we will miss greatly. She passed away in October of 1992, a week after she was interviewed for this book. Jay died in his sleep in their home some two weeks after Madonna's death.

5. There is great debate among Indian people about the usefulness of books, even accurate ones, and about whether this information should be shared with non-Indians. We have never heard of a religion dying from the spread of its philosophy or its contribution to human knowledge. More often than not, good books serve an important place in the lives of Indian people, just as they do in the broader world. Mark recently had the pleasant experience of having Lakota parents of a fifteen-year-old girl tell him that a copy of *Madonna Swan* was their daughter's dearest possession.

CHAPTER ONE

1. The Lakota occupy five reservations in western South Dakota, on what remains of the Great Sioux Reservation established by Congress through federal treaty in 1868. Increasingly over the last twenty years, the Sioux have made it known that they wish to be called by their own name for themselves, which is Lakota.

   The term *Sioux* is misleading because it has no specific reference within Lakota people's history. They call themselves Sioux when giving their tribe name to non-Indians but call themselves *Lakota,* which means "the Allies." Sioux is said to be a shortening of an Ojibwa word, *Naddowissi* ("lesser snakes," "adders," or "enemy"), with the French plural ending *-ioux,* thus becoming *Naddowissioux,* which was shortened over time to *Sioux.*

   In a real sense Sioux refers to all tribes of the loose confederation known as the *Oceti Sakowin,* or Seven Council Fires. Within this confederation (which may have been more philosophical than actual) were three main divisions, the Dakota, Nakota, and Lakota. Each of the three major subdivisions is characterized by differences in dialect and, to some extent, cultural orientation. The Dakota were Woodlands or Park Lands people with ties to other Woodlands tribes sharing some of their cosmology and worldview. The Nakota occupied a vast territory east of the Missouri River and shared traits with other river peoples, such as agriculture and occasionally earth lodges (Drifting Goose's band). The Lakota had in common with other high plains peoples a unique religious and philosophical system, including the Sun Dance and Vision Quest.

   The Dakota (eastern division) comprised four "seats"—the *Mide' Wakanton* (Spirit Lake People), the *Wakpe' Kute'* (Shooters Among the Leaves), the *Sissitoin* (Fish-Scale Dwellers), and *Whapeton* (Leaf Dwellers). These Dakota people live today on various reservations in South Dakota, North Dakota, Minnesota, Montana, and Canada.

   The Nakota (middle) comprised the two *Ihanktowan* or *Yankton* (End Dwellers) groups, which occupied two "seats" on the mythical council.

The final group, and the group from which most of the information in this book comes, are the Lakota. Although in earlier times they occupied only one "seat" in the Seven Council Fires they eventually grew in strength and numbers. By 1775 they had crossed the Missouri River and became subdivided into seven tribes themselves. Within that time frame they acquired the horse and became the buffalo hunting warriors of legend.

These bands or tribes, from largest to smallest, are as follows: the Oglala, on the Pine Ridge Reservation in South Dakota; the Sicangu (*Brule'*), on Rosebud and Lower Brule Reservations in South Dakota; and the Minnecojou (Plants by the Water People), of which Chief White Swan, Madonna's paternal grandfather, was a significant warrior and headman, in the large villages of Cherry Creek, Red Scaffold, and Bridger on the southern half of the Cheyenne River Reservation.

The Hunkpapa (Camps at the Horn, Sitting Bull's people) live in the South Dakota portion of the Standing Rock Reservation, near McLaughlin, South Dakota. The Itazipco (Sans Arc, or Bowless Band), who are the traditional keepers of the Sacred Calf Pipe, live along the Moreau River on the Cheyenne River Reservation.

The two smallest groups, largely intermarried today, are the O-ohe' Nunpa (Two Kettle), on the east end of the Cheyenne River, and the Si Sapa or Blackfeet Sioux, living in the northeastern part of the Cheyenne River Reservation and on Standing Rock.

The Lakota constitute by far the largest Sioux population today, numbering some seventy thousand.

2. Peter T. Furst, *Stones, Bones and Skins* (Toronto: Arts Canada, 1977), p. 24.
3. The Crow, Cheyenne, Lakota, Assiniboine, Arapaho, and Blackfoot are all classic Northern Plains nations. Historically, they shared methods of adaptation to the same harsh environment and, therefore, technological similarities. Because they share the same world, they also share some elements of worldview and thus religion. The Cheyenne and Lakota became military allies in the early nineteenth century because of their mutual enemy, the Crow, and still feel that allegiance, although old tribal animosities on the northern plains today serve mostly as a forum for teasing and joking among the various tribal groups.

The modern Southern Cheyenne are located in Oklahoma, while the Northern Cheyenne occupy a reservation with its agency at Lame Deer, Montana, in the eastern part of the state adjacent to the Crow agency. Their language is part of the Algonquin language group as are those of the Indian nations on the East Coast and all across Canada. The Cheyenne were, for instance, with their Lakota allies at the battle of the Little Big Horn in 1876 and sought refuge with the Lakota during their tragic flight north in 1878–79. Conservative by nature, the Northern Cheyenne are by economic standards poor but retain virtually all of their original reservation lands, ritual life, and language.

The Crow, who today live in southeastern Montana, and the Hidatsa, who live near New Town, on the Fort Berthold Reservation in central North Dakota, were a single people prior to the nineteenth century and speak a Siouan dialect. Originally a sedentary farming, hunting, and gathering people, the two groups split, with the Crows eventually adopting a typical buffalo-hunting nomadic lifestyle. The Hidatsa stayed in their earth lodge villages along the Missouri River and its tributaries. The Hidatsa and their cousins, the Mandan, occupied areas in what today is South Dakota and North Dakota. As the nineteenth century progressed, the Crow and Lakota increasingly warred against each other. Men from each tribe were anxious to win war honors by raiding and stealing horses from the other. This antagonistic stance culminated with the Crow serving as scouts for the U.S. military in its 1876 campaign of containment against the Lakota and Cheyenne, and they were present with Custer until he foolishly ignored their dire warnings on June 25, 1876.

The modern Assiniboine, a group linguistically and militarily allied with the Lakota/Dakota, live today in Canada, near Morley, Alberta, and on the Fort Peck Indian Reservation near Wolf Point, Montana. The Lakota call them *Hohe'* (which means "Speak Like Children"). So similar are their languages even today that a fluent speaker in either tongue can understand the other's language. All these groups shared basic spiritual concepts and had their own versions of pipe ceremonies, sweat lodge, and sun dance.

4. For further understanding of the Lakota Sun Dance, read Joseph Epes Brown's *The Sacred Pipe* (Norman: University of Oklahoma Press, 1953); or *Oglala Religion* by William K. Powers (Lincoln: University of Nebraska Press, 1975).

5. Madonna Swan, in *Madonna Swan: A Lakota Woman's Story* by Mark St. Pierre (Norman: University of Oklahoma Press, 1991), pp. 29–30.

6. John Sharkey, *Celtic Mysteries* (London: Thames and Hudson, 1987), pp. 82–83.

7. Furst, *Stones, Bones, and Skins,* p. 22.

8. Most books on the Lakota use such non-Indian constructs as sacraments to make comparisons to their native belief system. It is important not to let these comparisons cloud understanding or create misconceptions. Joseph Epes Brown speaks of the seven rites of the Oglala Sioux, leaving the Curing Rites out entirely. (It is of interest that he arrived at seven rites, exactly the number of Christian sacraments.) While the leadership of Yuwipi or Lowanpi doctoring rites may not be possible for most people, they are the most commonly used ceremonies for the good of the lay Lakota and certainly, unlike most books would indicate, fall within the mainstream of Lakota ceremonial life.

9. For further information on the central rites of the Lakota, see Brown, *The Sacred Pipe*.
10. Powers, *Oglala Religions*, pp. 130–34.
11. A number of good Lakota dictionaries exist, but we have used the *Lakota-English Dictionary* by the Rev. Eugene Buechel, published by the Institute of Indian Studies (at the University of South Dakota) and Red Cloud Indian School, Pine Ridge, South Dakota, in 1983. We feel it is the best and most complete dictionary of this language.
12. Kyle is a village in the north-central part of the Pine Ridge Indian Reservation. This reservation is as large as some eastern states and has many villages. The population of each village is descended from large extended families and headmen, who moved there when the reservation was formed, and carries with it a distinct identity. No one would say they were from Pine Ridge unless they were from that community.

CHAPTER TWO

1. James F. Walker, *Lakota Myth,* ed. Elaine Jahner (Lincoln: University of Nebraska Press, 1983), pp. 68–70.
2. Joseph Epes Brown, *The Sacred Pipe* (Norman: University of Oklahoma Press, 1953), p. 7.
3. Father Peter J. Powell, *Sweet Medicine* (Norman: University of Oklahoma Press, 1969), vol. 2, p. 444.
4. William K. Powers, *Oglala Religion* (Lincoln: University of Nebraska Press, 1975), p. 101.
5. Joseph Rockboy was a close friend who took Mark into his family as a grandson. He worked for the University of South Dakota Oral History Project as a field collector of Native American Oral History. He was respected as a very knowledgeable elder of the Yankton Sioux Tribe. Grandpa Joe was born before 1900 and died in 1981. Joe was raised by his Yanktonal grandfather, who was born in 1850. Joe was a linguist who spoke all the Sioux dialects fluently.
6. George Bird Grinnell, *The Cheyenne Indians* (Lincoln: University of Nebraska Press, 1972), vol. 1, p. 135.
7. Ronald Theisz, "Multifaceted Double Woman: Legend, Song, Dream, and Meaning," *European Review of Native American Studies,* 2:2 (1988): 9–15.
8. Ibid.
9. This society was formed in the 1980s. Debra Lynn White Plume and her mother, Bernice Stone, were two of its founding members.
10. Ray Dupris, now in his early forties, and Mark have been acquainted for twenty years. Ray was raised speaking Lakota and resides in the tiny Sans Arc village of Iron Lightning, on the northwest corner of the Cheyenne

River Reservation. He told this story half in English and half in Lakota; I hope I have recorded it accurately!

CHAPTER THREE

1. Marla N. Powers, *Oglala Women* (Chicago: University of Chicago Press, 1986), p. 53.
2. This "giveaway" remains a standard social ritual (with spiritual overtones) among the Lakota and other northern Plains tribes. Everyone in attendance is fed lavishly, with enough surplus for *watecha* (leftover) pails. Each person also receives a gift, the most important or those from farthest away receiving a star quilt or Pendleton blanket, and the less important receiving cloth, a dish towel, or cigarettes. The U.S. government outlawed this practice for many years. It has, however, persisted until the present.
3. Mari Sandoz, in *Crazy Horse: Strange Man of the Oglalas* (Norman: University of Oklahoma Press, 1961), tells us that the boy named Curly (the famous Oglala Crazy Horse) was a foundling whose father was named Crazy Horse. His father wished to give this name to his cherished son. When he did this, the father reverted back to his own childhood name, Worm.
4. Frank Linderman, *Pretty Shield: Medicine Woman of the Crows* (Lincoln: University of Nebraska Press, 1960), p. 19.
5. Frances Densmore, "Teton Sioux Music," *Bureau of American Ethnology Bulletin* 61 (1918): 65–66.
6. Linderman, *Pretty Shield,* p. 21.
7. There is a separate term for each type of kinship that defines the relationship. Out of formal respect, these terms were used when addressing relatives. In that sense, formal names were seldom used in the extended family. For a more complete list see the Rev. Eugene Buechel's *Lakota-English Dictionary* (Pine Ridge, S.D.: Institute of Indian Studies/Red Cloud Indian School, 1983), p. 39.
8. Cecelia (Shoots The Bear) Looking Horse is an important Lakota woman in her own right, because she has also been a Sun Dance leader (*Itancan*). A Hunkpapa from Kennel Community on the Standing Rock Reservation, she has made visitors to the Calf Pipe Bundle feel welcome for over thirty years.
9. Born in 1952, Mitchell Zephier, a lower Brule Lakota, reintroduced the metal jewelry tradition to his own people after it suffered a forty-year lapse in use. He briefly attended Dartmouth College and later Chicago Circle University, majoring in political science. In his early years he identified with the radical agenda of the American Indian Movement. Suffering a near-fatal gunshot wound, he discovered that he could express himself through the creation of jewelry. Mitchell has gone on to win every major award avail-

able in the field of American Indian jewelry making. He started and oper-
ates one of the few Indian-owned jewelry production facilities in North
America, Lakota Jewelry Visions in Rapid City. He is a bibliophile and a
self-taught expert on Lakota thought, history, and philosophy, and a Lakota
nationalist.

10. Mark St. Pierre, *Madonna Swan: A Lakota Woman's Story* (Norman: University of Oklahoma Press, 1991), pp. 40–43.

11. A woman who has been through the Isnati Ti Ca Lowan and taken a relative
(Hunkapi) has the right to appear in public with the part in her hair painted
red, her forehead painted red, and three vertical stripes painted on her chin.
In former times, these may have been tattooed. Lucy Swan was the last
woman Mark knew to use these marks, and shortly before she died she reminded Mark that she wanted these marks painted on her before burial, "so
that my relatives will know me on the other side."

12. While actually taking an older relative is not part of the Isna Ti Ca Lowan,
as Darlene Young Bear suggests, many Lakota people feel that it is; and it
often accompanies the coming-of-age rite. This new relative is usually an
older man or woman who is in need of a younger person to look out for him
or her.

13. Darlene (Knife) Young Bear was born in 1938 on the west end of the
Cheyenne River Reservation in the Hokwojo (Minnecojou) village of Red
Scaffold. She grew up very much connected with her traditions and later
married Kenneth Young Bear from the Fort Berthold Indian Reservation. In
his later years Kenneth evolved into a traditional holy man. Darlene supported him in this arduous role joyfully. She and Kenneth raised five children, the youngest born shortly before Kenneth's untimely death eleven
years ago. In the years since his death, Darlene has attended college, nearing
a degree, and has become a Catholic lay minister. She continues to be active
in the Catholic church while filling a role in the traditional religious life of
her people. Recently she conducted the Isna Ti Ca Lowan for a young lady
from her home community.

14. William. K. Powers, *Oglala Religion* (Lincoln: University of Nebraska
Press, 1975), pp. 100–103; and M. Powers, *Oglala Women,* pp. 194–95.

15. Joseph Rockboy was born in 1900 in Greenwood, South Dakota, on the
Yankton Sioux Reservation. Early in his life he became active in the newly
arrived Native American Church (sometimes called the Peyote Cult). Joe
was also a practicing Presbyterian and follower of the older Canku Luta
(Red Road) religion of his people. One of the last full-blood Yanktons, Joe
also claimed Cheyenne, Sicangu Lakota, Santee Dakota, Omaha, and Win-
nebago ancestry. Fully fluent in all three Sioux dialects, he was a natural for
selection as an oral historian and worked for many years collecting Native
American and pioneer history for the University of South Dakota Oral History Project. When he died in 1983, Grandpa Joe, as everyone called him,

was one of the most respected native elders in the upper plains region, having made friends, collected history, and attended or participated in ceremonies on many reservations. Mark's strongest memory of Joe is that he was ageless, always surrounded by younger people anxious to be with him and his ecumenical soul.

16. St. Pierre, *Madonna Swan,* pp. 5–6.

CHAPTER FOUR

1. Honesty is one of the core values of Lakota people, for it helps to reinforce many desirable communal behaviors. According to Lucy Swan, in the old version of the Lakota stick game, to decide which team would go first, a person from each team was selected to tell a story of his or her own personal bravery. No person would risk being disgraced by being caught making up or embellishing a story. The best story would determine who was first to hold the bones. In this way, both honesty and bravery were encouraged.

2. In traditional Lakota households, no son- or daughter-in-law would speak directly to his or her mother- or father-in-law. Refraining from doing so was considered proper etiquette and respect. It is essentially still this way in many households and helps to preserve family solidarity. If a daughter-in-law wished to tell her mother-in-law that dinner was ready, she would do so through her husband. On the other hand, teasing and joking and polite affection is expected among in-laws of the same generation.

3. Mark St. Pierre, *Madonna Swan: A Lakota Woman's Story* (Norman: University of Oklahoma Press, 1991), pp. 21–23.

4. Marla N. Powers, *Oglala Women* (Chicago: University of Chicago Press, 1986), p. 23.

5. Louise Plenty Holes, Oglala midwife, born approximately 1900. Translated into English by Tilda Long Soldier, from a video recorded in Lakota by the Oglala Lakota College, Indian Studies Department.

6. St. Pierre, *Madonna Swan,* p. 139.

7. The Lakota traditionally sponsor a memorial dinner on the anniversary of the death of a loved one. The first and fourth dinners are the biggest, and usually accompanied by a giveaway. All this is to honor the dead person, and is expected by others in the community and extended family. It is in a sense the extended family who will voluntarily prepare for these important feasts.

8. Mary Crow Dog and Richard Erdoes, *Lakota Woman* (New York: Harper Perennial, 1991), pp. 18, 19.

9. In a growing number of Lakota funerals, especially with, for example, a deceased respected elder or veteran, the traditional Christian funeral is altered by the addition of Lakota songs sung during the wake. Cedar and sweetgrass may also be used to smudge the body. In the procession from the church

to the cemetery, or from the hearse to the cemetery, additional old non-Christian songs in Lakota may also be sung. Four direction flags may be posted at the edges of the grave. Seashells and other objects are still left on the graves. On each Memorial Day the family is expected to visit and clean the grave and to bring fresh (and artificial) flowers. Small amounts of food may also be left.

Plains Indian people who are members of the Native American Church, the Peyote Church, have additional rituals they perform.

CHAPTER FIVE

1. Although we knew and spoke with Severt (he was Tilda's second cousin), this information came to us from charts drawn by Severt, through Ron Theisz at Black Hills State College, a few months after Severt's death. Ron has prepared a biography of Severt, *Standing in the Light* (Lincoln: University of Nebraska Press, 1994).
2. Mark St. Pierre, *Madonna Swan: A Lakota Woman's Story* (Norman: University of Oklahoma Press, 1991), pp. 166–70.
3. Lower Brule' people lived and moved as a separate part of the Sicangu, or burnt-thigh people, and are closely related to the Sicangu people on the larger Rosebud Reservation. They eventually found themselves on a separate reservation through the breakup in 1876 of the Great Sioux Reservation of 1868. Their reservation is on the west bank of the Missouri River, south of the South Dakota state capital, Pierre. They have been very successful in preserving most of their original land base.

CHAPTER SIX

1. Joseph Epes Brown, *Animals of the Soul* (Rockport, Mass.: Element Books, 1992), pp. 31, 32.
2. Ibid., p. 25.
3. Ibid., p. 42.
4. The second time is night, according to Lakota mythology. Day is the first time created, moons or months the third, and a cycle of seasons or of the year the fourth.
5. Brown, *Animals of the Soul,* p. 28.
6. Mary Crow Dog and Richard Erdoes, *Lakota Woman* (New York: Harper Perennial, 1991), pp. 24, 25.
7. From a booklet published by Oliver Brown Wolf. Oliver is a Lakota historian, and when he had finished telling us the story he said, in his humble way, "Oh, by the way, I could give you that story—I had it published." He was most helpful with other aspects of this project as well.

8. Mark St. Pierre, *Madonna Swan: A Lakota Woman's Story* (Norman: University of Oklahoma Press, 1991), pp. 27–29.
9. Frank Linderman, *Pretty Shield: Medicine Woman of the Crows* (Lincoln: University of Nebraska Press, 1960), pp. 165–66.
10. Father Peter J. Powell, *Sweet Medicine* (Norman: University of Oklahoma Press, 1969), vol. 2, pp. 209–10.
11. St. Pierre, *Madonna Swan,* pp. 163–64.
12. Michael F. Steltenkamp, *Black Elk: Holy Man of the Oglala* (Norman: University of Oklahoma Press, 1993), p. 125.

CHAPTER SEVEN

1. W. H. Over, "Late Joe Thin Elk: Lakota Holy Man to J. L. Smith, *Museum News,* 28, nos. 7–8 (1966, University of South Dakota, Vermillion, S.D.).
2. Father Peter J. Powell, *Sweet Medicine* (Norman: University of Oklahoma Press, 1969), vol. 2, p. 386.
3. Yellow Bird Woman is a full-blood Sicangu, enrolled on the Rosebud Reservation, where she returns on a regular basis for the Sun Dance. She has resided in Denver for over thirty years and has raised her family there. She works within the large urban Indian population providing many people with the kinds of spiritual and ritual help they would otherwise be able to get only by an expensive trip home. She was born into a well-known family and is fluent in the Lakota language, having taught it at a number of levels, including college.

CHAPTER NINE

1. William K. Powers, *Oglala Religion* (Lincoln: University of Nebraska Press, 1975), p. 151.
2. This song was used by the late Charles Kills Enemy and was found in an unpublished manuscript about Charles by Herbert Hoover. It is characteristic of these songs, and is only one from among a large repertoire that Charley had acquired. Some of his songs came to him through Isabel (Ten Fingers) Kills Enemy.
3. Also from the Hoover manuscript.
4. Powers, *Oglala Religion,* p. 152.
5. The spirits often give extra attention to the unfaithful. As we have witnessed it, one of the quilts used to wrap the holy person may be found folded in the lap, or thrown over the head, of the doubter. It is a source of embarrassment but also a gentle reminder that the spirits can read people's hearts, and results in humorous teasing.

6. John A. Grim, *The Shaman* (Norman: University of Oklahoma Press, 1983), p. 205.
7. Michael P. Steltenkamp, *Black Elk: Holy Man of the Oglala* (Norman: University of Oklahoma Press, 1993), p. 35.

CHAPTER TEN

1. Orville Mesteth is a Minnecojou from the west end of the Cheyenne River Reservation. Now in his late fifties, he is currently serving as the economic development director for his tribe. He has served in many capacities for his people over the years, including his early days as a Bureau of Indian Affairs dorm attendant. Orville was raised Catholic and sent his own children to a Catholic boarding school. Sadly, he lost a daughter at St. Joseph's, when her appendicitis was misdiagnosed by a dorm matron.
2. Mark St. Pierre, *Madonna Swan: A Lakota Woman's Story* (Norman: University of Oklahoma Press, 1991), pp. 63–64.
3. It must be remembered that overt racial discrimination existed in the early 1950s in South Dakota. Indians were treated largely as "coloreds" were in the South, in hospitals, hotels and motels, restaurants, and other public places. Governor Sigurd Anderson, himself an immigrant from Norway, purged the state of legal discrimination and became a one-term governor in the process.
4. Kenneth Young Bear and Mark met in late 1972. For the next four years Mark fasted and studied under him, spending significant time with him and his family. He called Mark "son." It is from him that Mark learned firsthand the songs and rituals used in doctoring. In that sense, Mark and all his other students are directly inspired from his grandmother, Iron Woman.
5. Assiniboine people speak a dialect of Dakota called *Ho' He'* that is very closely related to Lakota, sometimes also called the Sioux language.
6. Chauncey Dupris, insisting that he would lead one more Sun Dance, passed away in Cherry Creek at seventy-five, only months after this interview. He had inoperable cancer of the spine.
7. What Ted speaks of is the fact that his grandmother was first and foremost his grandmother and that at such a young age he would have had little involvement with the demands of her ceremonial life—and also that she was a female and thus he would not be as informed of her comings and going as he would if she had been a male member of the family.
8. Lucy suffered attacks of catalepsy, and in the Lakota idiom she was thought to have temporarily "died."
9. The reference to the specific colors of dust hark back to the colors that represent the four directions, or four winds. That she was able to make different colors of dust appear at will is an indication of the strength of her powers.

10. Giving cash or gifts to the healer is considered proper and respectful. It is a way to make an offering of thanks or *Wopela,* which is an important part of the reciprocal arrangement with the healer, the Creator, and the spirit powers called upon.

11. St. Pierre, *Madonna Swan,* pp. 17–20.

CHAPTER ELEVEN

1. Joseph Epes Brown, *Animals of the Soul* (Rockport, Mass.: Element Books, 1992), p. 54.

2. Within the oral tradition of Lakota people are stories of people whom the government called hostile or irreconcilable. These were men and women who refused to send their children to school, or who refused to give up the old ceremonial ways. They were sent to government-run mental hospitals (essentially political prisons). The records of one such hospital have recently begun to come to light. It was in Canton, South Dakota; and those who never returned home again—there were many—are buried beneath what is now a public golf course. A ceremony was recently held there by the Lakota/Dakota peoples and a plaque placed near that terrible spot.

3. These schools are run primarily by the Roman Catholic, Episcopal, and Mormon churches, although many other denominations run schools as well. (At one time forty-seven different Christian denominations were counted on the large Pine Ridge Reservation.) In all fairness, it must be said that attitudes toward the old beliefs have softened among some of the Christian clergy and that some of these schools, while funded through Christian charities, are run by Indian school boards. Schools like Red Cloud Indian School, formerly Holy Rosary, are attended by children whose parents are motivated by the reputation or quality of the school. These schools have also enabled those children who are from the reservation where the school is located to return home in the evenings.

4. Lucy Swan told Mark on numerous occasions her opinion as to why certain cultural practices were lost. The stick game, for example, is a traditional gambling game that is still held among most of the western tribes, but the Lakota no longer play it or remember the songs that accompany it. When Mark asked her about the absence of the Lakota stick game, she said, "When the boys came back from World War II many of them had drinking problems, and they would come around the public [during activities like the stick game] and scare people, so we stopped doing that." Lucy, however, did remember the songs and traditions that went with the game.

5. Ted Thin Elk, who has been made a chief by his Sicangu Lakota people, was one of the first students in the Alcohol Counselor Training Program, a four-

year program at the University of South Dakota for training alcohol coun-
selors. He also played the medicine man in the movie *Thunder Heart*.

6. Mary Crow Dog and Richard Erdoes, *Lakota Woman* (New York: Harper Perennial, 1991), p. 5.
7. Debra Lynn White Plume, *Cante' Ohitika Win* (Vermillion, S.D.: University of South Dakota Press, 1991), p. 67.

Index